THE

DINNER QUESTION

THE

DINNER QUESTION

OR

How to Dine
Well & Economically

(1860)

Tabitha Tickletooth

[Charles Selby]

A FACSIMILE EDITION
with an introduction
by
ALAN DAVIDSON

PROSPECT BOOKS
1999

Published by Prospect Books in 1999
at Allaleigh House, Blackawton, Totnes, Devon TQ9 7DL.

The original edition was first published in 1860 by Routledge,
Warne and Routledge.

British Library Cataloguing in Publication Data:
A CIP record for this book is available from the British Library.

Designed and set by Tom Jaine.

ISBN 0 907325 88 2

Printed in Great Britain by the Cromwell Press, Trowbridge,
Wiltshire.

Introduction

The author of this engaging work was a man, Charles Selby (*ca.* 1802–1863), an actor and dramatist. 'Tabitha Tickletooth' was not his only *nom de plume*; he also appeared as 'William Muggins, Natural Philosopher and Man of the World'. The playful disposition at which these names hint found fullest expression in the numerous theatrical farces for which he was responsible. *The Dictionary of National Biography* remarks that in the summer of 1844 no fewer than three of his farces were running in London simultaneously.

Indeed his life was devoted more to amusing the public than to enlightening them. However, these need not be alternative paths; there are authors and actors who have done both, and Selby himself, masquerading as Tabitha, carried out the double act with distinction in *The Dinner Question*. The extent of his achievement will be appreciated by anyone who compares the words of Tabitha with the contents of other little books or essays on gastronomy of the same period, e.g. those by Thomas Walker (1835)[1] and Hayward (2nd edition 1853).[2] These other works may still be perused with pleasure and interest, but they have little to offer in the way of practical information, their humour tends to be laboured and pompous, and their expected audience is one of 'toffs' who spend their evenings giving or attending dinner parties. Tabitha, in contrast, offers a great deal of practical information (some examples are given below) and the jokes which Selby puts into her mouth are of a sharper sort, served up with a dressing of light irony which puts them on a different plane from the ponderous anecdotes of competitors. Moreover, Tabitha aims her advice at a wider audience, not just upper-class givers of dinner parties, and willingly wanders out of the kitchen to deliver homilies on how a young married couple should furnish their home, the principals governing the use of curtains, the choice of towels (not ones like nutmeg-graters!) and soap, and the requirement of plunging the face into plenty of cold water after the soaping. Her denunciation of what 'old country house-wives call "cat-licking" in a teacupfull of warm water', raising the spectre of 'a sallow complexion and premature wrinkles,' is a little masterpiece. The term 'cat-licking' in this sense used to be widespread (and is even mirrored in Afghanistan, I am told), but it is possibly a further piece of evidence that Selby had a provincial and countryside origin in the north of England (a more direct piece of evidence being his reference on page 19 to the Yorkshire practice of 'siding oop').

Selby has a good eye for quotations; see for examples, the footnote on 'Pea taming' on page 73 and that on Dr Abernethy's 'blue pill' on page 111). A particularly surprising footnote is provided on page 128, where Tabitha, while discussing the nature of a soufflé, betrays her wide reading by attributing to Carême[3] a description of items in horseflesh dinners as 'filets de boeuf à la boot-heel' and 'soups à la wooden leg' – and is carried away by this reference into wondering what Carême would think of 'the wondrous *soufflées* of some of the present ... hangers-on to the edges of his imperial apron, who form them of crystallized snow, the dew of violets (not onions), and the pinions of butterflies preserved in their flour ...'

Generally, Tabitha shows herself well informed about French writing on food and cookery and about eating in Paris. However, she is far from being overawed by the French. Hayward, one of the authors referred to above, was content to reflect what Grimod de la Reynière[4] and Brillat-Savarin,[5] had written, in a manner which indicated that here was the true gospel to which English authors and cooks should pay heed, but without hoping that they could emulate, let alone surpass, its dicta. Tabitha, in sharp contrast, bends French authors to her own ends, is perfectly happy to quote them in an ironical way, and positively enjoys painting a lurid picture of the gastronomic fate awaiting British day trippers or holidaymakers in Paris (pages 141 to 143). In short, she is a true Londoner and a thorough skeptic.

Tabitha's remarks about France and French cuisine, had they come to the notice of French critics at the time, would have been treated as a piece of *lèse-majesté*. Now, however, almost a century and a half later, we find that Tabitha has begun to exercise a strong attraction on the French. An important *Colloque* was held in Paris in 1997 to discuss the influence of French gastronomic writing, especially but not exclusively the famous works by Grimod de la Reynière and Brillat-Savarin. I was the only non-French participant and it fell to me to describe the (limited) influence which these works had on writing about food in English. So I dealt with such evidence for this as I had been able to find, starting with *The Cook's Oracle* by the eccentric Dr Kitchiner and progressing all the way to the closing decades of the 20th century, when the influence of Brillat-Savarin was more prominent in Australia than anywhere else in the English speaking world.

Of the many tidbits of information which I conveyed to the audience, the only one which sparked off a truly vivacious response was my description of Tabitha Tickletooth. The French critics, savants and gastronomes were enchanted; and at the formal lunch which marked the end of the *Colloque* there was much talk about the possibility about translating Tabitha into French – the translation to appear, of course, with the same image of her on the jacket as adorned the original edition.

When I referred, above, to the practical nature of much of Tabitha's advice, I was thinking particularly of her remarks about potato cookery. My own training in this art was carried out under the guidance of a certain Catherine in Enniscorthy in Ireland and I recognise in Tabitha's prose (how to boil a potato and following passages, pages 96 to 100) many of the precepts which she instilled in me. It was only under her guidance that I learned to place a clean teacloth over the boiled and drained potatoes in their saucepan, with the saucepan lid on top of the cloth and the residual heat evaporating unwanted moisture and creating the 'floury' effect which is so desirable. It is noteworthy here, and in other passages about vegetable cookery and about boiling, stewing and frying, that Tabitha gives earnest attention to the principles governing the transmission of heat, and other scientific aspects of cookery. See, for example, the quotation from the *Encyclopaedia Britannica* and the accompanying remarks (pages 35 to 36).

It is true that here and in one or two other places we see that Tabitha, for all her independence of mind, was held captive by scientific terminology which has now for long been obsolete. The reference to 'osmazome' is one example. I note also that in common with other writers of the time she supposed whitebait to be a distinct species of fish, which it is not. In her defence I would say that the truth did not come to light until much later (*vide* my *North Atlantic Seafood*), and that Tabitha surely deserves credit for citing the article in *The Naturalist* which was at the time the *locus classicus* for the contention that whitebait should be classified as *Clupea alba*, and for drawing particular attention to the presence of whitebait in the River Dart (within miles, as it happens, of the place of publication of the present volume) during the months from March to November. I also applaud her frankness when she adds that: 'Whether they remain in the Dart throughout the year, has not been ascertained.'

The passage on whitebait serves to bring out one more aspect of Tabitha and her creator: the scholarly approach, manifest also in some other passages in the book. While I would not presume to offer a final analysis of Tabitha, I suggest that any such analysis would have to portray her as not simply a double act, but as a quintuple act, or perhaps something even more complex, the principal elements being: her talent for farce; her sharp wit; her practicality in the kitchen; her scientific approach to cookery; and her prowess as a scholar. Let her readers enjoy all these aspects of her character in the pages which follow.

Alan Davidson

NOTES

1. Thomas Walker (1784–1836) made his main career in law, studying the workings of Poor Law and becoming a police magistrate in 1829. In 1835, the last full year of his life, he published from May to December a weekly called *The Original*, in which essays of his own on 'Aristology or The Art of Dining', 'Suppers', etc., appeared. Several such essays, some on health and longevity, were published in book form by Philip Allan and Co, London, 1921. He urged people who felt faint for lack of food to 'take a little spirit of lavender dropped upon a lump of sugar'.

2. Abraham Hayward (1801–84) was a prominent essayist in Victorian times, contributing to the *Quarterly Review* and the *Edinburgh Review*. Articles which he published in the former periodical were collected into a small volume *The Art of Dining; or, Gastronomy and Gastronomers*, 2nd edition 1853. Besides quoting French authorities at length, he offers some native English anecdotes, including a couple about unsophisticated diners such as the Scottish officer who, at a formal dinner, found a large platter of wheatears (intended for the whole company) within easy reach and proceeded to work his way through the whole lot. When Lady Louisa Lennox tried to divert his attention to another dish, he replied, 'Na, na my leddy, these wee birdies will do verra weel.'

3. Antonin Carême (1783–1833) was and remains the most famous French chef of the 19th century, wrote a number of books and came to be regarded in the last few decades of his life, outside as well as inside France, as the ultimate authority on French haute cuisine.

4. Alexandre-Balthazar-Laurent Grimod de la Reynière (1758–1837), a highly eccentric figure, is often hailed as the first of the major French gastronomic writers. His annual *Almanach des Gourmands* (of which the first volume was published in 1803) was read attentively by English gastronomic writers.

5. Jean-Anthelme Brillat-Savarin (1755–1826), a lawyer, is famous for his book *La Physiologie du Goût: ou, Méditations du Gastronomie transcendante*, first published in Paris in 1825 and endlessly reprinted, also in English translations, thereafter. He can best be read in the admirable English edition, translated and annotated by M.F.K. Fisher (1972).

Bibliographic note

The publisher is grateful to Mr Alan Davidson for making his copy of *The Dinner Question* available for reproduction. The first binding was a yellow pictorial board, with a photograph of the author, identical to that reproduced opposite the facsimile title page, emblazoned on the front. The impression has been enlarged by approximately seven per cent to improve legibility. The original paper is quite acid; a certain amount of foxing had occurred. The printed impression is light. There is one printer's error of pagination: page 189 is numbered 9. The original copy is inscribed, 'Miss Allice Perkins from an Affectionate Fiend Febury 13th 1862'. This is further annotated, presumably by Miss Perkins herself, 'Who is a Fiend you impudent Hussy'.

THE FACSIMILE

FROM A PHOTOGRAPH BY HERBERT WATKINS, 215, REGENT-STREET

THE

DINNER QUESTION:

OR,

HOW TO DINE WELL AND ECONOMICALLY.

COMBINING

The Rudiments of Cookery

WITH

USEFUL HINTS ON DINNER GIVING AND SERVING,

AND OTHER HOUSEHOLD WORDS OF ADVICE:

GARNISHED WITH

ANECDOTES OF EMINENT COOKS AND EPICURES, AS WELL
AS WISE SAWS IN GASTRONOMY FROM THE
GREAT MASTERS.

BY

TABITHA TICKLETOOTH.

LONDON:

ROUTLEDGE, WARNE, AND ROUTLEDGE,

FARRINGDON STREET.

NEW YORK: 56, WALKER STREET.

1860.

[*The Author reserves the right of Translation.*]

CONTENTS.

THE DINNER QUESTION.

INTRODUCTION.

As man, in his civilized state, is supposed to eat above a thousand times in every year of his life, a work which will teach him how to vary his food, and prepare it skilfully, alike for the preservation of his health and the gratification of his palate, cannot fail to be highly interesting to *all* classes.

Brillat Savarin, in his world-famous *Physiologie du Goût,* has given us the foundation of everything connected with the "pleasures of the table." Carême, Ude, Francatelli, and a host of other renowned "ministers of the mouth," have endeavoured to instruct us how to produce an *Omelette Soufflée,* a *Suprême de Volaille, Poulets à la Marengo,* &c. &c. Mrs. Glasse in the olden time, Mrs. Rundle, Miss Acton, and Alexis Soyer in the present, have shown us how to deal with more substantial fare; while Doctor Kitchener, perhaps the most lucid and practicable of all, has initiated us in the chemistry of food, and revealed the more recondite mysteries of the culinary art; but none of them—and I say it advisedly—have given us the exact thing required by Housekeepers with small incomes—viz., *Plain instructions for the preparation of Plain Dishes, at the least possible expense.*

Soyer, in his *Shilling Cookery for the Million,* comes nearest the mark; but he is generally too French in his practice, and offers examples which many who have a natural love of simple and succulent English good cheer will never follow. The great fault of all the Cookery-books I have read (and their number has not been small), is, that their instructions are too complicated and vague, and address themselves principally to persons whose means permit them to keep up a good establishment, and *give* dinners.

Of what use to the wife of a clerk, at a salary of a hundred a year, or an artisan at five-and-twenty shillings a week, is a work profusely interlarded with French terms, describing dishes the cost of one of which would absorb half a week's earnings? neither, on the other hand, can such a person derive any advantage from what may be truthfully called *Workhouse Receipts for the Preparation of Pauper's Food*.

That the *Dinner Question* is one of great moment to the " higher classes," is proved by the shoals of letters which have lately appeared in the columns of the *Times*, in reply to a leader depicting the horrors of " dim soup, gloomy cod's head and shoulders, relieved by three or four evil side dishes, and followed by the inevitable haunch of mutton and pair of chickens ;" and calling the Matrons of England " to spits," to relieve Baker-street from the incubus of those set feasts, in which the same dishes are brought in in the same order, and apparently by the same servants.

Knight after knight of the spoon and fork has sounded his *appel* and shivered his lance in support of the transcendant merits of *La cuisine Française ;* while princely Amphitryons have rushed into print, and discussed the grand question of service *à la Russe*, at a length and with a spirit worthy the effort of repelling an attack on our liberties, or an infringement on our national rights.

What can be more exciting—in fact, heart-rending—to a poor man of only seven or eight hundred a year, to have all his moderate views of domestic comfort annihilated by the following awe-inspiring essay from a " Ten Thousand Pounder," who dates from Berkeley-street ?—

" Let a lady ask her guests to dinner at a quarter to eight (or seven, as the case may be), and let dinner be announced, *coûte qui coûte*, at eight.

" Let the guests in no case exceed ten in number, if there are ladies; if only gentlemen, the Roman rule, ' no more than the Muses.'

" Let some attention be given to the selection of the guests. Bring those together who like, or will like, each other—those who, you have heard, want to know each other—those whose tastes are the same, &c. This is too often neglected. I dined the other day at a party of twenty-six, when there was one young gentleman of twenty and myself, and not another creature under fifty-five or sixty years old.

" Let the lady settle every seat beforehand, with the same view in the selection; and let the husband direct each guest in succession to the proper seat.

" Let her have a round table.

" Let her have chairs with spring-seats and spring-backs, quite unlike ordinary dinner chairs.

" Let her table be covered, not with the bottoms of wretched side-dishes, of which the tops are wanting, but (apart from the usual accompaniments of silver, linen, and multi-coloured glass) with a grouped abundance of flowers, green leaves, French painted moss, and fruit according to the season.

" Let these be arranged, if possible, among Dresden or Sèvres productions, with a statuette here of a corbeille-bearing child (which corbeille fill with grapes), and another there of a shepherdess with strawberries or a pine in her apron; but, if these are not forthcoming, there are few houses where dinners are given that have not some pretty objects in silver, biscuit, or the like, to set off a table; and even an ordinary dessert-service may be made to look very pretty with the accessories of flowers, moss, cakes, and fruit.

" The two main objects of dessert (beyond those portions of it which will be removed from the table at intervals to form part of the dinner) are its fragrance and its effect by way of ornament. After dining properly, no one thinks, or ought to think, of stuffing dessert; and, with the exception of such parts of the dessert as naturally come in during dinner (and this I invariably make to embrace a good deal), as melon with roast lamb, *marrons* with capon, olives with ducklings, pine with *volaille sauté au suprême*, &c., few persons worthy of dining will do more than 'taste' dessert after dinner.

" Let the room have an overflowing light without heat, but not too much light on the table.

" Let the table, arranged with such an *entourage* as I have mentioned, have on it one vacant spot—and one alone—and that one before the host.

" Let the lady obtain a number of blank *menus*, and let each guest find one of these *menus* (carefully filled up in a lady's hand, and setting out the coming dinner) on his napkin before his seat, and if there should be a rose or a bunch of violets by its side it will only add to the beauty of the table, and still more increase the particular effect to be attained, which is as follows :—When conversation momentarily flags in any quarter, you will see the silent or stupid guest at once fly to his *menu*, or his rose, which are always there before him, and it is astonishing how soon he revives and joins again in the conversation. The pause is so much better occupied than by the ordinary process of munching bread.

"Let the dinner be served *à la Russe*—one dish at a time, and only one,—one soup, then one fish, and so on. The mistakes of ordinary dinners are too absurd to mention. You see two soups and two fish, the former often cold, the latter sure to become so while you are eating the former, and not one of the four properly adapted for any other. Then you see (as you graphically describe it) two great dishes and four or six side-dishes, all prepared at once, all coming up together, all rapidly losing their first and proper flavour, and the former of which (saddle of mutton and chickens!), if not cold already, must become cold while the latter are being handed about to everybody in the most incongruous confusion, one which, perhaps, you would like passing by because at the time you are eating another, a *vol-au-vent* offered you just as you finish *boudin de veau à la Richelieu;* a third, which you instinctively feel is the proper thing at that crisis, and unseen by you heretofore, replaced on an empty stand before you at the moment the saddle is uncovered, and it is too late; and a thousand similar absurdities—each dish probably very good, perhaps done by a real *chef,* but from the combined want of heat and of head the whole is an inextricable *podrida,* which is not ' dining.'

"Let, then, the dinner be served as I have mentioned, one dish at a time, and only one. Your correspondent of yesterday, who asks for a remedy, talks of giving people 'a choice.' In dining there is no choice. After one dish comes the proper dish. When offered to you, omit it, if you like ; you may injure the edifice; but don't substitute for it another which will also spoil all that comes after. Connoisseurs know that the true art, the difficult secret of each *cuisine,* are ' sauces ' and their attributes. Let me taste the productions of any cook in the way of three or four foundation sauces, as *Espagnol, Béchamel, velouté,* &c., and I will soon tell you if he is worthy to be, or ever will be, a *chef.* By consequence one of the secondary difficulties is ' soups.' Now, of course, it is impossible here to go at any length into the interior of those *menus* (varied as they must ever be) which I have recommended should be written out in a ladylike hand for each guest; but there are two or three things which if ladies will learn, they will soon know how to fill up their *menus* for themselves. Let them know, then, that the main importance of a dinner consists, or ought to consist, in the *entrées* (those hapless side dishes for which they, the ladies, so often think anything will do). The importance of the *entrées*, again, entirely consists in their sauces (not necessarily foundation sauces, but probably deductions from them), and according to the two or three distinguishing sauces which are adapted for the best forms of the different materials which the season of the year allows for the *entrées* ought to be regulated both the earlier and later parts of the dinners. Let a lady and her cook then devise how many and what *entrées* there shall be; and that being settled, let them think, on the one hand, of what fish is in season, and how to be dressed, whose sauce will not depend on the *entrées*, and what soup they can give, whose *consomme* or stock shall not be made of the *entrée* sauces; and, on the other hand, let them travel in the opposite direction, and think what *relevés* and *rotis*, and how dressed; and lastly, what game (the latter generally an easy choice) will best accord with the taste generated by, and yet be totally distinct from, the two or three leading sauces. In fact, begin with the middle of your dinner, and work outwards both ways.

"I very much doubt the existing routine being capable of much improvement, except the modifications I shall mention hereafter. You may begin with oysters if you like (a good thing, never exceeding from four to six), or with any other *hors-d'œuvre* of the same wooing nature (the Romans began with eggs); but next to any such *appas* I am satisfied the true foundation of dinner is soup. Soup used to come in as the fourth course, reigning Queen Anne, but without being *médecins malgré nous*, in a century and a quarter *nous avons changé tout cela*.

"Again, I only give one fish *as fish*, and that invariably after the soup. Other fish may come in as *entrées* after an interlude, but this again ranges to the higher branches of art. The Germans will give you many a fish *au naturel* after dishes such as stewed veal and the like, but such things are barbarisms, and in this country at least no one dines so well as with the ordinary and natural sequence of fish after soup.

Let each dish (where necessary) between the fish and the *relevés* be accompanied by its peculiar vegetable, and for ordinary English tastes you must have potatoes as well. As to this, I have generally at hand for all the softer kind of *entrées* a *gâteau aux pommes-de-terre*, almost as fine and light as sponge cake, and made of potatoes, cream, &c.; and for the severer class of *entrées, pommes-de-terre frites, maître d'hôtel*, &c., as the case may be. Plain potatoes (one of the best things in the world) are perfect with a few *relevés* and some *rotis*, but there are very few *entrées* that they will not absolutely and irretrievably annihilate. Let one of a lady's first lessons be to make a potato cake.

Let there come on after the game (and this invariably) one or two vegetables, by themselves. These must be particularly attended to, and many of them, as *salsifis à la poulette, artichaux à la Bordelaise*, or *à la Barigoule*, require some little trouble. Still, provided they are not a recurrence of anything gone before, the lady will find the trouble not misapplied, for they are the natural path leading to the *entremets*, and if they are good and appropriate, the *entremets* which follow (and which have generally given her so much trouble heretofore) need never be more than two in number.

" Let the *entremets* then succeed, and in the case of a dinner such as I have attempted to portray, one at least of those two *entremets* should always be of a light nature. A first-rate *soufflé* is very good for the second one; and if of *vanille* will suit most dinners. Never have a chocolate *soufflé* where a leading sauce has been *à la Batelière*.

" Finish between the months of October and May with caviare on buttered toast.

" Let the host carve each dish in succession except the final ices. This is not too much to do if the number does not exceed ten. Let the quantity given be small, and, above all, let the hot plates for each dish come in with the dish. Of course the dishes may be carved on the sideboard, but I have never found a dinner go off so well. Anything which gratifies the sight ' tells,' and each dish in succession ought to be a really pretty object. Supposing guests to be hungry (and why dine if you are not?) each dish, when uncovered, and still more when tasted, ought to be the very thing which the prior part of the dinner has led you at that moment to desire, and I have found

this effect is quite lost if nothing is seen but a small portion on the plate.

"Now, let any lady who has read so far, sit down and cal-
culate. She will have given one soup, one fish, three or four
entrées (never more), one *relevé*, one *roti*, one game (generally
enough, unless you have *ortolans* or *beccaficos* for a second),
two *legumes,* and two *entremets,* in all twelve or thirteen *plats,*
and equally twelve or thirteen courses. She will have probably
saved five substantial dishes at least, besides I don't know how
many other *entremets* and absurdities. She will have given a
dinner in which each dish is in its best ' form,' in which are
avoided the awkward cessations from all action and conversation
which so often occur during the change of the courses, and (cor-
rectly done) she will have improved her husband's temper and
gratified every guest she has. She will have done more—she
will probably decrease the length of her dinner, while she certainly renders it far less tedious, and she will (without fail, if
she can succeed in one other point) shorten the time that the
gentlemen sit alone after the ladies are gone.

"I remain, your obedient servant,

"Berkeley-street. G. H. M."

Who, after reading this wondrous *Arabian Nights' Entertainment* can be contented with a steak or a chop, a plain joint
and a bit of fish? Pimlico and the "Holborn-squares" are
blotted from the map, and the poor "humbler classes," like the
Chocktaw Indians, must inevitably be extinguished, did not
their old friend *Punch,* who is always on the watch to do "the
people" a service, thus feelingly advance to their aid.

ENGLISH DINNERS FOR SNOBS.

To the Editor of "Punch."

"SIR,—Since sending to the *Times* my letter, of a column
and a half in length, in which I laid down the true principles
on which dinners should be given (or rather exchanged, for I
need not say that a dinner creates a debt, due from those we
invite, except where a writer, buffoon, traveller, or other attraction is introduced as part of the *menu,* and, indeed, he ought to
be written down in it), I have been reminded that there are a
good many persons in this country who, though neither
millionaires, nor even possessing a decent income of three or

four thousand a year, arrogate to themselves, in this levelling age, the right to know what they are eating and drinking, and who complain of the present system of dinner-giving. I allude to those whom, without my being unnecessarily offensive, I may call Snobs, with perhaps six, seven, or eight hundred a year. I have been asked to give, for the benefit of such persons, a few hints in the spirit of the letter which I addressed to their betters. It is, I fear, almost insulting their wretchedness to advise them on such a subject, but it is our duty to help our inferiors, and endeavour to make them feel that the state of life in which Providence has placed them, to labour, and look up to us for direction, is as comfortable as they deserve it should be.

"Of course, I do not speak to them of 'dinner at 8,' when, if they have worked as they ought to do, they are yawning for bed; of chairs with 'spring seats and spring backs;' of 'Sèvres china,' 'abundance of flowers,' 'child with *corbeille* full of grapes,' 'French painted moss,' 'a rose or bunch of violets by the napkin,' 'ortolans and beccaficos,' or the other necessaries of civilized life. To mock the needy is the basest vulgarity. I will merely give the Snobs I have referred to a little counsel, derived from practical knowledge of their habits and wants.

"Addressing such persons, I would say,—

"You had better give no dinners at all. It is for your betters to dine; you have only to eat. Tea, at five o'clock, with plenty of muffins, Sarah Lunnes, and toast, is a more befitting repast for you to offer to your friends : and perhaps some bread and cheese, spring onions, or even a salad, afterwards, may not be regarded as extravagance. Beer is not an unwholesome drink for the inferior classes. I suppose that your females tolerate tobacco. Why not be content with the enjoyments natural to your order ?

"But, if you *will* imitate your superiors, and ask persons to dinner, attend to the following hints :—

"Always invite the wives of your male friends. These women will much abridge the evening, being desirous to get home to their children (for whom, of course, they have no nursery governesses and nurses), and they will in some measure check intemperate habits.

"Give your meal at 6, as persons of your class are unaccustomed to wait so long, and will have lunched, whereby you will save.

"Make your table pretty, by all means. A plaster cast of the Emperor Napoleon, or a Church with coloured windows, for illumination, can be bought for a few pence; and will lead the conversation to politics, or to religion, and kindred subjects on which your class imagines itself to have a right to speak.

"To have a *menu* would be a mockery, but as you, as well as we, have 'stupid or silent guests,' let your little boys write out on copy-book paper a few maxims, and lay a copy by each person. 'Gluttony leads to want,' 'Temperance profiteth much,' 'Let not your Eye be bigger than your bell-Eye,' and similar morals, may do good, besides improving your brats' writing. Instead of a rose or violet, place by each male person a cold saveloy, and by each female a piece of gingerbread, to be 'munched' instead of bread (as in high life) during the pauses.

"Never put tallow candles on the table. A lamp is cheap, and if the mistress of the house cleans it herself, will long keep in order.

"No soup that you can make is fit to eat. But oysters may begin your dinners as well as ours, only instead of 'four or six,' let each person have a couple of dozen, with roll, butter, and beer. This will materially help you with the rest of the dinner.

"There is no objection to cheap fish, and I have seen apparently good fish cried in the streets in which you reside. But a few fresh herrings, or sprats, will be the safest. Remember that fish should be eaten with the fork, even though made of steel. But albata is not dear, and looks nice, if the mistress herself rubs it with wash-leather.

"Instead of the huge, tough, gory joints in which you delight, try hashed mutton, Irish stew, or harico. Fried potatoes are a delicacy easily attainable. The mashed potato, with small sausage on the top, will wean many a husband— not from his club, for you have, happily for you, no such temptations—but from the chop-house. Marrowbones, when you wish to be particularly 'genteel' (as you call it), may be introduced.

"Why have a pudding course? Ugly, sloppy, or hard,

unwholesome things are your puddings. Go to a respectable grocer's, and ask him for an article called macaroni. He will tell you how to cook it. With a little grated cheese, you will find it a novel luxury. Treacle on toast will please the juveniles.

"Then your slatternly servant (by the way, insist on her washing her face, and wearing a cap—never let her come in with her bonnet on) will heave on to the groaning table a hemicycle of cheese like half a millstone. Keep this away, and have some slices handed round. Do not, from a foolish feeling of ' gentility,' deny yourselves onions, which you like. You will not be a bit more like us if you never touch another onion to your lives' end.

"By all means have what you consider dessert. Apples, oranges, and biscuits you have in your gallery at the theatre, why not on table? A drum of figs, covered by one of your girls with coloured paper, or stuck over with red wafers, will be a tasteful centre ornament, and to the sweet fig you may charge the bad taste of your wine. For I suppose you will give three-and-sixpence, or even four shillings, for this nastiness, though I advise (and your females prefer) brandy and water.

"I tell you frankly not to be ashamed of tobacco-pipes. We take a cigarette, and what is that but a tobacco-pipe of paper?

"Your best *chasse* is being driven up-stairs to tea. The sooner this is announced the better for the temper of your females, and for your own heads when you go to your work next morning.

"Keep your children up. If they are tired and cross, it is only once in a way. They materially help to break up a party, and my object has been to show you how, with your narrow means, you may in a humble and cheerful way, imitate your superiors, while exercising a wise economy. Let me add, never hesitate, if it be a wet night, to send your maid for cabs, instead of asking your guests to delay their departure. But give the poor girl one glass of spirits; remember what you save by dismissing your friends.

"If these hints are of any use to persons with not more than eight hundred a year, I shall have done my duty to the poor, and remain,

"Your obedient servant,

"Berkeley-street. G. H. M."

These " paper pellets of the brain" (for most of the writers who
have taken such hot part in the controversy, and dilated in such
glowing terms on the system adopted at *their* banquets, are
poor, hard-working *littérateurs,* who live in furnished lodgings,
and never gave a dinner in their lives) have done nothing for
the advancement of culinary knowledge, for their sublimest pe-
rorations are laughed at by those who keep great establishments;
while John Hobbs, the book-keeper at Messrs. Throgmorton's,
the ship-brokers, or James Clouter, the working-engineer at
Maudsley's factory, shrugs his shoulders, and says to his wife,
" Ah ! I wish instead of all this French flummery, some lady
or gentleman in *our* way of life would instruct us how to make
our two pounds or thirty shillings give us better dinners,
then I'd say something; but *dinners on paper, and dinners on
the table, are wofully different.*"

To pamper the appetite with foreign *kickshaws,* made gravies,
and condiments, is alike incompatible with economy and health.
*The skilful preparation of the meat, and not the variety of its
sauces,* should be the study of the poor man's wife.   To know
how to boil vegetables (particularly potatoes), fry or boil a
" bit of fish," broil a chop or steak, roast a joint or a fowl,
concoct a savoury hash, and make a wholesome family pie or
pudding on sound principles, is to possess a bank of useful knowledge, which never fails to return a very high interest.

It matters little to the young housekeeper seeking practical
instruction in the art of making her home happy, how the
banquets of Apicius, Lucullus, Prince Talleyrand, the Marquis
de Cussy, and other equally renowned pilgrim fathers in the
" Idolatry of the Stomach," were produced.*   This little work
professes nothing more than to point out to those who, as Dr.
Kitchener facetiously terms it, " have never shaken hands with
a stewpan," how to cook a plain family dinner, on the easiest
and most economical principles.   Fearing, however, that a mere
collection of receipts and dry instructions for their preparation
would not, in these days of light literature, be sufficiently
attractive to the public in general, I have thought it advisable
to season my narrative with occasional sprinkles of the *cayenne*

* To the curious in such matters, the pages of Brillat Savarin, Hayward's
Essays; " The Pleasures of the Table," in *Bentley's Miscellany; Paris à
Table,* by Balzac ; Count Romford's *Essays,* and the columns of the *Times*
in January, 1859, will afford the fullest information.

of anecdote, and a slight dash of the *sauce piquante* of the wit
and humour of the bygone great patrons of the gastronomic
art, whose happy thoughts have so brilliantly immortalized their
good dinners. I will begin by offering a few

HINTS TO THE NEWLY MARRIED ON THEIR FIRST FURNISHING.

We will suppose a "happy pair," just returned from their
wedding tour, cosily settled down in their second floor in a cheap
street in London, or their pretty "semi-detached" cottage in a
genteel row at Camberwell or Wandsworth. Of course they
have furnished, and everything has been made comfortable in
the "sweet home" under the active superintendence of mother,
mother-in-law, and unmarried sisters.

HOW FURNITURE SHOULD BE BOUGHT.

Do not rush in a hurry to cheap shops and buy everything
you are told you must want. Call a family council, and make
out a list of the *fewest articles* you can manage with at first
(you'll find dozens of little things you never expected you'd
require extend it day after day); then find out from the adver-
tisements in the newspapers where sales are about to take place;
go the day before and *carefully examine* the articles you wish
to bid for; let some friend who knows their just value mark
your catalogue, and if they are knocked down to you within a
shilling or two of your limit you may be sure you have your
money's worth. Take care, however, if you should have particularly set your mind upon something for which there is a lively
competition, that you are not "run up" by the Jew brokers who
swarm at all sales and take a special delight in opposing "money"
customers, as they interfere with the monopoly they wish to
establish for their trade. Beware also of cheap advertising
upholsterers—"veneered delusions," which, though very attractive to the eye, were never made to do service. You had much
better, if you cannot suit yourself at public sales, go to a good
tradesman and give a fair price for well made and properly
seasoned substantial articles, which, although they may be expensive at the beginning, are *always* the cheapest in the end.

BEDSTEADS AND BEDDING.

Modern improvement has given us iron bedsteads in lieu of

the old four-posters and the other varieties of wooden *bug pre-serves* of our fathers and grandfathers. Feather beds and the vermin-breeding straw *pailliasses* are fast succumbing to the French spring, wool and horse-hair mattresses.* Turn and beat your mattresses every day with a stick of moderate thick-ness, which will prevent an accumulation of dust, and keep their surfaces even. They should be carded, and thoroughly cleaned at least once in two years.

CURTAINS.

All you require is a head curtain to your bed, just large enough to shield you from draft from the door or window. It is obviously very unwholesome to sleep in an air-tight closet of six feet by three, which many do in their four-posters and tents, when comfortably tucked up with heavy blankets and quilts and voluminous closely-drawn curtains, very often carefully pinned together. Depend upon it the more pure air you can inhale during sleep the better.†

In summer, the window should be left open (at the top if possible) about a couple of inches. No bedroom should be without a green or blue blind or curtain to the window (it need not interfere with the pretty white dimity or chintz draperies we love to see in the country, as it may take the place of the usual sun-blind), for nothing weakens the sight so much as a glare of light on the eyes during sleep.

BED-ROOM FURNITURE.

Do not crowd together too many chairs, tables, chests of drawers, or boxes; and be very careful not to make a store-room, or, as they call it in Yorkshire, a "*siding oop*" hiding-place for boxes, bundles, &c. &c., *under* the bed, where, by the

---

* Open and examine an old mattress or feather bed, and you'll be astonished! The accumulation of dust, &c. &c. &c., after fifty or sixty years' constant service (for nine-tenths of both are heirlooms, or brokers' bar-gains), is so great, that it seems almost a miracle, inhaling as we necessarily must, during the hours of sleep, the vapours arising from the putrescent matter which has been so long collecting, and is nightly fused by the heat of our bodies, that we are ever free from illness. The well-known close, musty, fusty, stifling odour of a bedroom before the windows are opened in the morning may always be traced to the bedstead and bedding.

† It has been proved that a canary hung in its cage during the night within the area of a bed so closed has been found dead in the morning, the breath of the sleeper having exhausted the oxygen.

way, there should be no carpet—the bare boards, which should be often well scrubbed, will be found much more healthful. A bed-room should never be carpeted all over : slips round the bed are quite sufficient.

WASHING UTENSILS.

No bed-chamber should be considered furnished without a large tin saucer-like bath (a very large and good one can be had at any ironmongers for ten or twelve shillings), and its comfort when one stands in it and squeezes a sponge (filled from the washhand basin) over one's shoulders just after getting out of bed must be tried to be appreciated. No splash to wipe up on the floor—no trouble to keep in order. A towel-horse, and rough—but not *too* rough—towels (the make-believe Baden-Baden ones are nutmeg-graters), good yellow soap (Brown Windsor, Honey, and the whole tribe of scented emollients, are more or less irritating and injurious to the cuticle) plenty of

COLD WATER.

Mind, PLENTY, in a basin large enough to allow the face to be plunged into it after the soaping. What the old country housewives call " cat-licking" in a teacupfull of warm water, and a damask towel, is not only a dirty practice, but greatly tends to the production of a sallow complexion and premature wrinkles.

CARE OF THE TEETH.

Do not let your brushes be too hard, as they are likely to irritate the gums and injure the enamel. Avoid also too frequent use of tooth-powder, and be very cautious what kind you buy, as many are prepared with destructive acids. Those who brush their teeth carefully and thoroughly with tepid water and a soft brush (cold water should never be used, for it chills and injures the nerves) have no occasion to use powder. Should any little incrustation (*tartar*) appear on the sides or at the back of the teeth, which illness and very often the constant eating of sweetmeats, fruit, and made dishes, containing acids, will cause, put a little magnesia on your brush, and after two or three applications it will remove it.

While treating on the care of the teeth, which is a subject of the highest importance to those who have young families, and in fact every one who wishes to preserve them, I beg to remind my readers that as the period generally occupied by sleep is calculated to be about (at the least) six hours out of the twenty-four,* it would greatly promote the healthful maintenance of the priceless pearls whose loss or decay so greatly influences our appearance and our comfort, if we were to *establish a habit* of carefully cleaning them with a soft brush before going to bed. The small particles of food clogging the gums impede circulation, generate tartar and caries, and affect the breath. Think of an amalgamation of cheese, flesh, sweetmeats, fruit, &c. &c., in a state of decomposition, remaining wedged between our teeth for six or seven hours; yet how few ever take the trouble to attend to this most certain cause of tooth-ache, discoloration, and decay, entailing the miseries of scaling, plugging, extraction, and the crowning horror—FALSE TEETH!

FURNISHING OF SITTING-ROOMS.

The sitting-room, like the bed-room, should not be over furnished, the fewer knick-knacks and inferior engravings the

---

* There are many opinions about how much, or rather how little sleep is best for us. The advocates of early rising say " six hours are enough for any one if commenced before midnight;" on the other side, there are many hands uplifted for eight, and even ten hours, and there is an old country proverb which says—

"Nature for sleep five hours requires,
Custom takes seven,
Idleness nine desires,
And wickedness eleven."

The advocates for long rest argue that the time taken from seven or eight hours' sleep out of each twenty-four, is *time not gained*, but *time more than lost*. We cannot cheat ourselves, we cannot cheat nature; a certain amount of food is necessary to a healthful body, and if less than that amount be furnished, decay commences at once. It is the same with sleep; and any one who persists in allowing himself less than nature requires, will only hasten his arrival at the mad-house or the grave. The great Duke of Wellington's rule was to go to bed as early as possible, dismiss all thoughts, and rise at his first waking, no matter the hour; on the principle that nature was satisfied, and her functions were prepared for the labours of the day. This cannot in all cases be acted upon, for our domestic arrangements would be disturbed by the master or the mistress making their appearance in the breakfast room before the servants had arranged it; but it is worth bearing in mind, and will be found more beneficial than second sleep, which often engenders headache, and gradually leads to sluggishness. Old people (though by a strange contradiction they are given to rise early) require much more sleep than the young.

better; but I would recommend the cultivation of a few geraniums, monthly roses, myrtles, hyacinths, &c. These greatly tend to enliven the room, while they form pretty screens for the windows. I now come to

THE KITCHEN AND ITS FURNITURE.

This is the stronghold of the housewife, and a *comprehensive* attention to its means and appliances should be her first care; for when the kitchen shows symptoms of short-comings, the whole economy of the house is deranged. The efforts of the best of workmen are valueless without good tools; therefore, as a soldier looks to his arms, look to your kitchen furniture.

In large establishments, where "money is no object," the modern means and appliances of steam ranges, hot plates, and charcoal stoves, of course afford greater facilities for producing large dinners than the simple old-fashioned range, with its oven and boiler; but, as we are to suppose our young couple cannot afford to feast their friends, we will confine ourselves to the homely kitchen.

KITCHEN FIREPLACES.

One of the greatest comforts of the cook is to have the fireplace situated in a good light; but it is strange how little this very essential point is thought of by architects when they plan their chimneys, the kitchen fireplace being very often stuck into a dark corner, thereby obliging the cook to pursue her vocation by candle or gas-light. It is always easy, if the sun should now and then be too strong for the fire, to shut it out with a screen. We understand, then, that there is a good range, with an oven and boiler.

HOW AND WHEN COALS SHOULD BE BOUGHT, WITH A GLANCE AT COKE AND WOOD.

Buy as large a quantity from an old-established merchant as your purse can afford, in the months of June and July, when they are cheaper than during the winter season. Remember, if you buy them by the hundred from a small dealer, you will pay at least five-and-twenty per cent. more. A small quantity of coke is useful to assist in making a clear fire in the kitchen; but never use it in sitting or bed-rooms, for its vapour is unwholesome. Chunks of wood may often be purchased cheap, and they will give a cheerfulness to your fire on long winter evenings, and remind you at Christmas of the Yule-logs of our ancestors. Remember, however, that the constant use of wood is very injurious to the eyes, as it produces inflammation of the lids, and gradually weakens the sight. In many parts of the continent, where wood alone is burnt, red eyes are the rule, and not the exception. Now for your

FRYING-PANS.

A frying-pan stands first on the list of essentials for house-keeping. The young lady whose marriage portion consisted but of one, and a cradle, had by no means a bad idea of the articles most likely to be wanted in her new condition. The frying-pan is perhaps the most useful, though often the worst used, implement in the kitchen. Let it be large and well tinned; if it be small, it will not serve for general purposes, and in *all* cases requires greater care lest the articles cooked in it burn,* &c. &c. Before frying fish, dry your pan carefully, then put a table spoonful of salt in it, set it on the fire, and with a clean cloth rub it round for two or three minutes ; then throw out the salt, and put in your fat, oil, or dripping, which must be of a sufficient quantity to *swim* the fish.

THE GRIDIRON.

A common iron one is the next essential, and will serve for everything you have occasion to broil ; the patent ones, with enamelled channels in the bars and a reservoir for the fat, are mistakes, as they keep the meat too far from the fire, and when the enamel burns off—which it is certain to do in a very short time—burning and scoring the chop or steak naturally follow. Soyer recommends an assistant made of double iron wire, to hang on the bars before the fire ; this is certainly occasionally useful, but experience has proved that it is very apt to harden the meat, as in the progress of cooking all the juices, instead of being spread over a flat surface, are, from the upright position, drained from it.

* If you can afford it, have three pans. Keep the largest for fish only. for clean it as carefully and thoroughly as you can, it will flavour whatever you fry immediately after it has been used for soles, &c.; a middle size for meat, potatoes, &c.; and a small one for pancakes and fritters.

TEA-KETTLES.

A large iron one for the kitchen, and another of block-tin for the parlour (don't aspire to copper yet), and remember the good old grandmother's fashion of putting a marble in both to prevent the bottom and sides from furring.

SAUCEPANS.

You will require a dozen of different sizes, of iron and block-tin—avoid common tin and copper, and never buy them second-hand—a tin fish-kettle, and a large iron black pot, which you can keep continually on the hob, to boil anything and everything, from soup or a pudding, to a ham, a leg of mutton, or a piece of salt beef. This black pot is the brightest gem in the poor man's kitchen all over the continent of Europe.

TEA AND COFFEE POTS.

A metal pot (a very handsome Sheffield plated one, with silver edges, can be had at a moderate cost), from its retention of the heat, makes the best tea; as a cheap and nearly as good substitute for this, Britannia metal may be used, but earthenware has the double advantage of being still cheaper and of being more easily kept clean. The coffee-pot should be large and made of block-tin. The proper use of this will be explained further on. Biggins, Percolators, &c. &c., are fantastic delusions.

KNIVES AND FORKS AND SPOONS.

Have a good number of large and small knives (good Sheffield plated forks and spoons will do very well until you can afford to get silver), a large carving knife and steel fork with a guard for the parlour. By the way, never cut bread and butter, or attempt to carve anything, with a *small* knife, for it is not only dangerous, but from having little purchase in the hand, makes the operation tedious. Look into the windows of the cooks' shops, and notice the magnitude of their carvers.* A sharp-pointed knife or two for trimming meat, &c., in the kitchen, an iron ladle, with a long handle, to baste the roast, a bottle-jack, which can be hung on a bracket from the mantel-

---

* It is said that the celebrated *artiste* who was wont to cut ham at Vauxhall as thin as gold leaf, used a knife of such Brobdignag proportions that Grimaldi used to borrow it for the pantomimes.

piece or fixed in a tin screen (which should have a moveable dripping-pan), a sieve, a tin cullender, a funnel, a paste-board, a chopping-board, a dredging-box, a rolling-pin, a bread and nutmeg-grater, a dozen iron skewers, a Dutch or American oven, a wire toaster to hang on the bars before the fire, to toast bread, bacon, &c., a toasting-fork, an iron footman, a cinder-sifter, dish-covers, a wire cover to keep the flies from the meat, &c., and then you have almost everything you require to begin your culinary campaign. Now, recollect that " THE CAR-DINAL VIRTUES OF COOKERY ARE CLEANLINESS, FRUGALITY, NOURISHMENT, AND PALATABLENESS ;" let them preside over all your labours ; then, if you KEEP EVERYTHING IN ITS PROPER PLACE and USE EVERYTHING FOR ITS PROPER PUR-POSE, you will be half way on your road to become an accom-plished cook.

GOLDEN RULES FOR THE KITCHEN.

Never use any kind of utensil without being certain that it is *quite clean.* After you have used your frying-pans, sauce-pans, &c. &c., take the earliest opportunity of thoroughly washing them, and rubbing them dry with a clean cloth, pre-vious to putting them away in their *proper places* (which must be dry and handy to the fireplace).

Take care that your saucepan lids fit closely, and that they too are perfectly clean. If you are not attentive to this, the strength of your soups and stews will be lost by evapora-tion.

Be careful always to use earthenware vessels for putting aside gravies, soups, &c. Many persons have been poisoned by the carelessness of ignorant servants in using metal pots and pans which contained verdigris, caused by the action of the vegetable acids in the soups upon the metal.

Never cram a large piece of meat or fish into a small pot or kettle ; and on the other hand, never drown a small piece in a large one.

Regulate the force of your fire according to the work it has to perform. Coal is expensive, and a great deal is wasted by inexperienced or careless cooks, who imagine that nothing can be done without a " roaring fire."

Make yourself quite secure from windfalls of soot and from the risk of setting the chimney on fire, by having the sweeps every three months, and clearing the mouth of the chimney *every morning* with a long-handled birchbroom.

Do nothing by the "rule of thumb;" measure and weigh the articles you are directed to use in the receipts, so that you get the proper proportions, which is often of the utmost consequence to the flavour and palatableness of the dish.

Never be without a clock or watch in the kitchen to be *certain* of the time your joints, &c. &c., should roast, boil, bake, or stew. No *good cook* ever guesses her time, or trusts to her hand for weights, quantities,* &c. &c.

Let the cloth be laid and the table prepared at least half an hour before your dinner is ready, for, should this very important rule be neglected, all your labours in the kitchen will be in vain, as everything is more or less spoiled by being delayed in its serving up. Husbands should remember this, and always be home punctually to their time, or—the gentlest of wives cannot be silent on such a subject.

The furnishing of the kitchen being complete, I will now show the best methods of putting each article to its proper use; but as a first principle remember IT IS IMPOSSIBLE TO COOK WELL WITHOUT CONCENTRATING YOUR THOUGHTS ON YOUR WORK, AND GIVING IT CONSTANT AND PATIENT ATTENTION. Without this you will often have to lament over failures in the shape of over or under-done meat, burnt stews and gravies, spoiled vegetables and fish, heavy bread, and indigestible pies and puddings.

Never say "NEVER MIND," or "THAT WILL DO." Depend upon it, those who use these expressions are careless, ignorant persons, who always mean exactly the reverse. When a cook, through stupidity or idleness, has set fire to the chimney, or suffered her stews or joints to burn, she may grin, and say, "*Never mind*, it's a misfortune," and try to persuade herself that it *couldn't* be helped; but all the while she says to herself, "Oh, I wish it hadn't happened! how *could* I be so careless?" &c. &c.

---

* Doctor Kitchener says, "It is impossible to cook from the obscure directions of the old cookery-books. Who, for instance, can tell exactly what is meant by ' a bit of this, a handful of that, a pinch of t'other, a sprinkle of salt, a dust of flour, a shake of pepper, a squeeze of lemon, or a dash of vinegar?' "

Do not, to save yourself a little trouble, " make shift" with the first thing that comes to hand. A moment's reflection will tell you that A THING WHICH " WILL DO" CANNOT BE EXPECTED TO BE AS SERVICEABLE AS THE PROPERLY MADE AND SPECIALLY ADAPTED THING IT REPRESENTS.

BOILING.

Although this may appear to be the most primitive mode of cooking, it is nevertheless a fact, that as it requires the aid of fire-proof vessels of earth or metal, its use dates long after roasting, baking, or broiling. Frying is comparatively a modern invention.

GENERAL INSTRUCTIONS FOR BOILING.

Begin with a good fire and clean utensils, as before observed, and regulate the force of your fire by the size and weight of the joint you may have to cook. It is obvious that a small piece of fish does not require the same amount of fuel as a leg of mutton; but many make no difference.

Never let your saucepans boil at a gallop, but keep them at a steady simmer.

When your fire is well burnt up and ready for its work, and *not till then*, begin your operations. Select a saucepan or pot suited to the dimensions of the article to be cooked, which must be well covered, though not drowned, with *cold* water;* place it on the fire, and watch it until it boils; then skim it carefully, or the scum will break and stick to the meat. After skimming, put in half a teacupfull of cold water, which will throw the re-mainder of the scum to the top, which you must also carefully remove; then look to your clock or watch, and TIME YOUR MEAT, &c. FROM THE MOMENT OF BOILING. How long each joint, &c., will require depends in a great measure on the season of the year and the description of the article to be cooked.

Joints of meat in summer require twenty minutes boiling to each pound; in winter, if they are frozen, they must be thawed with warm water before being put into the pot; they will take

---

* Liebig recommends that the article to be cooked should be put into the pot when the water is *boiling*, as it keeps in the juices by rapidly coagulating them on the surface; but experience has proved that this process renders the meat tough.

five-and-twenty minutes. Salted meat at all times requires twenty-five minutes to each pound.

Observe that a thick solid joint, like a leg of mutton or pork, requires more time than a thinner piece of meat of the same weight, from the larger surface of the latter being sooner acted upon by the heat.

A large whole fish, such as a salmon or turbot, of ten or twelve pounds, put into *cold* water, requires twenty-five minutes to half an hour from the moment it boils.

Pieces of salmon and turbot, weighing about two or three pounds, should be put into *boiling water* with a little salt, and be allowed half an hour.

Mackerel, trout, haddock, soles, and plaice, put into boiling water, require only ten minutes.

Half a cod, weighing four or five pounds, put into boiling water, will take from twenty to five-and-twenty minutes.

Middling-sized lobsters and crabs, put into boiling water, will take from ten minutes to a quarter of an hour; large ones from twenty to five-and-twenty minutes.

Crimped skate, thrown into boiling water, only requires to boil up to be done. *Note.*—All crimped fish, from presenting so many surfaces to the action of the heat, requires but half the time that is otherwise allowed.

Shrimps and prawns thrown into boiling water (without any salt) have but to boil up to be done. To give them the brown colour, stir them in the pot with a red-hot iron (the kitchen poker is generally used), strain them, and throw a handful of salt over them.

Large fowls or Turkeys must be put into *cold* water with their *breasts downwards,* and be gradually (in about an hour) brought to the boil, after which they will require from twenty to five and-twenty minutes gentle simmering to be finished.

Small fowls take about half an hour to get to the boil, and a quarter of an hour to simmer.

STEWING.

As the action of the fire in this process requires to be spread over a *broad* surface, the pans should be shallow, with closely fitting covers; for if there be the slightest vent, the juices of the meat will escape in steam.

PREPARATORY BROWNING.*

Let the article you wish to stew be first slightly browned in the pan with a small quantity of butter (just enough to keep it from burning), then cover it with stock gravy (which I will by and by tell you how to make), the exact quantity of which must depend on the weight of the meat, &c.; but as a general rule, you cannot err in allowing a small teacupful to a pound. As in the case of boiling, the size of the pan should correspond with that of the article to be cooked. After you have browned your meat, pursue the same course with your vegetables, which of course must be cut into small pieces.

If you have no *stock*, after the preparatory browning, take out the meat, &c., put half a teacupful of hot water into the pan, set it on the fire, and let it simmer for a minute or two, shake the pan round (to mix the water with the gravy made by the browning), then put in the meat, &c., again, and proceed with your stewing.

The time required for a rump-steak or veal cutlet, weighing about two pounds, is about two hours. Thick pieces of meat will take from four to five hours. Bullocks' kidneys (which should be sliced) require no less than *twelve* hours.

No skimming is necessary in stewing; but, when finished, the fat which will rise to the top of the gravy must be carefully removed with a thin spoon.

ROASTING.

So important is this branch of cookery, that Brillat Savarin says, "You may be *made* a *cook*, but you must be *born* a

---

* This "good thought" is attributed to Carême (the ancestor of the Carême of our time), *chef* to Leo X., and like lithography and many other "great inventions," owes its existence to accident. He had entrusted the preparation of a stew to one of his numerous pupils, who from stupidity or carelessness, put the meat in the pan *without the gravy*, and set it on the fire; the fat supplying the place of butter, it was half fried before he discovered his error. Horror-struck, and fearing the anger of the great *chef*, he hastily threw in the gravy, and hoped the fault would not be discovered ; but Carême on supervising the *plat*, observing its extraordinary colour, tasted it in alarm lest any poisonous ingredient should have accidentally slipped into the pan, and liking the flavour, he questioned the trembling cook, and after repeating the experiment, adopted the process, it is needless to say with what *palate*-felt satisfaction to the whole of the civilized world.

roaster." As in boiling, you must have your fire quite ready and regulated in its force by the size and weight of your joint, *before you put it down.*

Hang your bottle-jack (if it be not fixed in a tin screen) *securely* on its nail or bracket in the centre of your mantelpiece, place your dripping-pan exactly under the spot where the fat falls; if you put it *close* to the fire it will catch the dust and cinders.

HOW TO MAKE UP A FIRE.

Let the centre be solid with large lumps of coal, well ignited (which they will be if put on half an hour before you begin your work); small pieces, mixed with a little coke, will do for the sides, and wetted cinders should be thrown on the top.

When you have fastened the hook in your joint, and tried the length of the string required to bring it into its proper position, stir your fire carefully, brush away the dust and flaming coals from the bars, and put down your joint, and you will have nothing to do but watch that it does not stand still and burn. Basting it frequently with a long-handled spoon is also essential, as it prevents the surface from growing too dry. THE GREAT SECRET OF GOOD ROASTING IS BASTING. Many persons flour the meat before putting it down; but this is an error, as by hindering the escape of the fat, the skin is very apt to be burnt, and the crispness of the meat destroyed.

TIME REQUIRED FOR ROASTING.

This, as in boiling, entirely depends on the size and weight of the joint or fowl, and the season of the year; but a quarter of an hour to each pound will not be too little for those who like their meat with the gravy in it.

A moderate sized fowl will take about an hour.

Remember that in roasting, as in every other branch of cookery, NOTHING IS DONE WELL WHICH IS DONE IN A HURRY. Particularly attend to this maxim; for by putting the meat too close to the fire at first the outside will not only be scorched, but by the too sudden setting of the juice (osmazome), it becomes hard and unpleasantly flavoured; therefore, DO NOT PUT YOUR MEAT TOO CLOSE TO THE FIRE, advance it gradually, so that every part may be slowly influenced by the heat.

It is better to scrape than wash your joints, &c., before putting them down, for water soddens the fibre and destroys the flavour of the meat.

After being well scraped and wiped with a clean dry cloth, the joint should be rubbed with a little salt, which assists the fire in drawing forth and distributing the juices.

BE CAREFUL IN STIRRING YOUR FIRE. If your fire should grow hollow, it will be necessary to stir it; but before doing so, take care to put back both the joint and the dripping-pan, to avoid the cinders and dust. The fire should be stirred when the meat is nearly done (which you will know by the steam rising from it), for the purpose of giving it a concluding browning, which cannot be effected unless the fire is bright and clear. Now is the moment, after well basting, to lightly dredge with a little flour; this (if you do not overdo it and make a paste) will slightly froth the joint and render it agreeable to the eye, which requires to be pleased almost as much as the palate.

GRAVY FOR ROAST MEAT.

When your joint is " done to a turn," dish it, and place it before the fire ; then carefully remove the fat from the dripping-pan, and pour the gravy into the *dish*, not over the meat, as is the custom of inexperienced cooks, who moreover, not content with this, ruthlessly drown it with a cupful of boiling water or highly-flavoured made gravy; this is a vulgar error, for *there is always a sufficient quantity of natural gravy in good meat to render the use of foreign sauces superfluous.*

If, however, the joint be small, and a large quantity of gravy be required, I recommend that *before* the meat is taken from the fire, the fat should be removed from the dripping-pan, a little simple stock gravy, made of a small piece of shin of beef (the shank if it be a leg of mutton), also a shalot and a little pepper and salt, stewed in a small saucepan, should be added to the natural gravy, and the joint *well basted* with it just before dredging. This, from long experience, I have found to be a far better plan than the old-fashioned one of soddening the meat with hot water, and destroying its flavour with catsup or acid sauces.

* Poultry, game, and veal, having but little juice, must be basted with fresh butter; or with clarified suet (for fowls, turkeys, &c.), to which may be added minced sweet herbs (for veal), and a little port wine (for hare and wild fowl); sucking pigs are often basted with cream.

Be careful, if you use a spit, to have it very clean, and run it through the centre of the joint, so that the action of the fire may be equal on all parts. Many use cradles for poultry and small joints, but as they make a mark wherever they touch, they are not generally liked. By the bottle-jack, with its tin screen and moveable dripping-pan, is the best method of roasting, as the meat can be attached to the hook by string and skewers, and the unsightly black mark caused by the insertion of a spit avoided.

There is another great disadvantage in roasting joints of meat with a spit; the wound it makes, by being passed through the centre, causes the juice to escape into the dripping-pan instead of being diffused through the meat. Spits are however very useful for game, poultry, sucking pigs, &c., as they can be passed through the bodies without touching the flesh.

BAKING.

Presuming that you use the oven of your range, take care about an hour before you put in your joint, &c., to make up a good fire in your grate, and clear the communicating passage to the oven. The force of the fire requisite to bring the oven to its proper temperature must, as in roasting and boiling, entirely depend on the articles you have to cook. The heat necessary for a large piece of meat would be too fierce for a fruit-pie, &c. &c.

YOU MUST BE INTIMATELY ACQUAINTED WITH YOUR OVEN BEFORE YOU CAN BAKE WELL WITH IT. For, so much depends on its construction, the position in which it is placed in regard to currents of air from windows, door, and chimney, and, which is very important, though seldom thought of, *the age and state of repair of the range.*

If it be an old servant, from work the plates of the oven have become thin, the heat is much sooner diffused than when it is new; besides, it often happens in the former case that the communicating passage and the door have, from constant use, ceased to be air-tight.

Let then one of your first steps in kitchen business be to test the capabilities of your oven, for it is only by being quite conversant with all its faults and virtues that you can properly use it.

Put your meat in a deep earthenware or tin dish, on a three-legged wire stand, with potatoes or a Yorkshire pudding under it, and place it in the centre of the oven, so that the heat may be equal on all sides, excepting that next to the fire.

To prevent the *fire* side from being done too quickly, you must occasionally turn your dish (all good ovens have a wheel trivet for this purpose), taking care to give all sides their share of the "post of honour," of facing the hottest fire.

A piece of meat weighing about six pounds will take nearly two hours, and a good sized meat pie about an hour.

Fruit pies, rice, and milk puddings should *always* be put into a brisk oven, and be turned every ten minutes, for the light crust is very apt to burn on the *fire* side. Allow them an hour.

BROILING.

Let your fire be clear and brisk, and your gridiron scrupulously clean in *every* part. Set it on the fire for a minute or two, to get warm, wipe it carefully with a clean dry cloth, then rub the bars with a piece of mutton or beef suet (to prevent the meat from sticking to them), set it on the fire again, and place the article you have to cook upon it, taking care, if it be a chop or steak, to let the fat end be in front; the gridiron should also have a slight inclination to the front of the grate, to prevent the fat from falling into the fire and making a smoke. You cannot turn the meat too often, for which purpose use a pair of tongs; to stick a fork into the flesh would cause the gravy to escape and destroy the succulence and flavour. Do not, for the same reason, sprinkle your chops and steaks with salt while they are on the fire.

The time required depends both upon the fire and the article to be cooked. A chop or a steak with the gravy in it will be done in about ten minutes or a quarter of an hour; but to eat these old English delicacies cooked to perfection you must go to the City chop-houses: there it is the custom to choose the meat that strikes your fancy, *and see it broiled* while you skim the newspaper and munch a hunk of bread.

Epicures from all parts of the town may be seen, even in the dog days, braving the furnace, which is but a few yards from them. So alluring are *the pleasures of the table* that (as in the case of Louis XVI. of France, who was captured at Varennes through stopping at Sainte Menehould to taste its celebrated pigs' trotters) fortune, life, and liberty, have often been risked for the gratification of the stomach.　Indeed it is astonishing, when we call to mind the uncomfortable, out-of-the-way, and often dirty places, to which the refined and wealthy resort in the pursuit of a dinner or a supper, or even a dish peculiarly well cooked and served.　Quin the actor travelled all the way to Plymouth to eat a " John Dory."　George IV is said to have dined at Williams' boiled beef house in the Old Bailey.　The great Napoleon visited Marseilles to test the merits of the famous *Bouillabaisse*.　All the gourmands of Paris some few years ago deserted Les Trois Frères Provençaux and Véry to flock to a small restaurateur's at Batignoles to feast on the *Mayonnaise d'Homard* of le Père Lathuile.

In the Tom and Jerry days, the chops and steaks, baked potatoes, and Welsh rarebits of the Coal Hole, the Cider Cellar, and Offley's, the tripe and onions of the Cadgers' hostelrie in St. Giles's, and the leg of mutton and trimmings at the sailor's rendezvous in Wapping, were patronized by the fashionable notorieties with the same gusto as at the present time, when their sons forsake the delicate *cuisine* of their clubs for " fish dinners " at Billingsgate, the turbot and saddle of mutton at Simpson's, the grilled chickens and devilled kidneys at Evans's, the Irish stew and pale ale of the Haymarket night-houses, and the sherry-cobblers and mint juleps of the American spirit stores.

I now come to perhaps the most important practical point of the family " Dinner Question."

FRYING.

The process is so simple, and its application so handy, that everybody can effect it, and almost everything can be cooked with it; but with all its primitive advantages, the proper use and management of the frying-pan is but little understood in this country, and its capabilities are often too indiscriminately tested.

The French are far before us in this matter.　Their pans are much deeper than ours (being in fact iron fish-kettles), and the quantity of oil and fat they use, by at once setting the juices of the fish or meat they immerse in it, preserves its nourishing properties, which by our process of cooking one side at a time escape into the pan.

The French method has besides the great advantage of sending fish, cutlets, &c., to table with a much better colour. I will, however, by offering a few hints on the management of the English frying-pan, endeavour to show how a careful and intelligent cook can overcome its natural difficulties.

In the first place, as a matter of course, the pan must be thoroughly clean and the tinning perfect; next, be careful never to use any oil, butter, lard, suet, or dripping, but what is quite clean, fresh, and free from salt.

Anything stale or having a bad odour spoils the flavour, and salt prevents browning.

Olive oil is the best medium for delicate French cookery; but for general purposes, especially for fish, clean fresh lard or clarified butter does almost as well: but when you use butter you must be very careful, for it is apt to burn.

Clarified mutton or beef suet, and good clean dripping, are equally available.

As frying is merely *boiling in fat* instead of water, it is essential that whatever kind of grease you use should be very hot before you put in your fish, cutlets, &c. The usual mode of testing the temperature is to throw a small piece of bread into the pan: if it be immediately crisped and browned, the fat is ready for its work; but if it burns the bread, or but slightly tinges it, you may be certain it is either too hot or not sufficiently heated, both conditions being fatal to good cookery.

Now, before I go any farther into the *practice,* I think it will not be amiss to say something on the

PHILOSOPHY OF THE CULINARY ART.

In illustration of which I cannot do better than quote a very remarkable paper in the *Encyclo. Brit. Edin.,* vol. iv. p. 244, article " Food."

To understand the *theory of cookery,* we must attend to the action of ·heat upon the various constituents of alimentary substances as applied directly and indirectly through the medium of some fluid. In the process of roasting and boiling, the chief constituents of animal substances undergo the following changes—

Fibrine is corrugated, the *albumen* is coagulated, the *gelatine* and *osma-zome* rendered more soluble in water, the *fat* liquified, and the *water* evaporated.

If the heat exceed a certain degree, the surface becomes first brown, and then scorched. In consequence of these changes the muscular fibre becomes opaque, shorter, firmer, and drier; the tendons less opaque, softer, and gluey; the fat is either melted out or rendered semi-transparent; the albumen is coagulated and separated; and they dissolve gelatine and osmazome; lastly, and what is the most important change, and the immediate object of all cookery, the meat loses the vapid nauseous smell and taste peculiar to its raw state, and becomes savoury and grateful.

Heat applied through the intervention of boiling oil or melted fat, as in frying, produces nearly the same changes; as the heat is sufficient to evaporate the water, and induce a degree of scorching. But when water is the medium through which heat is applied, as in boiling, stewing, and baking, the effects are somewhat different, as the heat never exceeds 212°, which is not sufficient to commence the process of browning or decomposition, and the soluble constituents are removed by being dissolved in water, forming soup or broth; or if the direct contact of the water be prevented, they are dissolved in the juices of the meat, and separate in the form of gravy.

To resume. The fire must be clear and strong; for to fry *well* is to do it rapidly; to *simmer* anything by a small slow fire is to spoil it.

Your fish being properly prepared (when I come to my Receipts I will give you full instructions for *egging, bread-crumbing, larding,* &c. &c.), put them carefully into the pan, taking care that there is on all occasions fat enough completely to cover, or, as it is technically termed, "swim" them; then with *a good light* and *undivided attention* watch your pan, for so uncertain and delicate is the process of frying, that if you take your eye off it for an instant, the "fat may be in the fire," or your fish, &c., may burn and be spoiled.

Having now, I trust, fully and clearly, although briefly, explained everything essential for the proper methods of Boiling, Stewing, Roasting, Broiling, Baking, and Frying, I will here offer a few observations on the reasons why our English mode of cookery has so long remained without improvement, and our dinners, alike in our families and our parties, are so undeniably inferior to corresponding entertainments on the continent.

In the first place, it has been truly said that one great impediment to culinary progress among us is to be found in the excellence of the raw material. We possess in abundance the finest kinds of meat, fish, and vegetables, and the consequence is that we do not think it necessary to heighten their flavour by any extraneous aid. On the continent, however, where nature has not proved so bountiful, necessity has been the mother of invention, and the result is seen in a variety of ingeniously concocted sauces which would render even horseflesh palatable.*

The next equally great mistake is the self-sufficient pride of the mistress of a house, who, forgetting the old saw of " a *little* learning is a dangerous thing," hermetically closes up her eyes and ears, and resolutely continues the old traditional " rules of thumb." Servants in the same manner will pertinaciously stick to their early training. " Well, ma'am," a cook is very apt to say, when her mistress ventures to suggest an improvement in her method of producing a dish, " your new-fangled style *may* be very good; but mine is the way I've been taught, and as it has always given the highest satisfaction in all the genteel families I have lived with, I'd rather be excused from altering it." Thus ignorance and vanity have continued from year to year to keep our kitchens " as they were," and as they ever will remain unless ladies of education and taste will, by giving their minds, and occasionally a small portion of their leisure time, to the practical elucidation of the *great question;* root out old prejudices and reform everything connected with the present hap-hazard system, in which " huge gory joints," " unpalatable soups," " fish boiled to jelly or fried black and swimming in grease," with gout and dyspepsia engendering " made dishes " and pastry, excite the ridicule of our foreign neighbours, many of whom still believe that all classes in England, excepting "*La grande aristocratie*," live upon nothing but half raw roast beef and steaks, plum pudding, and brandy " grogs."

But " to return to our muttons." Culinary reform is in the hands of the ladies : if they will determine to *qualify themselves* personally to superintend the operations of their kitchens, not only moderate housekeepers, but the possessors of large incomes who keep French *men* or professed English *women* cooks, will find it to their advantage to devote half an hour in the morning to regulating their bill of fare and consulting with their operatives on the general arrangement and production of their

---

* It is well known that at the cheap Parisian restaurants, great use is made of this equine beef, so abhorrent to English stomachs ; indeed it is *more* than suspected that half their *bif steks aux pommes, filets de bœuf,* soups, and ragouts owe their paternity to the denizens of the stable instead of the stall.

dinners.* To those who are not, as the newspaper advertise-
ments have it, "blessed with affluence," but are obliged to *do*
for themselves or manage with one servant, the *magical power
of culinary knowledge* will appear in the economical and skilful
employment of their limited means in procuring their husbands
and families superior home comforts and even luxuries, when
ignorance and unthriftiness would cause them, as is too often
the case, particularly in the houses of the working class, to
waste and spoil the good and wholesome meat, fish, poultry, or
vegetables, their Saturday-night cheap marketing has placed at
the mercy of their dilapidated and dirty kitchen furniture, and
their blind "rule of thumb" notions of how the various articles
should be treated to make them palatable and nourishing.

I have now arrived at the portion of the present work which
may be considered its main point—the

RECEIPTS.

Although the remarks I have made on the properties of the
saucepan, the stewpan, the gridiron, the fryingpan, &c. &c., are
necessary for the foundation of my system of cookery, without
full and practical receipts for the dishes to be produced, my
labours would be in vain. I therefore beg to submit the following few, but *personally tried and proved*

PLAIN RECEIPTS FOR PLAIN DISHES, IN WHICH ECONOMY IS BLENDED WITH PALATABLENESS.

I will by and bye say a word or two on *French Dishes* and
Dinner Giving, for those whose means permit them to entertain
their friends, but at present I will confine myself to the

---

* G. H. M., of Berkeley-street, who is good authority in this matter,
says:—" It requires a little education, but not more than any lady can
give to herself. It requires some practice, but not so much, if thought
accompanies it, as must grow upon you from the mere necessity of dining
more or less once a-day during nine months, or a year. It requires, above
all, imagination, or rather adaptation, but not nearly so much as every
lady exercises in her daily scientific discussions with her maid, or her
solitary and frequent reflections on dress. There is no reason why ladies
should not excel in this subject as well as in that of dress. That they do
not do so may, I think, be attributed to the fact that, first, other ladies do
not see the results and praise them so much; and secondly, that their dinner
parties come at intervals, whereas their dress comes before them every day
of their lives, and they will order anything for dinner or leave the whole
subject to the cook during the days when the family is alone."

KITCHENS OF HOUSEKEEPERS WITH SMALL INCOMES.

I have already shown you how to roast a leg of mutton, and broil a chop or steak; I will now instruct you in the best method of frying that great delicacy of country inns before the railroads sounded the " death knell " of the good old coaching times, a

VEAL CUTLET.

Let it be about half an inch in thickness; trim it carefully from hard skin and sinews, and remove also any small pieces of bone which may have stuck to the meat in the sawing, cut it into neat pieces of about three or four inches in diameter, then dip each piece in a soup-plate, in which the yolk and white of an egg are beaten up, then draw them through another soup-plate in which are some fine bread crumbs, taking care that every part be thoroughly covered with them ; then, after seeing that your fire is brisk and clear (you can do nothing if it be slow or flaring), and your pan in *working order* (you already know what I mean by that), put it on the fire with some thin slices of bacon (about the same number as those of veal), which you must fry briskly, and when done take out and place in your oven to be kept hot until the cutlet is cooked.

N.B.—If the bacon be tolerably fat, you will not require any more grease to fry the cutlet; but if it be lean, you must use a little good butter, for in either case the bottom of the pan must be well covered or the meat will be too brown, and perhaps burn.

Then with your slice put in the pieces of veal, and when they have been over the fire from three to four minutes, lift one of them carefully, and if it be *light brown* it is time to turn, which you must do, still with your slice, for to stick a fork into the meat (as in the case of the rump-steak) is to waste the juice. When the second side is light brown, dish up, and having previously mixed a small teaspoonful of flour with a small teacupful of stock (clear beef and veal broth kept in a jar for making good gravy for anything that may require it), or in its absence the like quantity of *cold* water, flavoured with a little mushroom or walnut catsup, pour it into the pan (of course you have removed the fat), shake it well over the fire until it boils, then pour it into the dish (*not over the meat*, for the reason I gave in my directions for dishing the leg of mutton), in which you have placed the pieces of veal in the centre, with the bacon round them. A "squeeze of a lemon" in the gravy gives it a pleasant flavour, and a little crisped parsley and a few thin slices of lemon, surmounting the bacon on the edge of the dish, and *your cutlet is cooked as near as possible to perfection.* But recollect that by some strange fatality a veal cutlet, or in fact anything you are frying, *always* burns if you turn your eyes from it for a single instant.

When you have mastered the veal cutlet, which I have placed first on the list of *Fritures* (fryings), for ladies to try on it their " 'prentice hands" before attempting a more delicate and difficult task ; for time-honoured as it is among us as one of our best English dishes, and every one who has a fryingpan can cook it, how very seldom, except in hotels, where it is still a staple and popular *entrée,* is it turned out in a creditable manner. It is either too thick and "knobbly," and fried in one piece, or partially burnt or sodden, with highly-flavoured gravy, thickened with flour into paste, or what is worse, swimming in a sea of melted butter. But with all its short-comings, its production is generally more satisfactory than that of *the great touchstone of the capabilities of a good plain cook,* as it is the highest triumph her fryingpan can achieve, a

FRIED SOLE.

This is the fatal dish that has driven hundreds of "well-to-do" husbands to dine at their clubs, and is looked upon by the working-man as analogous in its want of toothsomeness with the cold shoulder and sickly hash of washing days. Let me endeavour to show the wives of both conditions of housekeepers, who have hitherto by their want of knowledge in the preparation, and skill in the *pan*-ipulation, of this too-often spoiled homely dish, scared their liege lords from the domestic board, how, as Juliet says of her truant Romeo, to

"Lure the tassel-gentles back again."

Choose your fish (if possible) *yourself;* you will easily know if it be fresh (which it *must* be, or the best of cookery will be thrown away) by the edges of the mouth being " pinky" (they are white when stale), and the *fibre,* in kitchen parlance the *flesh,* being elastic. Take care, by the way, that you *have* the identical fish you choose, for fishmongers have been known occasionally to practise sleight of hand in the skinning ; beware also, if you buy a " pair," of having one fresh and the other stale—a trick too often played on the unwary.

PREPARATION.

After skinning, cutting off the tails and fins, and " *gutting*," which somewhat unpleasant operations are generally performed by the fishmonger, but I would advise you to effect them your-self *about an hour before you begin your cooking*, which will have the double advantage of keeping the " flesh " crisp and preventing the aforesaid sleight of hand, wash, and wipe your fish *quite* dry, with a *dry* clean cloth; then fold them in another cloth, equally clean and dry, dividing each with a fold, and place them aside until the time arrives for putting them in the pan.

Now cut out the crumb of a stale loaf (a penny one will be sufficient for " a pair" of moderate size*), put it in the centre of a fine clean towel, gather the corners in one hand (as you would when tying up a pudding), then with the other hand break up the bread and rub the pieces together (in the bag formed by the towel) until they are nearly reduced to powder. This you will find to be a cleaner and more expeditious method than grating, for the grater is seldom in *working order*, and does not do its work so evenly.

Put the crumbs into a shallow dish, and proceed to the next manœuvre, which is to beat up an egg (in the same way I have described for the veal cutlet), and the accessories are ready.

Your fire and pan being in *working order* (see cutlet direc-tions), unroll the cloth from your fish, give them a *slight sprinkle* of flour from the dredging box, to absorb any remain-ing moisture and form a foundation for the egg and bread crumbing, as painters size their canvas before they commence their colouring, then draw them (you may, if you prefer it, use

---

* Doctor Kitchener says, "When you want a great many bread crumbs, divide your loaf (which should be two days old) into three equal parts: take the middle or crumb piece, the top and bottom will do for table. *In the usual way of cutting the crust is wasted.*"

a paste brush) first through the beaten-up egg,* and then through the crumbs, taking care that every part be thoroughly covered with both. Then *half fill your pan* with the best Lucca oil, lard, or *sweet* beef dripping, and pray attend to the next most important piece of information.

THE GREAT SECRET OF FRYING SOLES WELL IS TO USE PLENTY OF FAT, *for if you do not have a full half inch of it above them when they are in the pan, they will either burn, be fried too brown, or be too greasy* †

Now take them by the heads and tails, and drop them carefully into the pan (you have been already told how to know if the fat is at the proper temperature), which shake to prevent sticking and burning. The *first* side will take about five minutes, and the *second* from three and a half to four ; but to make sure that all is going on well, you may now and then (after giving the pan a shake) lift the fish a little with your slice, to see if it be getting brown. When it is so (mind it must be *light* brown), it is time to turn, which you must do cleverly with your slice. Proceed in the same way with the second side, and then take up ; but before dishing, drain for a few minutes on a strainer, or a sheet of white blotting paper, then serve on a *hot* dish (with a strainer at the bottom).

---

* Of course you will use a *fork* for beating up the egg. I think it necessary to mention this for the benefit of *very young* housewives, many of whom I have known to use a knife or a spoon ; indeed, as may be seen by the following old country adage, such errors have often been run into :—

> " Beat with a knife
> Will cause sorrow and strife ;
> Beat with a spoon
> Will make heavy soon ;
> Beat with a fork
> Will make light as a cork."

For " frothing," or making cream for light puddings, you must whip up the egg with a whisk.

† As frying is *boiling in oil* instead of water, the culinary student will see that *by the fish being thoroughly covered with the fat, every portion of it is exposed at the same moment to the same action of the heat.* The albumen is *instantly* coagulated on the surfaces, which, with the egg and bread crumbs, forms a coating which prevents saturation. If, however, one side be left uncovered, the fat, by bubbling up and dashing over it in *small* quantities, sinks into the body of the fish, which is thus *gradually saturated*, and rendered so greasy that the flavour is destroyed, and its rankness is offensive to a delicate stomach.

Garnish with a sprig or two of crisped parsley,* and then you have your soles *dry, crisp, well coloured, delicately flavoured, and pleasing alike to the eye and the palate.*

Plain melted butter is the *best* sauce (for which see my receipt further on) ; but many prefer a more expensive one, like the tea at the cockney refreshment establishments at Gravesend, *made with shrimps* (for which also see my receipt).

Anchovy, Hervey, Worcester, or Reading sauces should be on the table to suit all tastes; but I would recommend, if you wish to have the sweet flavour of the fish, nothing but plain melted butter.

When you have dished up your fish, strain the fat you have fried it in, and put it aside in a jar, as it will serve several times (of course for nothing else but fish) ; but if you can afford it, have *fresh* material every time.

Very large soles should be cut into three or four pieces (before the egg and bread crumbing), or " filleted," which is effected by passing a sharp knife down the centre and the *inner* edge of the fins, and tearing the " flesh" from the bones. This is a French method, pursued in clubs and large establishments ; but for homely kitchens it will be found extravagant.

Plaice, flounders, eels, whitings, gudgeons, trout, small brill, fillets and cutlets of salmon, turbot, halibut, and cod, when fried, are cooked in the same manner as soles.

Mackerel, though generally boiled and served with a little fennel in melted butter, are very tasteful when split up the back, and broiled in the French fashion, with a small piece of cold butter and a little chopped parsley put on them when served. Eels (in pieces) are also very good when done on the gridiron.

Herrings and sprats should *always* be broiled.

Carp, pike, jack, mullet, and *river fish in general,* should be baked or stewed. *Eels* can be *stewed,* or *spitchcocked,* or dressed in the French fashion, *en matelotte.* The latter mode, as it requires numerous accessories, is expensive, but, as I wish

---

* Parsley is crisped by being taken out of cold water and thrown into the boiling fat for *half an instant,* after you have taken out your fish, which, as the old country housewives say; makes it

" As crisp as glass
And green as grass."

my book to contain receipts for dishes for "high days and holidays," as well as "working-days," I will give instructions for it hereafter; but I will first show you how to produce

STEWED EELS.

The first step to be taken is to *skin* the eels: now this is perhaps the most unpleasant task that falls to the lot of a cook; as the necessity for having them *quite* fresh requires that they should not be killed until a few minutes before they are to be dressed; and their tenacity of life is so great that it is very difficult for inexperienced hands to deprive them of it.

The following humane suggestion by Doctor Kitchener on this, to all housewives, most painful subject, will, I am certain, be read with great interest, and adopted by all *my* pupils:—

"*To kill eels instantly*, without the horrid torture of cutting and skinning them alive, pierce the spinal marrow, close to the back part of the skull, with a sharp pointed skewer: if this be done in the right place all motion will instantly cease."

Francatelli confirms this, and adds, "Then take a firm hold of the eel with a cloth in the left hand, and with the right proceed to detach the skin just below the gills with the point of a small knife; when there is a sufficient quantity of skin loosened, so as to gain a purchase, hold the head firmly with the left hand. and with a cloth in the right, force the skin to slide off the fish. Then cut off the head, make an incision about two inches in length at the vent, and the same at the neck, draw the gut, &c., trim away the fins, wash and thoroughly cleanse each fish, wipe them with a cloth, and then, after sprinkling them with salt, let them be in a dish for an hour or so previously to dressing them."

Returning to *my* directions,—After skinning, gutting, and thoroughly washing, cut into pieces of about three or four inches, place them in a stewpan with just water enough to cover them, stew *gently* for about five and twenty minutes, skim off the fat, then chop up three or four oysters, and throw them into the pan, mix two teaspoonfuls of flour with the oyster liquor, and add a little chopped parsley, which also throw into the pan; shake well round two or three times, and serve in a *hot* deep dish; flavour with a little salt and pepper, and grated or chopped lemon-peel; you may add for those who like the unfashionable, but very useful and cheap esculent, a small roasted onion minced very fine.

SPITCHCOCKED EELS.

This process consists of first lightly stewing and then broiling the eels instead of simply frying them. The preliminary preparation being precisely the same, viz., after you have skinned your fish (some recommend that the skin should not be taken off, but I have found the oil in it very apt to make the "*flesh*" rank), split them down the belly, and take out the bone, &c., wash them well, and cut them into pieces of three or four inches: then (here you *leave* the simple frying process), having put two ounces of butter in a stewpan, with a little minced parsley and thyme, a blade of mace, a leaf or two of sage, and a small shalot, chopped very fine. Having well egged and breadcrumbed your eels, put them in the pan, let them remain just long enough to set the coating with the butter and herbs on *both* sides, then put them on the gridiron (which of course is in *working order*), first rubbing the bars with a bit of suet to prevent the pieces from sticking, broil for a few minutes until *both* sides are *light* brown, garnish with crisped parsley, and serve with melted butter and anchovy sauce. If you would prefer a *sharp* sauce, see the directions given under that head.

EELS EN MATELOTTE.

This is a dish very often attempted, but for the want of a good and *intelligible* receipt is seldom well produced. In the French cookery books we read with dismay of " white *velouté* sauce," a " *roux*," an " *ambigu*," a " *suprême - grenadins*" " *blonde*," &c. &c., put into a " *bain marie*," with cray fish tails, the "*croustade*" to be garnished with a group of small " *quenelles*" of whiting, &c. &c., and with the best intentions, like one who feels for the door in a dark room, we frequently *knock our heads against the fireplace.*

The following plainly expressed and carefully composed receipt for this very delicate and savoury dish, will, I hope, be found useful:—Begin with half a pound of shin of beef, " score" it—that is, cut the piece nearly through in several places, so that by presenting several surfaces to the water, the juice may be sooner extracted; put it with a little salt into a stewpan with *cold* water, just enough to cover it; then slice a good sized onion, a small carrot, and half a turnip, and fry them, with an ounce of butter, light brown; put them into the stewpan with the beef, a blade of mace, and two bay leaves, and stew gently for four hours.

Now to make your force-meat balls. A couple of good fat oysters, half a teaspoonful of capers, a small piece of minced lemon-peel, the yolk of a hard-boiled egg, a small baked or roasted onion (this can be done by putting it before the fire in the tin of a cheese toaster), a sprig of parsley, a couple of button mushrooms, a sprig of dried marjoram, a couple of tablespoonfuls of bread crumbs, a small piece of cold veal or beef, raw ham or lean bacon, a " grate" or two of nutmeg, and a little cayenne—chop very fine; then beat up an egg, and mix all the above with it, taking care not to make the paste it will form *too* wet; roll into balls about the size of a small walnut, which roll in flour; put them in the oven to bake for ten minutes, and set them aside until your eels are ready to be dished.

When your beef is sufficiently stewed, take it out, and strain off the gravy; return the latter into the stewpan, and put your eels into it (they must be cut into pieces of about three inches), stew about twenty minutes; skim off the fat, and then put in your force-meat balls, with half a dozen *whole* button mushrooms, half a dozen small oysters, without their beards, and their liquor mixed with a teaspoonful of flour; stew five minutes more, then put two tablespoonfuls of port wine, a teaspoonful of essence of anchovy, and half a teaspoonful of soy, in the *dish;* do not put them in the stewpan, or you will injure your flavour; shake the dish round for the wine, &c., to mix, and turn the eels and their gravy into it; the pieces should be taken out of the pan with your slice, to prevent splashing the gravy; lightly sprinkle the whole surface with cayenne; garnish with a few pieces of fried eels, sprigs of crisped parsley; and there you have your *matelotte,* which, I am confident, you will find so good that you will not say of it, " ONE TRIAL WILL SUFFICE."

Now, while my hand is in for " holiday" dishes, I'll give you a receipt for one of my own invention, which I call

FILETS DE SOLE A LA TICKLETOOTH.

"*Fillet*" a good sized sole, making, by dividing each *fillet*, eight pieces, dredge these lightly with flour, put them in a *thin* cloth to dry, then put the head, fins, and bones (the *fillet* being taken from the centre of the fish, the shoulders and tail should be fried for garnishing) into a small stewpan with the beards of two or three oysters, two button mushrooms, a small roasted onion, two slices of carrot, a piece of lemon-peel, and a little salt, all chopped very fine.

Now put the *fillets*, which must be slightly egged, but not bread-crumbed, into another pan with an ounce of butter; fry them quickly light brown, then add the gravy (which of course has been strained ; stew a quarter of an hour, take off the fat, and add a few small force-meat balls, made in the same manner as for the *Eel Matelotte*.

Put into the *dish* just before you serve half a glass of Sherry or Madeira, and a teaspoonful of walnut or tomato catsup.

Garnish with the shoulders and tail (cut in small pieces) of the sole, gudgeons, or smelts, fried, and "diamonds" of spinach, either plainly boiled, or beaten up with a little butter or cream, and a teaspoonful of chopped capers.

This is simply a variety of the *matelotte* previously described, but it possesses an advantage from the sole being less rich than the eel, and its preparation is also less expensive and troublesome.

Nothing more need be said at present on *frying, broiling, baking*, or *stewing* fish, as you are now no doubt perfectly able to deal with all the "smaller fry ;" but, when I come by and bye to French cookery receipts, I may perhaps introduce you to a few more "holiday" extravagances. The general directions already given have shown you how to *boil* and to *time* accurately the various kinds of fish ; if you attend carefully to them, you need have no fear for the result of your experiments.

I now come to the dish which has so long been the terror of husbands, and is quoted by stomach-loving old bachelors as one of their most powerful reasons against venturing on matrimony.

HASHED MUTTON.

"Oh words of fear!
Unpleasing to the married ear."

What a vista of steam, soap-suds, and the soles of his old boots swimming in greasy hot water, rises to the mind's-eye of a poor *Paterfamilias* when the "partner of his bosom" an-

nounces to him that he must manage to-morrow with the
" hashed mutton !" and how many " artful wretches," suspecting
that they are to be trepanned into dining on this Spartan
black broth equivalent, have held a colloquy with their servant
after this fashion :—

MASTER OF THE HOUSE.—" Oh ! Mary (*affecting to ignore
the soap-suds, and the entrance of the washerwoman with
something very like a bottle concealed under her apron*).
By the bye, what is there for dinner to-day ?"

MARY.—" Dinner, sir ? (*innocently pretending ignorance*)
I think it's hashed mutton."

MASTER OF THE HOUSE.—" H'm. Oh ! tell your mistress
when she comes in, that I may possibly be detained in the city
to-day on business, and she is on no account to wait dinner for
me. (*Aside as he goes out :*) Ough ! hashed mutton again !
I'm sick of that nauseous mess. I'll drop down to Greenwich
with Jawkins, and try the whitebait."

Although such hashed-mutton-eluding excuses have become
almost as general as " severe indisposition," or " I'm obliged to
go to Manchester to settle that confounded law business" on the
Derby-day, I hope to show that by employing a little skill and
contrivance this hitherto unsavoury dish is capable of being
made one of the nicest and most nutritive that can be placed on
any *plain* table. But bear in mind that meat, or any other
alimentary substance which has already been cooked, does not
possess sufficient *osmazome* to make gravy, and that you must
supply the deficiency with fresh juices extracted from foreign
sources. Ignorance of this very obvious necessity for creating
succulency as the first principle is the cause of our dislike to
hashing ; re-cooking in *any way* being moreover not only
generally repulsive to the palate, but equally often devoid of
nourishment.

The French, our superiors in the theory and practice of the
culinary art, never attempt a *réchauffée* without especial observance of this principle. They first *restore* the juices of the
foundation they have to work upon, with *strong* stock, and
then proceed to obtain flavour and appearance. This is my plan
for preparing hashed mutton.

Put half a pound of shin of beef, scored as I have before
explained, into a stewpan with half a pint of cold water, and
any cold gravy that may be left from the first cooking ; simmer

gently two hours, then lightly brown in the frying-pan, a moderate sized onion, a small carrot, and half a turnip cut in thin slices. While the beef is stewing, cut the mutton from the bone in *neat* slices, about four inches square, and a quarter of an inch thick (taking care to trim off the gristle, burnt skin, and sinews); if it be underdone, so much the better, as it will have more natural juice; should, however, the joint have been *boiled*, you must lightly fry the slices with a little butter.

About an hour before you want to serve your dinner, strain the gravy from the beef and vegetables,* and put it in the stewpan, to which add the slices of mutton. Here, let me say, is a correction of one of the greatest errors in hashing—the usual method is to put the mutton into the pan about *five minutes before dishing !* thereby just giving it time to warm; the consequence is, by being merely *scalded* with the poor broth which has been obtained by stewing the bone with an onion and a large quantity of water, it is *sodden, tough, and totally flavourless !*

By *my* plan, the meat is gradually saturated with the good and strong gravy formed by the fresh beef and vegetables, imbibing their flavour of course, and rendered tender at the same time from the stewing.

When just ready to serve, carefully skim off *all* the fat, mix a teaspoonful of flour with a tablespoonful of the gravy, which you must put aside and save for the purpose at the time you strain it from the beef, and add them to the hash; put a tea-spoonful of mushroom catsup, and (if possible) two teaspoonfuls of port wine into the *dish*; sprinkle lightly the whole surface with cayenne pepper; garnish with thin triangular sippets of toasted bread; and *there you have your hashed mutton;* which I can confidently say, particularly if it be eaten with currant jelly, is *equal, if not superior, both in flavour and nourishment, to the general run of venison.*

MINCED VEAL.

This is another "family dish," which, from its natural insipidity, and unskilful treatment in cooking, bears even a

---

* The best way to extract the juice of the vegetables is to press them between two plates; but if you are catering for a family, I would recommend you to leave them untouched in the pan, taking out nothing but the beef, which will be stewed to rags.

worse character than hashed mutton. Let me endeavour to point out a method of rendering it as agreeable, if not as nutritious, as its fellow-sufferer in reputation.

Prepare a gravy with shin of beef and vegetables, as for hashed mutton; mince the veal very fine, taking out all the sinews, skin, and burnt pieces; put it in the pan with the gravy; stew gently three-quarters of an hour; skim carefully; then add half a dozen oysters, cut in quarters, a little of the stuffing left from the roast, a teaspoonful of flour mixed with the oyster liquor, and a "grate" of nutmeg; squeeze a lemon in the dish, and garnish with sippets of toasted bread.

Believing that the minute instructions I have given you for the preparation of the foregoing two "standing dishes" at all plain tables will be sufficient to guide you in re-cooking anything which should be done in the stewpan, I will here observe, that every kind of cold meat, particularly salted beef and roast pork, can be made very palatable by being fried with slices of onions, carrots, turnips, parsnips, &c., or à la "BUBBLE AND SQUEAK," with the cabbage or greens of the preceding day's dinner chopped up with a bit of butter, pepper, and salt, and a cold potato or two, mashed with a little milk; or, in what the old cookery books delight to say,

ANOTHER WAY WITH POTATOES A LA MAITRE D'HOTEL.

I once saw in a newspaper account of a civic banquet, "slices de cod broiled," and "saddle de mutton à la Wales," so I hope to be excused for mixing my French titles.

This very popular and tasteful vegetable *réchauffée* is effected by cutting already cooked potatoes into small pieces, and frying them with a little butter, black pepper, salt, and chopped parsley.

FRIED POTATOES,

Which the French do so well, and travelled English always associate with "*clumpy*" beef-steaks, cut from the under part of the sirloin, are prepared thus—cut some good sized raw potatoes into slices a "*little more*" than the eighth of an inch thick, dry them in a cloth, and put them into a *good quantity* of boiling lard or dripping, shake them well; in about three minutes turn them, fry the other side the same time, then take them out, strain them, and serve them round the dish.

All these accessories, particularly the fried potatoes, are of great use in *second* cookings, whether they wait on the frying-pan or the gridiron, and should therefore be looked upon by the thrifty housewife as her best elements for rendering " Banyan" or make-shift dinners agreeable.

To enumerate the many dishes which can be artistically, and at the same time satisfactorily, turned out from second-hand materials, would far exceed the limit of this work. I shall therefore confine myself to but two more examples, and pass to receipts for more important productions.

The first of my concluding "twice laid" or "warming-up" receipts is a very tasteful method of

RE-ROASTING.

It is simply to cut your cold beef, mutton, veal, or pork, into neat slices of about the third of an inch thick, and the whole length of the sirloin, rib, or whatever other part you may have to work upon, and place them in a dish, on a hanger in front of the fire, covering each slice with as much as possible of the gravy left from the first cooking, or should that be wanting, a little strong stock. Sprinkle lightly with cayenne, turn, and baste with the gravy until *thoroughly* hot, then serve immediately on a very hot dish. You can garnish with *fresh* fried or *à la maître d'hotel* potatoes, spinach, plain or beaten up, warmed-up greens or cabbage.

This, particularly if the cold meat be underdone, is a mode of *second* cooking by no means to be despised.

DEVILLING,

Or broiling with cayenne, is also a good expedient to coax the palate when you have *relics* of poultry or game. Fish can likewise be " devilled," or egged and fried with a small piece of butter and bread crumbs, mixed with a little dried thyme, marjoram, and *fresh* parsley crumbled and chopped very fine.

TOMATO SAUCE.

Which is made by skinning a ripe tomato, beating up the pulp, and stewing it, in a small pan, with half an ounce of butter, a little cayenne, and a small shalot, half an hour.*

---

* This sauce can also be made to be kept in bottles, and used in small quantities as anchovy, Reading, and other sauces, for flavouring ; for

Served in a butter-boat, mixed with a little vinegar, it will be found an excellent *sharp* sauce for cold meat, hashes, and devils of every description.

Here I conclude my instructions for *second cooking*, which have occupied more space than I intended at the outset of my work to devote to them, but feeling as I progressed that to *re*-dress the remnants of the preceding day's dinner with appetite-creating and stomach-satisfying results is a point of importance, I have made my information as minute and extensive as possible.

HARICOT MUTTON.

This dish is nothing more than mutton chops browned in the frying-pan, and then stewed in just water enough to cover them, with pieces of onion, carrot, and turnip (also browned), cut into dice and placed upon them, flavoured with mushroom or walnut catsup, tomato or Reading sauce, and served with a slice or two of pickled gherkins.

IRISH STEW.

Another variety of stewed mutton; but "although," as an Irishman observed, "it is the sister of the haricot, it's another individual, and must be differently educated to be pres*in*table; for, in the first place, the mutton's half beef, and in the next, the carrots and turnips are repealed for potatoes!"

The following is a receipt I obtained in Ireland, and repeated trials have proved it to be a "purty invintion."

Put a rump-steak into a good-sized stewpan, and cover it with slices of a Spanish onion, sprinkle with salt, then place on the onions a cutlet of mutton, with the bone taken out, or two or three not too fat chops; cover the mutton with another layer of onions, a sprinkle of salt, half-a-dozen black pepper corns, and *one* clove; barely cover with water, and stew *gently* two hours. In the mean time, peel half-a-dozen middling-sized *good mealy* potatoes, and boil them in a saucepan for *ten* minutes; then take them out, and (having previously removed every eye of fat from the pan) place them on the top of the

which purpose purchase in the months of August or September a quantity of the love-apples, and prepare them as follows :—Take off the skins, and beat the pulp with vinegar—reckoning about half a pint to three apples—stew a quarter of an hour, add a little more vinegar, and bottle; but do not cork until the sauce is cold.

second layer of onions, cover with a closely-fitting lid, and simmer for *twenty minutes,* when your stew will be ready for serving in a deep dish, with the meat and onions in the centre, and the potatoes, as a guard of honour, surrounding them. After you have taken out the meat and vegetables, put two teaspoonfuls of catsup and a teaspoonful of flour into the gravy, give it a concluding boil, and then pour it upon the meat.

The advantages of this Irish method over the usual English one of filling the stewpan at the commencement with alternate layers of mutton, onions, and potatoes, are, that the beef foundation adds strength and flavour, and the potatoes being boiled in a separate saucepan, can be freed from their *white froth,* and moreover will not be " stewed to death," and converted into pulp.

STEWED BEEF.

Under this head a greater number of dishes may be classed than can be furnished by any other kind of meat, for it comprises every part of the ox, from the tip of its nose to the last joint of its tail. The shin, however, distancing even the sir-loin and the round, leads the van in the homely kitchen ; for in addition to its being the foundation of a host of soups and gravies, it forms in its integrity, when its juices are extracted for its *own* advantage, and the " *ragging"* of its flesh is mercifully eschewed, one of the best family dishes that England rejoices in, fully carrying out the qualities enumerated by the old proverb, " Of all the *fowls in the air* commend me to the SHIN OF BEEF; for there's marrow for the master, meat for the mistress, gristles for the servants, and bones for the dogs !" It is prepared and cooked as follows :—

Procure a nice fleshy shin, weighing about six or seven pounds with the bone, which the butcher should saw into three or four pieces ; put it in your iron " black pot," for you may probably not have a stewpan large enough, and just cover it with cold water.

As soon as the broth begins to bubble, skim carefully, and put in a little salt, allspice, black pepper, cayenne, three cloves, a blade of mace, a large onion, two or three small carrots, and a head of celery cut in pieces; stew (with the lid on) for four hours ; then take out the meat, cut it in neat slices from the bone,* and put it in a hot deep dish, while you mix, for "thickening," a teacupful of the gravy and three tablespoonfuls of flour; skim carefully, *then* add the thickening, stir round, boil up half a minute, and pour the gravy, flavoured with catsup, Harvey, or tomato, and (if within your reach) a glass of port wine—over the meat.

This is a plain yet very savoury family dish, and as the meat can *always* be had for *five pence* per pound, and often for less, the cost is very moderate.

STEWED RUMP OF BEEF.

The treatment of this dish is nearly the same as that of the preceding; but the quantities of the vegetables, &c., being slightly different, I will give you the receipt with the variations, in order that you may be *sure* you are right; for *much of the success of this and every other made dish depends on the nice calculation of the quantities, and a judicious employment of the proper vegetables and condiments.*

Put four pounds of the top of a rump of beef (hung a sufficient time to have become tender) into a stewpan, with a quart of cold water, then add three English or six small French carrots (the latter need only to be cut down the middle, but the former must be halved and quartered), one turnip cut in quarters, one whole good sized browned onion, half-a-dozen whole button mushrooms, half a teaspoonful of salt, and a dozen black pepper corns, and let this stew gently four hours; take out the meat, place it in a deep dish, with the vegetables round it, skim the fat from the gravy, thicken with two teaspoonfuls of flour, mixed with a tablespoonful of walnut, tomato, or mushroom catsup; boil up for an instant, and pour over the meat. This is also a plain but tasteful dish, and can be produced with very little more trouble than the stewed shin.

BEEF STEAKS PREPARED LIKE IRISH STEW.

Cut two pounds of steaks from a rump or round of beef, which has been hung until it is tender, about three-quarters of

* If you wish to preserve the marrow as a *bonne* (I had nearly written *bone*) *bouche* "for the master," according to the proverb, cover the ends of the bone with a little flour-and-water paste, over which tie a piece of coarse muslin to prevent the marrow from escaping into the pan. Served on a slice of toast, with a little salt and Cayenne, this is a delicacy fit for an epicure.

an inch thick, and divide them into pieces of four or five inches square; cover the bottom of a stewpan with part of them, then strew over them a thin layer of pounded spices and finely chopped vegetables, composed of a good sized onion, a small carrot, half a turnip, two sprigs of fresh parsley, a strip of celery, a dozen black pepper corns, half a teaspoonful of salt, three cloves, and a blade of mace; over this put another layer of meat, and alternate layers of the vegetables and meat until all your materials are disposed of.

Then put a *little more* than half a pint of *cold* water, or "stock," if you have it in store; cover closely, and stew gently (shaking the pan frequently to prevent burning) for about two hours; season and thicken with a tablespoonful of walnut, tomato, or mushroom catsup; a teaspoonful of flour, mixed well with a teacupful of the gravy taken from the pan; simmer for two minutes, to set the thickening, and serve in a deep dish.

Having given, in the three preceding receipts, the plain and economical methods of stewing beef, I will now offer one for a "holiday" effort, which, although it is more elaborate and costly, is still within the limit of the "*homely kitchen*," and ought to be at the "fingers' ends" of the thrifty housewife for grand occasions. It is the rival of the veal cutlet of our English taverns, and is very nearly allied to the famous "*filets de bœuf sauté*" of the great Vatel. I scarcely need say it is a

STEWED RUMP-STEAK.

To cook this well will not only tax your skill, but your patience; therefore pay particular attention to *all* my instructions.

Of course the meat must have been hung a sufficient time to have become tender. For a substantial dish you will require two pounds of evenly cut rump-steaks, about an inch and a half thick; these must be cut in half, for your pan will not be broad enough to receive the steaks in their whole length.

Take care that the butcher does not give you "knobbly" corners, or one end thin and the other thick, for if the surface on either side be uneven, or one part thicker than the other, your steak will not stew "cleverly."

This observation may probably appear needless to those who are not practised in the *niceties* of the art, but every experienced cook well knows that, *in all cutlet stews, evenness, both in surface and thickness, is of the greatest consequence.*

Now, to make *sure* of an *even* surface, and improve the tenderness of your steak, give it two or three smart blows on both sides with a flat wooden bat, made and kept for the especial purpose of beating, or, in kitchen parlance, " tendering" cutlets, steaks, &c. &c. ; do not use the rolling-pin, for that is a slovenly make-shift which does its work imperfectly.

As a stewed steak should be dark in its colour, and *crisp* as well as tender, you must brown well (or rather half fry) *both* sides four minutes, with a few thin slices of onion, carrot, turnip, and a strip of celery ; then, having stewed for an hour and a half in a small saucepan, half a pint of small onions in a *little more* than half a pint of water ;* pour their liquor into the pan (reserving the onions in the oven for dishing) ; add a dozen corns of black pepper, and stew (with the cover on) an hour and a half ; skim carefully ; then take out the meat while you pass the gravy and vegetables through a fine sieve ; when this is done, put it (the gravy) in another small *sauce* stewpan, with a tablespoonful of mushroom catsup, a quarter of a spoonful of cayenne, and a glass of port or claret (on this occasion one or the other *must* be had) ; put this pan on the fire, mix well, and thicken with flour to the consistence of *thin* paste ; then pour the whole into the other pan, over the, meat, and simmer for two or three minutes.

Serve in a hot deep dish, with the small onions, previously browned in the oven, encircling the meat and the gravy.

The above will be found to be the plainest, easiest, and cheapest way of producing this very delicious dish ; but should you desire a higher and richer flavour, and don't mind the trouble and expense, instead of flavouring your gravy with the articles I have enumerated, substitute half a teacupful of

ESPAGNOLE SAUCE.

Which is thus prepared :—Brown in the fryingpan with an ounce of butter, a slice of lean ham, two thin slices of veal, and half

---

* Whenever the phrase " a little *more*" than a pint, a glass, a pound, &c. &c., occurs, it is meant to convey that the *measure* should be " *brimming,*" and the *weight* " *lumping.*" Too little is as bad as too much in delicate cookery ; to hit the happy medium should be the study of the intelligent practitioner.

the back or leg of a rabbit; then put them in a stewpan with a teaspoonful of essence of anchovy, another of mushroom catsup, a clove of garlic, and as much beef stock as will cover them; stew gently until the meat is reduced to rags ; then strain the gravy through a fine sieve. When you serve, you *must* add a glass of port or claret.

There are various " *other ways*" of stewing beef, mutton, veal, &c., but as they all embrace nearly the same elements as those I have detailed, they do not need any special mention.

EVERY RECEIPT IN THIS BOOK IS FOUNDED UPON MY PERSONAL EXPERIENCE, my aim being not to offer a mere alphabetical list of a great number of " fancy" dishes, many of them impracticable or too expensive for those who only possess small means to produce, but A FEW PRACTICAL, SIMPLE, AND HOMELY DIRECTIONS, AS THE GROUNDWORKS OF ALL FAMILY COOKERY, by which the novice in the art may easily become acquainted with the properties of the various materials employed (which professed cooks rarely dream of inquiring into), and acquire from the plain rules here laid down, the best methods of preparing them for the table.

When you know how to fry a sole, to make a matelotte, to hash, mince, roast, broil, bake, and stew beef, mutton, veal, pork, and vegetables, on proper principles, you are in possession of the stem from which all the more elaborate and costly varieties branch.

I have purposely endeavoured not to confuse the choice of the student, nor record my own want of faith in my directions by introducing variations on each theme, under the customary phrase of ANOTHER WAY; I point out but *one* which I have personally proved to be " the best of all ways," and leave to the growing knowledge, experience, and taste of my pupils to improve upon it, or invent " *other ways*" for themselves, according to their means or fancy.

I will now give a few *foundation* receipts for making soups, gravies, and plain pies and puddings, and pass to the conside-ration of another most important division of the subject— THE DINNER QUESTION IN CLUBS, RESTAURANTS, DINING-ROOMS, AND CHOP-HOUSES.

In the late war in the Crimea, when our soldiers had un-roasted coffee and scanty rations of salt beef and pork served out to them, to be cooked in any way their ingenuity could contrive, which in general extended no farther than the use of a frying pan, and a ramrod as a toasting-fork, the French had attached to every file of men a "*batterie de cuisine*," in the shape of a "*pot au feu*," or "*black pot*," in which they clubbed their rations (inferior both in quantity and succulence to ours), and with the addition of a few carrots, turnips, onions, potatoes, and even *sorrel and nettles* (gathered on the spot), produced several quarts of nourishing soup and a savoury dish of meat, proving that in cookery, as in everything else, "knowledge is power."

To make soup well is a branch of domestic economy of no little importance, for it is often the *one dish which forms the entire dinner of the workman and his family*. The good housewife should, therefore, make it her first study to render herself mistress of everything relating to it.

The first step is to produce what is called in the language of cookery,

STOCK,

which is a strong essence, or meat broth, to serve as the foundation of soups, gravies, sauces, made dishes, hashes, &c. &c. There are two kinds of this very valuable assistant—viz., "brown," which is made from brown meats, and "white," which is composed from veal, chickens, turkeys, and rabbits.

The materials for producing each should be collected in what is called a

STOCK POT,

which is simply an iron kettle or saucepan, with a closely fitting lid. Subordinate to this regular stock, both kinds of which are indispensable in great kitchens, is the

POT AU FEU, OR BLACK POT,

so long the "poor man's friend" in every part of the Continent, and which *no English kitchen should be without*. Into this *careful* housewife's "*save-all*" should be thrown all the pieces and trimmings of every description of meat, poultry, and vegetables that may have been prepared for roasting, frying, &c., with liquor from "boilings," *uncooked* bones, gristle, and sinews of mutton, beef, veal, lamb, and pork, heads and feet (previously scalded to take off the small feathers and outer skin), necks, livers, gizzards, and hearts of poultry and game, and

every clean and succulent scrap that may be left from anything you have prepared for the fire.

The pot should be gently " seethed " on the hob for four or
five hours, and the " scum" carefully taken off two or three
times, when the liquor should be strained off and put aside in
a tureen, or any other *earthenware* pan (without a cover), and
kept in the larder until needed.

As the fat will have formed a coating over the surface of the
broth (which ought to form a jelly), and there will be a sediment at the bottom, for even the finest sieve will not entirely
clear it, you have only to cut out as much jelly as you have
occasion to use, and remove from it the fat and the sediment,
leaving the remainder to be dealt with in the same manner.
In hot weather *you must boil up the jelly every day*, or it will
turn sour and be spoiled; but in cold weather you may keep it
two or three days at a time.

Soup, respecting the nutritive merits of which doctors
disagree, has been proved, by its generally suiting the
delicate stomachs of invalids, and many persons whose digestive
organs are either temporarily or permanently impaired, to be a
most palatable and digestible aliment; witness the chicken soup,
which gives the old, or the long suffering weakened, strength
to bear the fatigues of the day, and then who can deny the
comfort and benefit of a basin of plain mutton broth or beef-
tea when out of sorts, from whatever cause ?

Throughout the continent of Europe it is the chief support
of the poorer classes, and its non-adoption in England is perhaps
chiefly attributable to the fact that there has not been, until
Doctor Kitchener first, and subsequently Soyer, took the subject
in hand, any good and cheap practical receipts for making it.

Long before I thought of turning my culinary experience to
account in this way, I had endeavoured to discover some good
and palatable method of making the liquor left from a boiled
leg of mutton, a fowl, or a piece of salted beef or pork, available
for the foundation of the next day's dinner. I consulted
cookery books in vain, for I gleaned nothing but expensive
receipts, somewhat resembling the following :—" Take two or
three quarts of strong clear *consommé*, add to it four or five
pounds of good gravy beef, a tough old hare (good for nothing
else), or an old partridge, a pound or two of fat bacon, the legs
and *wings* of a rabbit, a gill of port wine, half a teacupful of

mushroom catsup, a fagot of sweet herbs, and some carrots, turnips, and onions, cut in fanciful devices." I am not ashamed to say I have been obliged to try other and more attainable ways, and have at last arrived at the knowledge how *good*, *wholesome, and palatable soup, fit to be served on* ANY *table, can be made*, and this may be called

WINTER VEGETABLE SOUP AND BOUILLI.

Put five or six pounds of the top of a rump of beef into a large iron saucepan, or pot, with three quarts of cold water, and a teaspoonful of salt, and to prevent the side of the meat which covers the bottom of the pan from burning, place it on a wire trivet, which will also have the advantage of bringing it to an equal action of the heat from having the water all round it —the trivet should be used for all kinds of meat you have to boil—so treasure up this as a valuable hint.   Let the soup simmer gently until the scum rises ; you must then skim carefully, and put in another quart of cold water, which, when the saucepan is placed on the fire, will after a few minutes cause more scum to rise.   When you have taken this off, your soup will be clear of all impurities.   Now put in your vegetables, which should consist of two large onions, lightly browned *before* the fire in a Dutch oven, four carrots, six turnips cut in quarters, two heads of celery cut in pieces about two inches long, two bay leaves, two dozen pepper corns, two cloves, half a clove of garlic, a bunch of sweet herbs, formed of sprigs of marjoram, lemon, and common thyme, and winter savory, a large broiling mushroom broken in pieces; simmer (with the lid of the pot closely fitted) for four hours, when you must take out the meat, and after carefully skimming off the fat, strain the vegetables from the liquor, and reduce them to pulp by beating them with a wooden spoon, then replace the liquor and pulp in the pan, thicken with a teaspoonful of flour, mixed with a cupful of the soup, a teaspoonful of walnut, mushroom, *and* tomato catsups.   Give the soup a concluding boil up, and serve it with the vegetables in a tureen.   You should in the mean time have boiled some cabbage, Brussels sprouts, or spinach, which you must strain and press, and place at the bottom of a large hot dish ; upon this you must put the meat, and keep it before the fire until the soup is despatched, then serve it, and with the soup and some plain boiled potatoes you will have a very good dinner for a small family. You may, if you please, have some fresh tomatoes, beaten up and made into sauce (see my receipt), served with the meat in a butter boat.

You will observe that this is not put forward as a very *cheap* soup, for it is made entirely of *fresh* materials; you can, however, produce another for a great deal less money by using the liquor from the "Stock Pot," in place of the meat.

In families where strict economy is imperative, the "Black Pot" will be found a most valuable assistant. I therefore again earnestly recommend its adoption. I am well aware that "poor people" assert that they have nothing to put into such a "hog's wash" receptacle, for they eat everything, to the smallest scrap, at first hand; but no thought is ever given to the morrow by the preservation of any of the *many* good and wholesome "trimmings," "boilings," "drippings," &c. &c., which have resulted from the preparation and production of their not unfrequently "hot dinner."

"Goodness knows, we are not extravagant," said the wife of a mill-man at Bradford; "I, and my master, and the children, all work hard, and we want good nourishing things to support us. I don't pretend to be a grand cook; but this I *do* know, that I make our bit of meat and vegetables, and such like, go as far as they can be made to go; for there isn't a bit of fat, nor a crumb of bread, nor a scrap of anything that's *eatable* left after we've done our dinner."

Have then in every kitchen a "Black Pot," and do not grudge to bestow upon it a little time and attention. I have already spoken of the preservation of *un*cooked remnants in the kitchens of those who have moderate means; I will now recommend those who *must* be careful to go a step further, and add *cooked* scraps (of course it is understood that everything must be clean, sweet, and wholesome), such as the bones (which should be broken) of joints, poultry, and fish—the clearings of plates and dishes, dripping, rinds of ham and bacon, stale pieces of bread (toasted brown but not burnt), scraps of paste, and scrapings of flour from the rolling-pin and paste-board, &c. &c. The tops (not the green leaves) of carrots, parsnips, leeks, and celery, peelings of onions and turnips; pea-shells can also be made available. In fact, the careful housewife should throw nothing away that can by any means be turned to account; for if the strict economy I have pointed out be not necessary for

her own family, she will have the means at hand of providing,
with the addition of one or two shillings for a little fresh meat,
a good dinner for several of her poorer neighbours.

With this view I will, in the hope of its being found valuable alike to the poor man's kitchen and the charitable, who
have but little to spare, give the receipt for a

GOOD AND CHEAP VEGETABLE SOUP.

Chop the tops, peelings, and shells of your vegetables into
small pieces; brown them in the frying-pan with a good piece
of dripping; then put them, with the dripping, into your black
pot, having previously removed and strained off the liquor of
the articles you have collected during two or three days (remember, I have already told you to give the pot a "boil up"
every day, or the broth will turn sour). Put this liquor back
into the pot and add an ox-cheek, or two or three pounds of
shin of beef, or a bullock's kidney in thin slices. Stew gently
until the meat be tender, but not in rags.

About half an hour before dinner-time, strain off the liquor
(beating the chopped vegetables, which will be reduced to a
pulp through the sieve), and return it to the pot, with the peas
you have taken from the shells (old ones will do), and stew
again half an hour, or if the peas are very old a trifle longer.

You must (as in *all* boilings and stewings) take off the scum
as it rises from the meat, and remove the fat before you serve.

Thicken with a little flour, and flavour with mushroom or
walnut catsup. A few flour-and-water or suet dumplings may
be advantageously added when you put in the peas, to be served
on a separate dish with the meat. Should there not be sufficient liquor from the stock-pot to make the quantity of soup
the weight of your meat should produce, you must add cold
water. The pieces I have named should make four quarts.
This is a very cheap but by no means a *poor* soup; and if the
persons for whom it be provided will look at its *foundation*
without prejudice or false pride, it will be found not only a
great help to a slender purse, but a most palatable and satisfy-
ing lining for a hungry stomach.*

---

* The late Alexis Soyer, who was a true friend of the poor, and indeed
many others who needed advice for the better management of their
kitchens, never ceased to impress on careful housekeepers the necessity of
using up, as they do in France, every article that could afford nourish-

Leaving the "Black Pot" and its homely virtues for "metal more attractive," I will give you a receipt for

MOCK TURTLE SOUP.

Have the head, with the skin on, split by the butcher (he will of course have scalded off the hair); remove the tongue and brains; cleanse the head thoroughly, and lay it in salt and water with the tongue (the brains must be put in a basin by themselves) for an hour and a half. Then put the head, with a tablespoonful of salt, into a stewpan or iron pot, with just cold water enough to cover it. When it has simmered gently half an hour, take it out (I'll tell you presently what to do with it), and skim the pot carefully, for a great deal of scum will rise, and put in three pounds of skirt or four pounds of shin of beef; a large Spanish onion, with half a dozen cloves stuck in it, a teaspoonful of salt, two bay leaves, a tablespoonful of black peppercorns, two carrots, two turnips, a head of celery, all cut in pieces of about two inches. Now with a sharp knife cut the meat and skin from the head, break the bones with a hammer, and put them into the pot with the beef and the vegetables (still keeping out the pieces of meat and skin of the head), and a small bunch of sweet herbs and a parsnip cut in pieces. Stew for three hours; then take out the bones, strain off the liquor (of course you have previously taken off the scum), pound the vegetables, the beef, and the spices; mix them with the liquor, simmer again for half an hour; then strain through a hair sieve, and put the gravy only into the pot, in which you must now place the meat and skin of the head, cut into pieces of about two inches square, with two teaspoonfuls of salt and two dozen button mushrooms. Simmer three hours and a half; then skim carefully, and twenty minutes before dinner-time put in some small forcemeat balls (see my receipt for veal stuffing), which have been "setting" in the oven for ten minutes. Serve in a tureen, with half a pint of sherry or Madeira, a tablespoonful of essence of anchovy, the same of soy, and half a teaspoonful of cayenne.

The tongue may be either cut in pieces and stewed with the soup, or be kept for a side dish with the brains.

ment; but when he went on his mission to Ireland, his advice was ungraciously received,—"He's taching us to make stone soup," and "It's making pigs of us to tell us to stew offal and scrapings."

In addition to the forcemeat balls, the yolks of hard boiled eggs (put in whole, at the same time as the balls), will be found to improve the flavour of the soup. If you have more meat and skin than you require for your soup, take out a part, and set it aside with two teacupfuls of the liquor for the next day's dinner, for which it will make an excellent dish by the following treatment:—Put the liquor and a dessertspoonful of curry-powder into a stewpan; mix them well; simmer for a minute or two, and put in the pieces of skin and meat, with a dozen button mushrooms. Simmer half an hour more, and serve with the juice of a lemon squeezed into the dish.

The foregoing is *my* way of making this very popular English soup, with as little expense and trouble as possible, and I can answer for its giving satisfaction; but, as more luxurious feeders might perhaps like to try a higher flight, I will give a receipt (from Doctor Kitchener) for

MOCK TURTLE, AS IT IS MADE AT BIRCH'S.*

"Endeavour to have the calf's head and the broth ready for the soup the day before it is to be eaten.

It will take eight hours to prepare it properly.

Cleaning and soaking the head	1 hour
To parboil it to cut up	1 „
Cooling, nearly	1 „
Making the broth and finishing the soup .	5 „
	8 „

Get a calf's head with the skin on (the *fresher* the better), take out the brains, wash the head several times in cold water, let it soak for about an hour in spring water, then lay it in a stewpan, and cover it with cold water and half a gallon over; as it becomes warm, a great deal of scum will rise, which must be immediately removed. Let it boil gently for one hour, take it up, and when almost cold, cut the head into pieces about an inch and a half by an inch and a quarter, and the tongue into mouthfuls, or rather make a side dish of the tongue and brains.

---

* This establishment, which is a remarkable relic of " Old London," was first opened in the year 1711, and has continued up to the present time to hold a high reputation for its turtle soup and pastry. The original shop-front and door-plates are still preserved, and present a strange contrast to the modern gilding and plate-glass.

When the head is taken out, put in about five pounds of knuckle of veal and as much beef, add all the trimmings and bones of the head, skim it well, and then cover it close, and let it boil five hours, and let it stand until the next morning, then take off the fat, set a large stewpan on the fire with half a pound of good fresh butter, twelve ounces of onions sliced, and four ounces of green sage, chop it a little, let these fry one hour, then rub in half a pound of flour, and by degrees add your broth till it is the thickness of cream, season it with a quarter of an ounce of ground allspice, and half an ounce of black pepper ground very fine, salt to your taste, and the rind of one lemon peeled very thin; let it simmer very gently for one hour and a half, then strain it through a hair-sieve—do not rub your soup to get it through the sieve, or you will make it grouty; if it does not run through easily, knock your wooden spoon against the side of your sieve; put it in a clean stewpan with the head, and *season it* by adding to each gallon of soup half a pint of wine (Madeira, or, if you wish to darken the colour of your soup, claret), two tablespoonfuls of lemon-juice, the same of mushroom catsup, and one of essence of anchovy, a teaspoonful of curry-powder, or a quarter of a drachm of cayenne, and the peel of a lemon pared as thin as possible; let it simmer gently until the meat is tender—this may take from half an hour to an hour—*take care it is not overdone ;* stir it frequently to prevent the meat sticking to the bottom of the stewpan, and when the meat is quite tender the soup is ready.

A head weighing twenty pounds, and ten pounds of meat, will make *ten quarts of excellent soup,* besides two quarts of stock, which you can put away for made dishes, &c.

Observe.—If there is more meat on the head than you wish to put in the soup, prepare it for a pie, and with the addition of a calf's foot boiled tender, it will make an excellent ragout pie : season with sharp sauce, and a little minced onion; put in half a teacupful of stock, cover it with puff-paste, and bake it one hour ; when the soup comes from the table, if there is a deal of meat and no soup, put it into a pie-dish, season it a little, and add some little stock to it, then cover it with paste, and you have a good *mock turtle pie.*

This soup was eaten by ' The Committee of Taste,'* with

* This committee was composed of the *élite* of the " Grands Gourmands"

unanimous applause, and they pronounced it a very satisfactory substitute for 'the far-fetched and dearly-bought TURTLE,' which is entirely indebted for the title of SOVEREIGN OF SAVOURINESS to the rich soup with which it is surrounded.

Without its paraphernalia of subtle double relishes, a STARVED TURTLE has *not more* intrinsic sapidity than a FATTEN CALF: friendly reader, it is really neither half so wholesome nor half so toothsome.

While the soup is doing, prepare for each tureen a dozen and a half of mock-turtle forcemeat balls, made as follows :—Pound some veal in a marble mortar, rub it through a sieve, with as much of the udder as you have veal, or about a third of the quantity of butter; put some bread crumbs into a stewpan, moisten them with milk, add a little chopped parsley and eschalot, rub them well together in a mortar till they form a smooth paste; put it through a sieve, and when cold pound and mix all together with the yolks of three eggs boiled hard; season it with salt, pepper, and curry-powder or cayenne, add to it the yolks of two raw eggs, rub it well together, and make small balls ; ten minutes before your soup is ready, put them in with a dozen of egg-balls.

Brain balls, or cakes, are a very elegant addition, and are made by boiling the brains for ten minutes, then putting them in cold water, and cutting them into pieces about as big as a large nut-meg ; take savory or lemon thyme dried, and finely powdered, nutmeg grated, and pepper and salt, and pound them all together; beat up an egg, dip the brains in it, and then roll them in this mixture, and make as much of it as possible stick to them, dip them on the egg again, and then in finely grated and sifted bread-crumbs ; fry them in hot fat and send them up as a side dish.

A *veal sweetbread*, previously parboiled, and fried with sweet herbs, cut into pieces the same size as you cut the calf's head, and put in the soup just to get warm before it goes to table, is a superb *bonne bouche*, and pickled tongue, stewed till very tender, and cut into mouthfuls, is a favourite addition.　　We order the

and wits of the day, who met at the Doctor's table to test the merits of his recipes.　Long will these most agreeable réunions be remembered for their generous hospitality and hilarity.　Speaking of the unremitting zeal of the committee, the Doctor facetiously says, " They were so truly philo-sophically and disinterestedly regardless of the wear and tear of teeth and stomach, that their labour appeared a pleasure to them."

meat to be cut into mouthfuls, that it may be eaten with a spoon. *The knife and fork have no business in a soup-plate.*

Some of our culinary contemporaries order the *haut goût* of this (as above directed sufficiently relishing) soup to be be-devilled with a copious addition of anchovies, mushrooms, truffles, morels, curry-powder, artichoke bottoms, salmon's head and liver, or the soft part of oysters or lobsters, soles cut into mouthfuls, a bottle of Madeira, a pint of brandy, &c.; and to complete their surfeiting and burnt-gullet *olio*, they put in such a tremendous quantity of cayenne pepper, that only a fireproof palate lined with Asbestos, or indurated with Indian diet, can endure it.

N.B.—In helping this soup, the distributor should serve out the meat, forcemeat, and gravy, in equal parts; however trifling or needless this remark may appear, the writer has often suffered from the want of such a hint being given to the *soup server*, who has sometimes sent a plate of mere gravy without meat, at others of meat without gravy, sometimes scarcely anything but forcemeat balls.

Observe.—This is a delicious soup within the reach of those who 'eat to live,' but if it had been composed expressly for those who only 'live to eat,' I do not know how it could have been made more agreeable; as it is, the lover of good eating will 'wish his throat a mile long, and every inch of it a palate.'

N.B.—Cucumber on a side-plate is a laudable vegetable accompaniment."

I have given the facetious Doctor's receipt in its integrity; for it is so good, and his observations are so amusing, that I am sure both will be read with interest.

I will here observe that

GRAVY SOUP,

which in the language of the kitchen is called "clear stock," is used not only for the *potage* bearing its name (which is the "*bouillon*" or *consommé* of the French *cuisine*), but is the foundation of all kinds of meat sauces and gravies, and of the following soups, the different flavours being supplied by the cook according to order.

In the kitchens of the Parisian *restaurants*, small stewpans containing macaroni, vermicelli, sliced vegetables (*Julienne*), carrot pulp, the pulp (*purée*) of peas, also crab, &c. &c.. are kept beside the "*grande marmite*" of stock to be mixed with the foundation gravy in order to meet the tastes of the various customers.

I shall by-and-by give you the French receipts for producing both brown and white stock ; but, as they are too expensive for the family kitchen, it is sufficient to observe in this place that a small quantity of shin of beef, stewed with browned vegetables in the manner I have before detailed, is all that is required for English brown stock ; and for white, knuckle of veal, rabbit or chicken, with a very small quantity of *unbrowned* carrots, turnips, white onions, and the hearts only of lettuces—you may, if you wish to " stretch "* the quantity, and at the same time add to the strength of your soup, use the liquor from your "*pot au feu*," which term I will in future use when I wish to refer to *general stock*.

Although I warmly advocate the introduction of this great economizer to our kitchens, I wish it to be clearly understood that I do not recommend it to be used on *all* occasions. Soups made from *fresh* materials are undoubtedly to be preferred; but it is by no means a bad resource to fly to, when the purse is slender.

CARROT SOUP.

Carefully scrape some good carrots—then slice off the outside red portion (the yellow inside is not used for this preparation, as it is often hard), cut the slices into small pieces, and brown them with a little butter or dripping in the frying-pan. Observe, as a general rule, that all vegetables intended to be used for *brown* soups, stews, and hashes, should be so treated, as it adds to their flavour. Stew them in a covered pan in cold

---

* This word was significantly used some years ago, at the Old Ship, at Brighton ; an habitué complaining to the landlord that from some mysterious cause the Turtle soup gradually decreased in quality towards the end of the week, received the following candid explanation of the phenomenon: " As you are an old customer, sir, I'll frankly confess that when the demand exceeds the supply, we are obliged to ' *stretch*.' Turtle soup with *us* has, like the year, four seasons ; the first day it is fresh and strong, that's its *spring*; the second day, we throw in a little Cayenne to increase its piquancy, that's its *summer*; the third day we strengthen with additional forcemeat and catsup, that's its *autumn*; the fourth day, we ' *stretch*' with aqua pumpo, that's its *winter*."

water, or "stock," until they are quite soft, then strain, and
beat them with two wooden spoons, through a hair sieve, and
mix the *purée* or pulp (over the fire) a few minutes before you
serve, with as much stock as you may require.   Season with
catsup and Reading or tomato sauce, a little salt, and Cayenne
pepper.

SPRING VEGETABLE SOUP.

Stew gently for three hours a knuckle of veal weighing four
or five pounds in two quarts of cold water, a little salt, a small
carrot, two turnips, and one small onion—remember that in all
white soups the vegetables should not be browned—skim carefully so as to remove the *scum* at the commencement, and *fat*
at the conclusion.   When the meat has simmered for about an
hour, add the hearts of two lettuces, the *white* of a head of
celery, the heart of an endive, a small white onion (all chopped
in small pieces) a few thin slices of cucumber, and as much
small asparagus as you can grasp in one hand, sliced in pieces
as far down as tender.   Season with white pepper.   The meat
should be served with a portion of the vegetables, melted butter,
a little chopped parsley and a few slices of boiled or toasted
bacon, or a small piece of pickled pork.

GREEN-PEA SOUP.

For this also, knuckle of veal is the best foundation, as it is
more delicate in flavour than beef, and harmonizes better with
the vegetables, which should be the same as those used in the
spring soup ; but with the addition of a peck of peas, carefully
sorted after shelling, in three sizes, large, middling-sized, and
small, and put in separate basins.   The first should be put into
the pot as soon as the meat begins to simmer and the scum has
been removed; the second about three quarters, and the third,
one quarter of an hour before serving.   When you put in the
last instalment of the peas, add a little chopped green mint
and parsley.

OTHER SORTS OF VEGETABLE SOUPS.

Turnip, Celery, Cabbage, Asparagus, &c. &c., are made in
the same manner as the "Spring" and Green-Pea soups, the
"stock" being either beef or veal; but if the French plan of *purée*,
or pulping, be preferred, follow my direction for carrot soup.

CHICKEN SOUP.

Cut off the feet and legs, scald them to take off the outer skin and nails, and place them at the bottom of the stewpan with two small onions, the white of a head of celery, and half a dozen button mushrooms (chopped in small pieces), split the chicken down the back, scald the inside well, and *take out every-thing that may have been forgotten in the trussing*, then divide the back from the breast, and cut the first into four pieces and the latter into two; then just cover the pieces with cold water: stew gently, with a close cover, for an hour and a half; if longer, the chicken will lose its colour; skim carefully, and take out the feet; just before serving, mince four oysters (without the beards) mix them with their liquor and a teaspoonful of flour, and throw them into the pot—a tablespoonful of rice stewed with the chicken will thicken the broth without flour. This will make a pint and a half of strong soup. The meat should be dished up with either melted butter and parsley, oyster, or onion sauce, and should be garnished with slices of toasted ham or bacon; but take care the fowl be young, for whatever *old* women, or all the *old* cookery books may say in favour either of *old* fowls or *old* hares, they are both very sapless, unsatisfactory foundations to work upon.

The pieces of chicken may be served up with rice and curry sauce, as an Indian Pillau.

MULLIGATAWNEY SOUP.

There are many fanciful varieties in the ways of making this soup; some recommend veal only, others chickens, others a *mélange* of beef, veal, chickens, rabbits, and pickled pork; others insist on fried ham, or bacon, being included in the olio; but the *native* method is unquestionably the simplest and the best—viz., a strong white stock made from veal or kid, a *young* fowl, cut in pieces, and browned in a little butter or clear dripping, with the "*four friends*" (carrots, turnips, onions, and celery), to which must be added the "GENERAL SAHIB," *id est*, two good tablespoonfuls of curry-powder, and a table-spoonful of rice. Reckoning the "stock" to weigh five pounds, you will require three quarts of water. Every particle of the scum must be carefully skimmed off, and then the curry-powder (mixed in a cup with a little of the *cold* stock or cold water) put in with the rice, and the soup should then be simmered, with a close lid, for two hours.

A rabbit, or a partridge, or perhaps a pheasant, cut in pieces, can be advantageously used in place of the chicken.*

Serve with rice, boiled and dried in the Indian fashion (see my receipt farther on). It is always the better plan to make your stocks *the day before you require them*, as the fat can be more easily removed; and if you have to add fowls, &c., you need not "rag" them by too much stewing.

HARE SOUP.

If you cannot get a *young* hare, you must put up with an *old* one, although in the latter case you will in all probability, as in the analogous experiment of "pig shearing," often obtain more leather than juice; for according to Jack of Newbury,† *old* hares are when stewed "naughte but shoe leathere;" but as the toughest natures can be softened by gentle treatment, I will show you how to extract goodness from the most venerable "furrier" ever snared by a poacher. After it is skinned and *well* washed, take off the legs and shoulders (this will try your temper if puss be very ancient) and cut them into four pieces, the back into six, and divide the head; next place a stewpan on the fire, containing four ounces of butter, a carrot, two onions, a head of celery, cut into small pieces; fry these, as usual, light brown; then put in the pieces of hare; over which, when also fried brown, shake a good handful of flour, and *moisten* (for you have not yet put in any water or stock) with *half a bottle of port wine* (*hare* bears a strong affinity to the celebrated *stone* soup), add a teaspoonful of salt, two bay leaves,

---

* A literary friend, who is well read in gastronomy, remarking on this European innovation, observes:—" I have occasionally lighted upon a small island of partridge or pheasant floating on this aromatic Eastern sea, whose limpid rivulets of saccharine juices have agreeably lulled the ebullition of my capsicum-excited palate."

† This "worthy" flourished in the sixteenth century, and he says in the "Hystorie of hys Life:"—

"If any of ye men shoulo catche, ano bringe in an olde hare, you will have a prize; albeit, he is very harde eating, stewe hym as longe as you will, ano hys fleshe will be naughte but shoe leathere, he will, with a sheepe's heade, ano a little stuffe from ye garden make very good supping ano chewing, ano bye these means you will save much money in ye yeare, wherebye you mighte better maintaine your wife's French hood ano silke gowne."

three cloves, a blade of mace, a bunch of sweet herbs, and two quarts of white veal stock. Stir the whole on the fire until it boils; then remove the pan to the side to simmer gently for an hour and a half, taking care to remove the scum as soon as it rises, and the fat when ready to serve. Now take out the pieces of hare, and place them in a dish; select the finest pieces of meat (if the hare be young, they will be very tender and palatable, but if it be old, "naughte but shoe leathere"), remove the bones, and set these pieces aside in a soup pot; strain off the liquor, then clear the remainder of the meat from the bones, and pound it thoroughly with the vegetables in a mortar. When this is done, mix the "pulp" with the soup, boil up again for a few minutes, then strain through a fine sieve (gently rubbing the pulp with a wooden spoon), and pour the now rich gravy over the pieces of hare reserved in the soup pot; season with a little more salt, a quarter of a teaspoonful of cayenne, a teaspoonful of soy, another of catsup, and serve *hot*, but not boiling.

You may add forcemeat balls, made with the brains and liver (boiled and chopped up), and the herbs, &c., I have directed to be used for mock turtle. These must be put in, with a few button mushrooms, when you give the concluding " boil up."

WINTER PEA-SOUP.

This is the natural sequence of boiled beef, mutton, or pork, and is, if properly made, another of our most popular English soups; the subjugation of those too often unrelenting " swan-shot" peas being the only obstacle to success in its production; but soak them half a day, stew them a week, " ill trate them with bating till they are as spoony as male," they will *not* be mollified; in fact, your best efforts to that effect only increase their obduracy. But as intractable peas, as well as intractable men and horses, have a weak point in their natures, which, when skilfully attacked, can make them as ductile as Mr. Rarey's Cruiser, I will show you how to *persuade* the *hardest* pea that was ever grown to obey your wishes.

Most housekeepers know that there are two kinds of dried peas—the grey and the yellow, the former being whole and the latter split. The grey being only used for *purée*, or pulp, to accompany boiled pork or bacon, I will dismiss them with a direction *always* to soak them at least six, and boil them ten or twelve hours before beating them through the sieve. Upon the yellow or split peas I have more to say.

First, you must endeavour to procure YOUNG ONES; *this is as necessary for their boiling tender as when they are green;* in fact, *it is the secret of the puzzling toughness so often complained of.* You'll know them by the transparent brightness of their colour; as cornchandlers have always two qualities, of course you will endeavour to buy the best; still you may light on patriarchs, or a bad sort. In either case, there is no alternative but to grind or pound them before you put them in the pot, and when they have been stewed a very long while, pulp them through a sieve.

*The young ones require no soaking, as they are naturally tender.**

To proceed with my receipt. Having saved the liquor in which you have boiled a piece of meat, take off the fat, and put it in a pot with as much water as may be required to take off the "*saltness*" and make up the quantity of your soup (which for *two* days' consumption of six persons should be about four quarts); then add a pound of shin of beef, a pound of *Pork rinds* (which can be bought at fivepence a pound at any pork-shop); the "four friends" (I will in future use the term when I have to speak collectively of carrots, turnips, onions, and celery), two parsnips (all browned in the usual manner), a little *un*chopped parsley, and two dozen black peppercorns. When the pot boils, remove the scum, and put two quarts of carefully picked and rubbed split peas. Boil gently for three hours; skim off the fat and strain with a fine sieve, beating the vegetables through with a wooden spoon.

The pork rinds must be removed, but the pieces of meat

---

* The following apposite remarks on "pea taming," by J. H. P., in the *Cottage Gardener*, are worthy of quoting:—"We frequently hear our cottage friends complain of peas being 'bad boilers,' and taking many hours stewing before they break, and sometimes not doing so at all. Now, under the following treatment, peas that would take twelve hours to break them in the usual way, may be broken in less than one:—Pick them and clean them, if necessary, by rubbing them in a *dry* cloth; have a vessel containing a sufficient quantity of water to cover them, boiling very hard, strew the peas into it from the hand, a few at a time, so as not in the least to check the boiling of the water, and when boiled nearly dry add cold water, and after boiling a few minutes they will break. If the water be very hard, a bit of washing soda may be put in."

This process may answer with middle-aged peas, but I have always found the old ones inexorable to everything but the mill and the mortar.

should be put back into the pot with the liquor and the pulp; boil up for a minute or two, and serve with some dried mint, and toasted bread cut in small pieces.

If the saved liquor should be from *fresh* meat, you must have *three* pounds of beef, and throw in a little salt.

PEAS-PUDDING.

I will give instructions for this now, in order that my remarks on the treatment of old and bad peas may be remembered. If you are at all doubtful of the age or quality of your peas, soak them overnight in cold water; but if you know them to be young and a good sort, they will not require it. Tie them in a clean cloth, leaving room for them to swell, and put them into the pot with the joint you are boiling; but as a *quart* pudding will take but three hours' cooking, you must be guided in your time for putting it in by the weight of the meat. Many boil the pudding in a separate pot lest the brine, if it be corned beef or pork, should *harden* the peas; but by so doing they not only lose the *flavour of the meat*, but the *vegetable strength* of the soup is diminished. I have always found it best to boil them together.

Ten minutes before dishing, take up the pudding, turn it out of the cloth into a large basin, and beat it up well with a wooden spoon; season with a little pepper and salt, an ounce of butter, and the yolk of a well-beaten egg; then turn it into a dish, and set it in the oven or before the fire to keep it hot.

If you should find, when you turn the pudding into the basin, that the peas are *refractory*, "bate them into good timper" with your wooden spoon (separating the *ringleaders* from the others, and consigning them to do penance in the "*pot au feu*"); then flour the cloth well, put the pudding into it again, *tie it up as tight as possible*, and boil it another hour.

Doctor Kitchener says, "To increase the bulk and diminish the expense of this pudding, the economical housekeeper who has a large family to feed may add, when it is being beaten up, two pounds of potatoes that have been boiled and well mashed. To many this mixture is more agreeable than peas-pudding alone."

GIBLET SOUP.

This is a very rich soup, and *its use is more general than it is acknowledged to be,* particularly in hotels and *restaurants,* figuring under the guise of Mock-turtle, Ox-tail, Bisque, Colbert, Bouillabaisse, Raviolis, &c. &c. Nevertheless, although its foundation be uninviting to the sight (why do poulterers persist in conspicuously exhibiting these " remains " huddled together in their shops?), there is no doubt of its possessing great nutriment, and (for those who like it) a peculiar flavour.

To make three quarts of soup will require four " sets" of giblets, of any kind of poultry (those of the goose are principally used, and they must be *quite fresh*), two dozen chicken's feet (which can be bought at the poulterer's for threepence), two pounds of shin of beef scored, " the four friends" (browned as usual), three cloves, a blade of mace, two dozen black peppercorns, a bunch of sweet herbs, composed of a sprig of lemon thyme, winter savory, and marjoram, *two* sprigs of parsley, two or three leaves of *green* sage, and two teaspoonfuls of salt. Stew for four hours, skim, strain, and serve in a hot tureen, with a teaspoonful of soy, and a quarter of a teaspoonful of cayenne.

Now prepare the giblets thus: pick and clean the heads, wings, and gizzards (with goose and duck giblets you will have the liver, which, when *the gall* is carefully removed, you must chop up in pieces of about an inch square), then scald and *skin* the feet, chop the bills off close to the heads, cutting the latter in two, cut the gizzards into four, six, or eight pieces, according to their size, and the wings and necks into four pieces each. Wash the whole *thoroughly* in two or three waters, and put them on the fire with just sufficient water to cover them.

Considering it to be perfectly understood that you will always remove the scum and the fat at the *proper times,* I shall in future cease to repeat this caution, leaving you to " walk alone" in the strict observance of this important rule.

When the soup has stewed half the proper time required, add as much cold water, or stock, as may be needed to make up your quantity. Remember, by the way, that any *cold* fluid put into the hot broth *always* causes fresh scum to rise; so be on the alert to deal with it.

When you have strained off to serve, take the pieces of gizzard and liver from the sieve, and put them in the tureen with the soup. A wine-glassful of sherry will improve the flavour; and a few forcemeat balls, made as for mock turtle, may be added.

OX-TAIL SOUP.

Three tails (which must be jointed by the butcher) will produce, by stewing in three quarts of cold water for four hours, five pints of strong soup, no more meat being required, but you may advantageously add a pound of bullock's liver, cut into three thick slices, fried in a little butter or dripping, with "the four friends:" but as the tails are *always* very fat, it is essential that this soup be made the day before it is required, for in spite of the greatest care in skimming, it will be too rich.

The vegetables should be the same in kind and quantity as for giblet-soup; but in place of the bunch of sweet herbs put in a couple of bay-leaves.

After straining, the meat should be taken from the bones, and put aside until the soup is ready for serving, when it should be put in the tureen, together with two glasses of port wine and two teaspoonfuls of soy. Do not serve the liver; and take care that the tails be not stewed to rags. The mock turtle forcemeat and egg-balls may also be added to improve the flavour.

I have purposely omitted re-stating the mode of treatment, as I hope by this time you will be quite perfect in the practice of all that relates to browning, skimming, mixing, thickening, straining, and serving: take my WINTER VEGETABLE SOUP as your general guide, and you cannot greatly err.

GAME SOUPS

Are nothing more than pheasants, partridges, grouse, quails, snipes, woodcocks, &c. &c., cut into small pieces, added either to brown or white stock ; the only thing to be attended to is, that when the pieces of the birds are stewed tender, they should be taken out while you strain off the liquor; then, as I have directed in the receipt for " hare-soup," select the best pieces to serve in the soup, and pound the inferior ones with the bones into pulp, which you must mix with the vegetables, and beat through the sieve with a wooden spoon. A glass of either port, sherry, or claret is *necessary* to *confirm* the flavour.

FISH SOUPS

Have all a strong family resemblance, and there is one general instruction applicable to all varieties, viz., to cut your fish, whatever it may be, into small pieces, and brown them with the sliced vegetables, as in meat soups ; but as in some instances a special important mode of treatment is indispensable, I will here point out the exceptions to the above simple general rule.

FISH SOUP STOCK

Must, however, be first considered, for it is *supposed* that you do not use any meat for your foundation, therefore clean and cut in pieces a pound of skate, four or five flounders, or any cheap *fresh* fish you can procure, brown the pieces in the pan with a sliced onion, a head of celery, a sprig or two of parsley, a couple of dozen of black peppercorns, and a bunch of sweet herbs. Simmer in a quart of water with a close lid for one hour, and put the broth to cool. You already know how to deal with the fat and sediment of *cold* broths and gravies, so here also I leave you *alone.* The French *cuisine* has a great variety both of " shell" and "scale" fish soups, but as I do not in this part of my work purpose to give expensive or difficult receipts, I shall confine my examples to the treatment of two or three of the most popular kinds.

WHITE EEL SOUP.

Skin, and cut off the heads and tails of three or four pounds of eels, put them in a stewpan with a quart of cold water, a small teaspoonful of salt, a dozen *white* peppercorns, a blade of mace, a good-sized onion (whole), the beards of a dozen oysters cut in pieces, a little chopped lemon peel, a parsnip cut in four pieces, the heart of a *white* head of celery, six button mush-rooms, and half a dozen chickens' feet ; stew for an hour ; when the soup begins to simmer, strain—then put in the bodies of the eels cut in pieces three inches long, let them stew half an hour, when they should be taken out and kept hot to be stewed *after* the soup, either with *white* sauce (which I will presently tell you how to make) or brown stock, half a dozen chopped oysters, and a glass of port wine, if with brown gravy, and sherry with white ; next take off the *oil* from the soup (there will be a large quantity of it), then put a tablespoonful of the essence of anchovies, a glass of Madeira, sherry, or port, twenty drops of garlic vinegar, and the remaining six oysters (cut in small pieces), into the tureen, to which add the soup. You may also throw in, when you give the concluding boil up after straining, a few small

FISH FORCEMEAT BALLS,

which are made as follows:—a tablespoonful of fine bread-crumbs, a teaspoonful of finely-chopped suet, another of parsley, half a teaspoonful of dried marjoram, a small piece of lemon peel, a tablespoonful of picked shrimps, a small piece of cod liver (boiled), three oysters, the yolk of an egg (boiled hard), all finely chopped. Season with cayenne, salt, and nutmeg, and mix with a beaten egg. Roll the balls to the size of a small walnut, with a little flour, and " set " them in the oven for ten minutes before you put them in the soup.

N.B. This forcemeat will serve for all kinds of fish soups.

LOBSTER SOUP.

Procure one fine *hen* lobster, take out all the meat, break up the shell, and put it (the shell) with the small claws (bruised) and the heads and shells of a pint of shrimps, in a stewpan, with just water enough to cover them. Stew half an hour, strain and set the liquor aside—to be used by-and-by.

Lightly brown two small onions, half a carrot, and a turnip cut in slices, a blade of mace, a dozen black or white pepper-corns, two cloves, two bay-leaves, a sprig of parsley, another of marjoram, and two strips of celery tied together—put them in a stewpan with six chickens' feet (scaled and skinned as I have before directed), and a quart of fresh veal or fish stock. Stew an hour and a half more; meanwhile prepare your lobster. The meat of the tail and claws must be cut in pieces the size of dice, and then put them aside for a time. Take out all the cream and meat of the head, and the coral; pound them well in a mortar with a pint of picked shrimps. Season with cay-enne and a little grated nutmeg, moisten with a few drops of garlic vinegar, and mix the liquor you have set aside from the shells with the pounded fish. When ready to serve, put a tablespoonful of essence of anchovy in the tureen; skim and strain the soup, and mix with it the small pieces of the lobster you have reserved, and also the pounded ingredients, boil up, and pour the soup into the tureen, adding, as in mock-turtle, the yolk of six eggs boiled hard, and a few fish forcemeat balls,

the receipt for making which I have given above with the white
eel soup.

OYSTER SOUP.

Stew two dozen chickens' feet in a quart of water two hours,
with a middling-sized onion and half a parsnip, sliced, and very
lightly browned, an anchovy, a blade of mace, two cloves, two
dozen peppercorns, the rind of half a lemon, a dozen button
mushrooms, and the *beards* of four dozen oysters; strain, take
off the fat, and put the *oysters* in the stewpan with the liquor,
leaving out a little to mix with two tablespoonfuls of flour for
the thickening. Simmer the oysters at most six or seven
minutes (if longer, they will become leathery). Put a glass of
sherry in the tureen, the juice of a lemon, a tablespoonful of
essence of anchovy, fifteen drops of garlic vinegar, the same of
tarragon vinegar, and a quarter of a teaspoonful of cayenne.
Serve with the "fish forcemeat balls." The cream of a crab,
mixed with the hard part of a dozen of the oysters, pounded in
a mortar, and put in the soup a minute or two before the concluding boil up, will greatly add to its richness and flavour.

The above examples being quite sufficient for the production
of every special kind of fish soup, I will pass on to the meat
soups remaining to be treated on, after observing that the FISH
SOUP STOCK may be used, in place of the fresh materials, or to
increase strength and flavour.

BEEF-TEA.

This is the simplest of all soups, being but a pound or two
of shin of beef cut in small pieces, and gently stewed, with a
little salt, in a pint of cold water to each pound of meat, without either vegetables or spice, for three hours. It is generally
served in a basin, with toasted bread.

PLAIN MUTTON BROTH,

Is my concluding example of English soups; and although it
is almost as simple as "beef-tea," it requires a good deal of
attention in its preparation. To preserve the sweet "nutty"
flavour of the meat so grateful to the palate of the invalid is
the first consideration; the next should be the strength of the
potage; and lastly, the happy amalgamation of the vegetable
flavour.

I had once an opportunity of proving the virtues of this purely English *panacea*. Calling on a sick friend, who, in addition to very limited resources, had a "fine lady" wife, totally ignorant of everything relating to household comfort, I found him sadly prostrated in strength and spirits, his appetite entirely gone, so that he quite loathed animal food; his doctor had therefore, in the ordinary off-hand, matter-of-course manner of a fashionable physician, prescribed soup.

To *make* the soup was never for an instant thought of, so the lodging-house servant was despatched to a neighbouring pastry-cook's for a basin of mock turtle. I shall never forget the poor invalid's shudder and look of disgust when it was placed before him—the aroma of the herbs and spices, the colour of the Stygian lake of paste, and above all, the nauseating appearance of the lumps of *variegated* fat, completely overpowered him. "Take it away," he said, averting his head; "it would kill me to eat it." My knowledge of domestic cookery enabled me in this instance to do a good service. I went out and bought a "chump" of mutton and a few vegetables, and in an hour and a half I made him a basin of mutton broth, with a chop in it, which he could and did manage to eat both with relish and appetite.

The following I have found to be a very satisfactory method of producing

GOOD FAMILY MUTTON BROTH.

Half a dozen shanks of mutton, cleanly scraped and washed, but *not* broken (for the marrow which would in that case *all* boil out, would make the broth too rank), should be laid at the bottom of the pot, two middling-sized carrots, "halved and quartered," a middling-sized *uncut* onion, *one* quart of cold water, a small teaspoonful of salt. Stew them gently two hours and a half: then put in *two* quarts of cold water, and three pounds of the middle of the neck cut in three pieces, but *not* chopped, for the small bits of bone will adhere to the meat and be dangerous to the teeth; and a "chump" of the loin of mutton weighing two pounds, with another spoonful of salt (remember here the first point on which you are "walking alone"); add six turnips "halved and quartered," half a head of white celery cut in small pieces. Cover closely, and simmer two hours more; then take out the meat and *half* of the vegetables and place them on a hot dish, the meat in the centre and the vegetables round it.

Having previously mixed in a cup two teaspoonfuls of flour, a quarter of a pint of water, and an ounce of butter, put the paste into a small saucepan and stir it until it boils ; then *take off* the saucepan and throw into it a teaspoonful of chopped capers, and another of their vinegar ; mix these well and pour part over the meat, reserving the remainder to serve in a sauce boat. Remember, the capers must not be mixed with the butter *over the fire*, or they will lose their flavour and the sauce will be *" curdled."*

The remainder of the vegetables should be "pulped" through a fine sieve, when you strain off the liquor. You know *when* to take off the fat.

After the strained liquor has boiled up, throw in a tablespoonful of chopped parsley, and serve the broth in a hot tureen.

For invalids you may (according to their taste and strength of stomach) make the broth without vegetables, or you may use but half the quantity. Should appetite for solids be returning, a nice evenly-cut chop from the best part of the neck or loin, carefully divested of the fat, and stewed just long enough to be *very tender*, should be served in the basin with the broth. Small pieces of toasted bread should also be sent up in a plate or round the saucer of the basin.

With this (excepting beef-tea), the simplest of our English decoctions, I conclude my examples of soups. I might have much extended the list, but as I wish each division of this work to form the *solid basis* on which the "plain cook" can eventually become thoroughly proficient, I have confined myself to essentials. Those who can produce the *foundation soups* I have enumerated, will find it easy to raise a superstructure of almost endless variety thereon, and may on "holiday" occasions successfully attempt to vie with the elaborate productions of the French *cuisine*.

It may be just hinted that the *"pot au feu,"* or black pot, although not adverted to in the instructions given for the foundations of my stocks, still " holds its place in my dear love ;" *it can be used to add to or even to supply the fresh material in every one of my receipts ;* therefore, never cease to cherish it, and carefully endeavour to " increase its store."

F

There is another important point in soup-making I wish particularly to impress upon the " culinary mind "—viz., that as there is always much fat to be removed from the surface, the careful housewife should, if it be in her power, make all her soups overnight, as the fat and other impurities can, when cold, be so much more easily and completely separated from the soup.

I have said nothing on barley, rice, sago, tapioca, and other seed broths, as you will know they are only flavourings for stock soups ; and their preparation consisting merely of washing and picking, it would be wasting space to go into minute details.

By way of conclusion to this subject, the following extract from *La Cuisine Française*, by Monsieur A. Gogué, head cook to the Comte du Cayla, Lord Melville, &c. &c., an *artiste* of rising reputation, may perhaps not be considered inappropriate, as it shows, particularly to dinner-givers, the very important position *good* soup should hold in the bill of fare.

It has often been maintained that soups are barbarous destroyers of our alimentary enjoyments ; that soup is but the preface to the dinner, and that a good work does not need a preface ; but these, and many similar depreciatory phrases, prove absolutely nothing, being merely so many individual opinions, frequently, indeed, nothing but random shots fired by a wit in wanton sport to raise a laugh at convivial moments.

The most celebrated cooks and epicures have always been hearty advocates of the just claims of soup against the objections of its detractors. " Soups," says Antonin Carême, " are, and always will be, the provocative agents of a good dinner."

Soup (remarks also Grimod de la Reynière) is what a portico is to an edifice, and it is not only the first object of attraction, but it ought to be well combined, with a view to give a true foretaste of the temple itself, just as the overture of an opera shadows forth the subject of the work. Soup, moreover, should be regarded as a preliminary test of the artistic knowledge and talent of the cook.   For my own part, I will confine myself to saying, plainly but earnestly, that a *good soup* is a most excellent thing, always much relished by guests, and in a well-ordered bill of fare it ought to hold an important place, from its just claims to be considered as an object of particular attention.

A bad soup, which, however indifferent it may be, we are often out of politeness obliged to swallow, will so disturb our equanimity as to dispose us to find fault with every dish subsequently served up, and thus we dine badly owing to a foregone conclusion.   Let me fully urge upon you who are mistresses of establishments and good housewives, carefully to attend to this opening act of your dinner; for just as an author is naturally anxious that the commencement of his work should conciliate the minds of his readers, so you should look to your soup to impart good-humour to the stomachs of your guests.

There is no doubt that a failure in your *potage* when you give a dinner, jeopardizes the success of the whole of the feast, particularly if it be burnt, or too highly seasoned, in both of which cases the palate can scarcely recover its serenity until the appearance of the second course, the flavour of the fish and of the delicate *entrées* being almost undistinguishable. If, therefore, you do not wish your guests to be in the position of the man who, swallowing his dinner in a passion, was unconscious whether he was eating boiled cabbage or stewed umbrellas, follow Monsieur Gogué's advice, and spare no pains in making your soups as perfect as possible.

GRAVIES AND SAUCES.

" England has a hundred religions, but only one sauce," said Talleyrand ; and in the Life of that renowned wit, Sydney Smith, it is stated, that on hearing a lady exclaim, " No gravy, if you please," he turned to her and proposed to swear eternal friendship on the instant, saying that he had been looking all his life for a person who, on principle, rejected gravy.

These dicta are emphatic rebukes on the enormities we have so long been content to put up with under both heads, *melted butter* being an utter abomination to the gourmand Prince, and *hot water and catsup* the " favourite aversion" of the facetious divine ; and although many meritorious efforts have been made to eradicate these national reproaches from the kitchens of our wealthy dinner-*givers*, the old-established *paste* and *aqueous acid* are still to be found in all their pristine repulsiveness occupying a post of honour at our family tables, and fully justifying the severest animadversions that can be passed upon them.

It is by no means necessary that " melted butter" should be made by beating up a large quantity of butter with cream and eggs, till it becomes a custard ; neither should gravy for roast meat be the essence of mock turtle, or a mixture of the juices of half a ham and a dozen pheasants and partridges, stewed down to a teacupful of " Espagnole" or " Béchamel." But they should, on the contrary, both be plain, wholesome, palatable, easily to be produced, and inexpensive adjuncts, which neither sicken us with their mawkish insipidity nor destroy the flavour of the natural juices of the different meats, either by a profusion of spices, or a too liberal infusion of that mysterious product waggishly called by the London dairymen the " *cow with the iron tail.*"

As all gravies are founded on meat, and all sauces on butter,[*] the natural process is to produce the former by stewing, and the latter by melting; but civilization has thrown in a difficulty. We are not, like the savages of New Zealand, contented with "boiled missionary" *au naturel;* our educated palates have been taught to require a gravy or a sauce fit to rival in succulency and piquancy the famous " Sauce Robert," which, according to *L'Almanach des Gourmands*, when well composed, would make one eat one's grandfather or an elephant.

It is thoroughly understood nowadays that every gravy or sauce should be skilfully adapted in flavour to the peculiar aliment whose palatableness it is intended to enhance : but ignorant and idle housewives prefer the beaten track to the study of principles, and tenaciously cling to the " good old ways" of their grandmothers, or are content with the old-fashioned cookery-books, which direct them to

" Take a piece of butter as big as a walnut or your thumb, and two or three tablespoonfuls of flour ;" or " Pour from the teakettle over the joint when you dish a goodish quantity (according to the number to partake of it) of boiling water, and a large teacupful of flavouring made of catsup, soy, garlic, vinegar, anchovy sauce, and cayenne."

In the English kitchen we trust, and I think wisely, more to the natural flavour of our meat than to the foreign juices and condiments which are essential to *la cuisine Française*.

Can a " *Gigot braisé* " or " *à la Provençale*" ever be eaten with the same *gusto* as a leg of " Southdown" or Welsh mutton, hung a fortnight, and served with a gravy formed solely from its natural juice ? What " *Filet de Bœuf à la Napolitaine*," or " *à la Sauce Poivrade*," or *à la anything*, was ever half so toothsome as a plain Old English Sir-loin with a Yorkshire pudding under it ? What English palate has ever preferred " *Perdrix aux Choux*" or " *à l'Estoufade*," or " *Faisans à la Dauphinoise*," or " *à la Financière*," to our plainly dressed birds, with bread sauce and simple beef gravy for their *aides-de-camp?*

---

* Cream cannot be considered a *foundation*, as it is always joined either to meat stock, as in the instances of " Béchamel," &c. &c., or to strong flavouring essences, such as vanille, pine apples, &c. ; butter and beaten-up eggs are also very general adjuncts to sweet white sauces.

The flavour of fish and vegetables is also too often destroyed in French cookery by the craving for rich sauces and gravies. Even the famous " *Sole à la Normande*" and " *Saumon à la Maintenon*," although they may be relished as an occasional *bonne bouche*, cannot successfully cope with our plain frying and boiling, when carefully done. Can Phillippe or Les Trois Frères Provençaux find anything in their " *répertoire*" of *Entrées de Poisson*, to match our leviathan Dover turbots and Severn salmon, boiled and served whole, with lobster sauce for *epicures*, and plain melted butter for *true fish eaters?*

What sauce can improve a potato? Is spinach beaten up with eggs, cream, and vinegar, equal to the crisp leaves plainly boiled?

Does a fresh cauliflower require "*Gratin*" and *Sauce à la Soubise?* And, to conclude these instances of culinary sophistication, do green peas need boiling with sugar, or stewing *à la Française*, with onions and lettuces, combined with the yolks of eggs and "*Beurre noir?*"

It is clear, then, that in *English* cookery the fewer gravies and sauces we employ the better; but it is also clear that these few should be composed with skill, and *only taste of the materials from which they take their name.*

For instance, Anchovy should not predominate in lobster, nor Vanille and mushrooms in oyster sauce. Carefully attend, therefore, both to the quantity and quality of the different ingredients I will set before you. I will commence with

PLAIN GRAVY FOR ROAST POULTRY AND GAME.

About half an hour before you put down your fowl, cut off the feet and neck (the lower part of the legs, I never could understand why, unless it be to make the bird look ugly and give additional trouble to the carver, are always retained in the trussing), scald them well, take off the skin and the feathers, and put them into a small stewpan with half a pint of cold water, half a teaspoonful of salt, half a dozen black peppercorns, a small shalot (cut in half) three whole button mushrooms, a "nose" or crusty corner of a loaf, or an end of a French roll toasted *very brown*, but *not burnt* (for colouring), and half a pound of scored shin of beef.

When the fowl is done remove the fat from the gravy in the

dripping-pan, and mix it with the "*made*" gravy (of course properly skimmed and strained), then pour a small quantity into the *dish* (you know *why*), and serve the remainder in a sauce-boat. *This is the simple method of supplying the want of natural gravy without destroying the flavour of the bird;* but if you would make a rich or

A FLAVOURING GRAVY,

in addition to the materials I have already enumerated, brown a slice of lean *uncooked* ham (about two ounces), with half a turnip, half a carrot, and a quarter of a head of white celery, cut in thin slices; a sprig of winter savory, another of parsley, three thin slices of chopped lemon-peel, and a dozen berries of allspice; skim and strain as usual. If you wish your gravy to be thick, mix a little flour—you know how.

For game you may add, *when you serve*, a tablespoonful of port, claret, or sherry, and a little cayenne.

Either of these gravies may be used for roast meat, and if you are not providing for company, the *pot au feu*, with a little attention to flavouring, will save you the expense and trouble of a special concoction.

SAUCE FOR WILD DUCKS.

Mix a teaspoonful of salt, half a teaspoonful of cayenne, two teaspoonsful of lemon juice, the same of pounded sugar, and the same of catsup, a tablespoonful of Harvey sauce, and three table-spoonsful of Port wine.—Warm in a small saucepan, and pour over the bird, which should be previously sliced, so that the sauce may mix with its own gravy.

SAUCE PIQUANTE FOR GRAVIES, STEWS, HASHES, MINCES, &c. &c.

Pound a couple of shalots, a teaspoonful of capers, and put them into a stewpan with a tablespoonful of vinegar, half a teaspoonful of mustard, and a quarter of a teaspoonful of cayenne.

When the shalots and capers are dissolved, add as much of the *Espagnole* sauce (for which I have given instructions at page 56) as you may require for your flavouring, mixing well over the fire.

From the above receipts you may easily form every variety of the " brown" gravies, which are generally given in cookery books ; the " white" kinds require a different treatment.

WHITE SAUCE.

This in the French kitchen is called "*Velouté*," taking its name from its " velvety appearance;" and as it is a very delicate " holiday" sauce, the utmost care and skill must be bestowed on its preparation.

Much of its sightliness, smoothness, and artistic finish (a very important consideration with most French " *chefs* ") depending on the "*Roux*" or thickening, that is the first point to which you must direct your labours : therefore, put a quarter of a pound of fresh butter into a stewpan over a slow fire, and when it is melted, put in by degrees, and mix with a wooden spoon, five tablespoonfuls of flour : then moisten, also by degrees, with a teacupful of cold clear stock, mixing and stirring and *lifting** until your thickening becomes a pale sherry-coloured paste of moderate consistency, for if it be either too thin or too thick, or too deep in colour, it will not do you credit; put it aside to cool while you prepare your gravy, which should be made as follows :

If you have any uncooked trimmings of veal or poultry, put them into the stewpan with two quarts of cold water, or, if you have it, white stock; a thick slice weighing about a quarter of a pound of lean uncooked ham, a pound of veal cutlet, and if possible the legs of a fowl or rabbit cut in pieces; a small carrot, a parsnip, three button onions, half a head of white celery, a small turnip, three *clear* button mushrooms, half a shalot, a bay leaf, a sprig of thyme, and another of green parsley sliced and chopped.

N.B.—A preparatory light browning with a quarter of a pound of butter, although it may slightly heighten the colour, will greatly add to the flavour. I therefore leave it to your taste to adopt or omit it.

Simmer, with a close lid, for two hours ; then strain off the gravy and replace it in the pan. Now is the moment to display

* This is a French process to bring the sauce to its proper consistency and colour, and make it *perfectly smooth*; it is effected by taking out spoonfuls and letting them fall again from a slight elevation into the centre of the pan.

your "artistic finish." While the gravy is gently simmering, with your wooden spoon put in a small quantity of the thickening, and stir it round until it is well mixed with the gravy, then put in a little more, and more, and "*lift*" until your sauce arrives at its culminating point of consistency and colour; then take it off, *coax* it through a very fine sieve, and set it aside in an uncovered basin to get cold and be in readiness to use as the FOUNDATION OF ALL WHITE GRAVY SAUCES, the first on the list being the famous

BECHAMEL SAUCE.

Understand, however, before I give the receipt for it, that it is not put forward as belonging to plain English cookery, but as a " holiday" effort, should means and occasion justify its use. You have merely to put into a stewpan a pint of cream, or in its default the same quantity of good milk; as soon as it begins to simmer add to it as much of the "*Velouté*" you have in store as the quantity of *Béchamel* you wish to make will require. Stir until well mixed and about as thick as plain cream; then strain through a tammy (a worsted cloth made expressly for straining sauces), and it is ready to serve.

This, with the exception of

DUTCH SAUCE,

which is another " holiday" variety of great merit, is the last example I will give here of foreign sauces.

Put into a stewpan a quarter of a pound of butter, a dessert-spoonful of flour, the yolks of two beaten-up eggs, half a teaspoonful of salt, a quarter of a teaspoonful of ground and sifted black pepper, a " grate" of nutmeg, a wine-glassfull of water, and the juice of a lemon; mix well and simmer over a slow fire, stirring and "lifting" continually with a wooden spoon. Let it be tolerably *thick*, and when you put it into the sauceboat add a few small pieces of *cold* fresh butter, which will give your sauce, according to the highest authority, a more exquisite finish.

This is a very popular composition on the Continent, particularly for fish; but it is used like the " *Béchamel* " for fricassees, boiled poultry, &c. &c.

The preceding full and particular instructions for the preparation of these important delicate sauces have been introduced in order that those who complain that *no cheap English cookery-book is to be found containing a practical method for making them*, may take advantage of my experience.

"Once more on English ground," I will proceed to show you how *properly* to make *our* foundation sauce.

PLAIN MELTED BUTTER.

The chief defect in its ordinary composition is insufficiency of the very article from which it takes its name; in fact the flour and water, to use a familiar expression, "drown the miller," the flavour of the "bit of butter" being entirely destroyed by the lumpy, wishy-washy paste with which it is incorporated. As the perfect production of this most useful sauce is of great importance, I will give directions for it under three heads; the first under the title of

BUTTER SAUCE A LA TICKLETOOTH.

Put four ounces of fresh butter, cut in small pieces, into a saucepan; when they are melted, shake in gradually with the left hand a tablespoonful and a half of best flour, stirring all the time with a wooden spoon; then add a teacupful and a half of cold water, put in by spoonsful with the left hand, while you continue stirring the butter with the wooden spoon with the right (all one way) until it boils; then take the pan off the fire, and stir and "lift" until your sauce be as thick as cream and a *full straw colour.*

N.B.—If the quality of the flour (and there is often a great difference) should not enable you to obtain the proper thickness, put in a little more. You will find by properly stirring and "lifting" that your sauce will be beautifully smooth and sightly. If the sauce should chance to oil, put in a small piece of cold butter and a teaspoonful of cold water, stir well and "lift" (off the fire) and all will turn out right.

This I have by long experience proved to be the best method of making plain melted butter: it will serve for the stock of all butter sauces. The next example is

FRENCH MELTED BUTTER.

This is formed with four ounces of butter cut in pieces and melted in the pan, to which is added by little and little, stirring all the while, the yolks of two eggs well beaten or whipped up with three tablespoonsful of good milk, and a "grate" of nutmeg—just as the sauce begins to simmer take the pan off the fire, and stir and lift.

This is a good foundation for sweet sauces, although it is used on the Continent as a leading feature in many Béchamel varieties.

ARROWROOT BUTTER SAUCE.

Mix well a tablespoonful of arrowroot in a quarter of a pint of milk, with a little grating of nutmeg, as well as of dried lemon-peel, then mix them in the pan with four ounces of butter, in precisely the same manner as the Tickletooth and French melted butter.

All the above may be flavoured according to fancy, with wine, vanille, pine apple, &c., and finished with a few small pieces of cold butter when in the sauce-boat.

I have been the more particular in my instructions for the production of this very common, but too often very ill used parent of so large a family of sauces, all of which more or less depend for their success or failure, on its being properly prepared; for if the "melted butter" be oily or ropy, or economically thinned with too much water and flour, our fish, white meats, vegetables, and pies and puddings, lose rather than gain flavour when it is made use of.

How often has it happened when poor Mr. Bartholomew Lane, the stock-broker, has sent home a fine turbot and lobster from Billingsgate, with a note to his *more than* "*better half*," timidly requesting that they may be dressed with "the birds," and a cabinet pudding, at seven, for a friend he would bring with him, that he has "looked daggers" at the brick-dust coloured, thin, lumpy, essence of anchovy abomination, on which floated in pale fragments the "pride of the market," which cost him, he would be sorry to confess to Mrs. L. how *much;* the lobster, which, if it had been converted into proper sauce, he hoped his friend Jawkins (his companion at the Trafalgar, at Greenwich, on "hashed" mutton days) would have smacked his lips at, and said, "capital, capital, worthy the turbot; so creamy, so piquante, yet withal so '*lobstery.*'" "No butter, thank you," when it is proffered to flavour the cauliflower, and when bread-sauce to the birds, and *wine-paste* to the pudding, are also eschewed by " that dainty Jawkins," who is supposed, from " dining so often with Mr. Lane at Greenwich and at the French houses," to like nothing plain and wholesome, complete the annoyances of the poor Amphitryon, who inwardly determines that unless Mrs. L. will look to the kitchen herself, or find a cook who will not disgrace him, he'll never bring a friend home again.

Look, therefore, good housewives, to your " melted butter."

Having shown you how to build a good foundation, I will now point out the best methods of dealing with a few of the most simple and useful fish and sweet sauces.

The first on the list is :—

LOBSTER SAUCE.

Wipe carefully the shell of a hen lobster before you crack it, save any liquor which may run from it—take out the meat of the tail and claws, cut them in pieces the size of dice, and put them aside. Scoop out all the cream and small pieces of meat from the head and the coral, pound them well together with a little salt and cayenne in a mortar ; break the shells in pieces, and put them into a saucepan with just water enough to cover them, a blade of mace, and six black peppercorns. Let them boil ten minutes, then strain, and when the liquor is cold mix two tablespoonsful of flour with it, and put it into the stewpan with four ounces of butter cut in small pieces, shake the pan till the sauce boils, then gently stir in the pounded lobster and let it just boil up, add the pieces of lobster you set aside, and boil up again. In this manner you will have the pure flavour of the lobster ; but if you wish to make it stronger, add a teaspoonful of anchovy sauce, half a teaspoonful of catsup, and half a teaspoonful of soy, stir well, and " lift " to mix and bring the sauce to its proper consistency (mind, it should be tolerably thick) ; *before* you put in the pieces of lobster, add, *in the sauce-boat,* a few small pieces of cold butter.

SHRIMP SAUCE.

Pick half a pint of shrimps, and mix them in a saucepan with as much melted butter (brought to the thickness of cream) as you may require, and a teaspoonful of essence of anchovies.

For a family sauce, the heads and skins should be boiled up

in a separate saucepan and the liquor which is strained from them mixed with the butter; but as it is apt to give too strong a flavour, if you wish to make a delicate sauce you had better not use it.

OYSTER SAUCE.

Put the beards cut from two dozen oysters into a small stew-pan with a little chopped lemon-peel, a small piece of shalot, six white peppercorns, and a quarter of a pint of water; stew them gently twenty minutes. Then dissolve four ounces of butter in another stew-pan, thicken gradually, in the same way as for melted butter, with a tablespoonful of flour, and half a teacupful of good milk or cream, using the liquor of the oysters and the soup strained from the beards instead of water. When smooth, and of the proper thickness, put in the oysters (with the gristle removed) either whole or cut in small pieces. Boil up and serve.

To flavour oyster sauce with anchovies, vanille, &c., is simply to spoil it.

SCOLLOPED OYSTERS.

If scolloped oysters you would make,
Fine, fresh-caught oysters you must take ;
From shells detach, on fire boil them—
Not too long, or else you'll spoil them.
The fish then strain, and save the juice—
You'll find it of the greatest use;
And then, to be as nice as wise,
The oysters you must *barberise*.*
Now put your beardless oysters whole
Into a nice clean casserole ;†
Add parsley chopped, and nutmeg grate,
With juice of oysters inundate,
Make rich with butter, with pepper hot,
And taste if it wants salt or not.
If stronger *goût* you now would wish,
Add fine-chopped onion to this dish ;
But, as the onions tales do tell,
To leave them out would be as well.
'Tis now all in that you require,
The next thing—place it on the fire.
As on the fire it now doth quicken,
With flour and butter mixed you thicken.
Two minutes' boiling will suffice—
Taste, and I think you'll say " It's nice."
If lips you smack, and nod your head,
The cook's approving *yes* you've said.

* To take off the beards.　　　　† Stew-pan.

'Tis all perfection if once more
You taste, and nod, just as before.
So far so good, you've come good speed ;
Some scollop-shells you now will need.
But, if you have no scollop-shell,
A China dish will do as well.
Strew on the dish some crumbs of bread,
Then on the dish the oysters spread.
With crumbs you now the oysters crown,
And with a knife you smooth them down.
Before the fire now place the dish
Until it's browned—just like fried fish.
To table send—delay it not,
For oyster scollops eat best hot.

G. F. C., in *North British Advertiser*.

CAPER SAUCE.

Chop two teaspoonsful of capers, and mix them with a table-spoonful of their vinegar mixed with melted butter.

PARSLEY AND BUTTER

Is merely a little chopped parsley mixed with melted butter ; but if it be used for boiled fowls or veal, the butter should be mixed with milk.

EGG SAUCE.

Boil two eggs hard, chop them into small pieces, and mix them with a little pepper and salt, with melted butter. If you wish the sauce to be *piquante*, add a quarter of a teaspoonful of mustard and the juice of a lemon.

CELERY SAUCE.

Cut the hearts of two heads of *perfectly white* celery into small pieces, stew in a pint of cold water one hour, then strain off the liquor (which is too strong and dark for a deli-cate white sauce), add to the celery half a pint of milk, and stew for another hour, then " pulp " through a fine sieve, and mix the liquor and pulp, by little and little, with " melted butter," which should be prepared with milk. When in the sauce-boat add a " grate" of nutmeg.

For a " family" sauce, stew at once in a pint of milk and water (in equal quantities) two hours, use part of the liquor to mix the " melted butter," and instead of " pulping " the celery, chop it in smaller pieces and let them *appear* in the sauce-boat.

ONION SAUCE.

Melt an ounce of butter cut in small pieces in a saucepan, and gradually mix it with a tablespoonful of flour, then add also gradually, a quarter of a pint of milk, and a moderate sized Spanish onion (boiled for three-quarters of an hour) chopped in small pieces ; mix well with half a teaspoonful of salt, and a quarter of a teaspoonful of ground black pepper, give a concluding boil up, and serve in a sauce-boat.

This is the best sauce for roast mutton, boiled rabbit, tripe, and boiled veal; it is also used with rabbit pies; indeed, in Cornwall and Yorkshire, where all kinds of pies are in the ascendant, it is popular with everything that wears a crust.

BREAD SAUCE.

Put the crumb of a stale twopenny French roll, broken in small pieces, into a basin, and pour over them half a pint of boiling milk, beat up well with a wooden spoon, then add a middling sized roasted onion chopped in small pieces ; mix well with the bread and milk. Next melt an ounce of butter in a stewpan, and put into it the paste from the basin, with a little salt and cayenne, stir round for a couple of minutes over the fire, thinning if necessary with a little more milk.

I have always found it best to make this sauce *thick and bready*, but as many prefer it *thin and milky*, the tastes of those for whom it is prepared should be consulted.

If onions are objected to *in body*, instead of serving them in pieces, use only their juice.

With this I conclude my examples of English sauces; but before entering upon another branch of my work, it is neces- sary to observe that I have studied to make all the receipts as plain and economical as possible, so that they may be within the means of all classes of housekeepers.

I will now turn to

VEGETABLES.

Under this head is comprised what may truly be called the *better half* of all plain English dinners ; for what table is ever without them, and how many thousands of the labouring com- munity from year's end to year's end depend almost solely on them for their support? What country housewife ever dreams of dishing up a joint without " garden stuff " of some kind; and what plain cook would venture to serve either fish, flesh, or fowl without their natural adjuncts, vegetables ! vegetables ! vegetables ? Yet, notwithstanding the important position they hold, not only as accessories, but as principals in the composition of a good dinner, how do we cook them ?—do we not continually hear and read of, as well as *see*, potatoes with the " bone "* in them, or boiled to pulp ? Is not cabbage often served up greasy and yellow ? are not green peas sometimes half swan shot and half *squash ?* Whitey-brown stringy turnips which *wont* be mashed, sluggy cauliflowers fringed with scum, gritty spinach, and many other equally unpleasant products of a carelessly conducted kitchen.

How comprehensively suggestive was the question the eminent gastronomic divine, who, when deputed by the committee of his club to examine the candidates for the vacant *cuillère de " chef de cuisine,"* which, like the *"Baton de Maréchal "* that every French soldier believes to be hidden in his knapsack, every scullion of the meanest " *Gargotte* " is certain he will some day find at the bottom of one of his stew-pans, at once put to the aspirants, " Can you boil a potato ?" That is the touchstone of a cook's talent; everything else, like Dogberry's reading and writing, " comes by nature." Well cooked vegetables do much for all classes of dinners. Smoking hot potatoes with " their jackets on," " the laughing maley vagabonds," have given an epicurean relish to many a cold shoulder ; a young summer cabbage has more than excused hashed mutton ; mashed potatoes have banished all sinister speculation on the foundation of sausages. Who has not been " a pig at beans and bacon ?" to say nothing of the miracles worked by early green peas, new potatoes, and asparagus, on ducklings, spring chickens, and house lamb.

All good housewives take advantage of their knowledge of the seasons, when the flavour of every variety of root, plant, or pod is enhanced by being presented to us for the first time. " Don't forget we've new potatoes with the salmon to-day, Alfred," one will say; or another will make " the first of the season" the principal feature of a family festival. " James,

---

* *"Au ghealeach"*—*i.e.* with the bone or the moon in it—is an Irish expression, arising from the moon-like disk and halo the centre of a half-cooked potato presents when cut in two.

dear, peas are in, you shall have a peck with a roast duck for your birthday." Or another " domestic treasure " will say, " I'm watching the asparagus, John, and as soon as it gets down to *our* mark, I'll treat you to a bundle."

" *Primeurs*,"* though seldom possessing their full flavour, and are often disadvantageously introduced after the appetite has been satisfied, are always looked upon as important components of a set dinner ; in short, *vegetables in their natural seasons are cheap luxuries at everybody's command*, and need but skilful treatment greatly to increase our zest for the " *plats de resistance* " alike of our homely and more pretending prandial meals.

So, like Shakspeare's " French falconers," flying at everything relating to " garden stuff," I will endeavour to show how best to employ every variety of it, whether by plain boiling, stewing, frying, roasting, or baking.

The " first horse in the team " is the " Irish fruit." I will therefore open the ball with instructions

HOW TO BOIL A POTATO.

This appears at first sight to be, next to boiling the tea-kettle, the easiest of all culinary efforts ; but daily failures, or " perishings in the attempt," show us that in dealing with this tuberous root, we often parallel the proverb of " one man can lead a horse to the water, but a hundred cannot make him drink ;" for although a child may put it into the saucepan, a brigade of the most illustrious " *chefs* " that ever wore white caps, men who, like " *le Grand Vatel*," would die for the honour of their profession, cannot force or coax it to boil well, *if nature has determined otherwise*.

This is the cause why so many good housewives are often in despair when, in spite of plain boiling, steaming, with or without their jackets, drying, &c. &c., the cleanest, smoothest, and best looking farinaceous warranted Yorkshire regents, pink eyes, cups, or apples, turn out " waxy, sad, or bony," and dropsical. " To begin with the beginning," then, in your efforts to merit the reputation of a good cook, let your first

---

* This is a term of the French kitchen for which we have no technical parallel, saving " the first of the season ;" it is generally applied to forced productions.

care be to procure good materials, for without good quality your greatest skill will prove unavailing; but experience will teach you that there are many sorts of potatoes which will " steam " although they wont boil, others which require quick boiling, others slow, others which should be peeled, and others which should retain their skins.

No certain rule can be laid down to be generally adopted among the various methods I have detailed; nothing but constant practice will enable you to judge of the "natures of the craytures," and how to deal with them accordingly. The best guide I can offer is to select those with rough skins, and eschew those with numerous large eyes; and if you have doubts of their soundness, break off a small piece, and if the inside be spotted or honeycombed, reject them as worthless. To proceed with my receipt. Buy your " fruit " in the mould, for the scrubbing and washing as practised by the potato merchants several days before use, greatly injure their crispness and freshness. Scrub them well with a hard brush, but do not cut out the eyes, or partially pare them, as by so doing you will let the water into the heart, and produce all the bad boiling qualities you desire to avoid. Carefully select them of an equal size, and put them into a saucepan with a tablespoonful of salt, and just sufficient cold water to cover them ; for if there be too large a quantity they must necessarily remain in the water long before they boil, and consequently break before they are done. When they have boiled five minutes, pour off the *hot* water and replace it with *cold** and half a tablespoonful of salt. Neither simmer nor " gallop," but boil steadily (with the cover on) three-quarters of an hour, some kinds (which you will discover by watching, and gently testing with a fork, *if they be not cracked*), will not require more than half an hour. When you are sure that they must be done (if you are in doubt, probe them with a fork) drain them dry, and put a clean cloth (kept for the especial purpose) upon them, cover closely with the lid, and let the saucepan stand on the hob until you are ready to serve

---

* The reason for this innovation on the general practice is, that the heart of the potato being peculiarly hard, the outside, in the ordinary course, is done long before it is softened. By chilling its exterior with cold water, the heat of the first boiling strikes to the centre of the vegetable, and as its force gradually increases when the water boils again, by the time the outside has recovered from its chilling, the equilibrium is restored, and the whole potato is evenly done.

your dinner, when you must take them out with a spoon, for if you use a fork for that purpose, you will in all probability break them if they are floury.

N.B. The sooner a potato is eaten after it is done the better.

Cooking and serving in the skins is unquestionably the best method, if the quality of the vegetable will warrant it; but, when peeling is necessary, on the Irish principle of "killing a sick pig to save its life," you must make the most of it.

STEAMING

Is merely putting the potatoes, either pared or in their skins, in a saucepan with a colander bottom made for the purpose, on the top of another saucepan full of *cold* water.

TO BOIL POTATOES IN THE LANCASHIRE WAY.

" Pare the potatoes, cover them with cold water, and boil them slowly until they are quite tender, but watch them carefully, that they may not be overdone; drain off the water entirely, strew some salt over them, leave the saucepan uncovered by the side of the fire, and shake it forcibly every minute or two until the whole of the potatoes appear dry and floury. Lancashire cooks dress the vegetable in this way to perfection, but it is far from an economical mode, as a large portion of the potato adheres to the saucepan; it has, however, many admirers." —*Modern Cookery*, by Eliza Acton.*

BAKED POTATOES.

Clean, scrub, and *dry* carefully some large ones, and bake them in the oven of your range, or in what I have heard called the "American Dutch," before the fire; if very large, they may be parboiled before being put in the oven. With a pat of fresh butter, and a little salt and pepper, they are worthy their great popularity.

MASHED POTATOES.

Peel and boil according to previous directions the quantity you may require, and when done, pour off the water; let the

* In giving insertion to this most excellent receipt, I gladly avail myself of the opportunity of offering my testimony to the great talent of a contemporary, whose book on cookery is perhaps one of the most comprehensive and useful works on the subject that has ever been published.

saucepan stand on the hob, with the cover off, for a minute or two for the steam to evaporate, then with a three-pronged wooden fork either simply break the potatoes, or, as many cooks do, "pulp" them through a colander, or they may be mashed into a paste with a wooden spoon; but I have always found breaking with a fork to be the best process, as it does not destroy the roughness of the flour, which is an agreeable element in the flavour of this dish.

Carefully take out all obstinate and black pieces, then put in an ounce of fresh butter cut in small pieces, half a teaspoonful of salt, and a quarter of a teaspoonful of black pepper, to every pound of potatoes; mix well, and add in the same proportion two tablespoonsful of milk; mix and stir well over the fire, and serve in a very hot dish.

You may for variety "brown" in the Dutch oven.

A mild Spanish onion *boiled until tender*, chopped in pieces and mixed with the potatoes, also forms an agreeable variety.

NEW POTATOES.

It is essential to have these fresh from the ground; wash well, and rub off the skins with a rough cloth (in some instances they must be scraped), put them with a little salt into a saucepan, with just enough of *boiling* water to cover them; boil quickly, with the lid on, from ten minutes to a quarter of an hour, according to size and quality; pour off the water, and hold the saucepan over the fire for about a minute that the potatoes may dry, then serve in a hot dish, in which you have placed an ounce of butter cut in small pieces.

N.B.—New potatoes should be eaten as soon as possible after they are taken from the saucepan, for if they are allowed to stand, their unevaporated steam will make them watery.

POTATO BALLS.

Mash with a little pepper and salt some well boiled potatoes, first with butter (an ounce to each pound), and then with three tablespoonsful of milk, or two of cream, in the same proportion.

Make the paste into balls, roll them in flour or egg and bread-crumbs, and fry them either with butter or good dripping until they are light brown.

The Dutch oven may be used instead of the frying-pan for browning.

SAVOURY POTATO BALLS.

These are made by adding to the above, if you wish for herb
flavour, two sprigs of chopped parsley, one sprig of marjoram,
and another of lemon thyme; if you like onions, substitute a
" mild Spanish," boiled and chopped in small pieces; if you wish
a force-meat flavour, add to the onion and herbs a slice of fried
ham finely minced; the ham may also be used alone.

OYSTER POTATO BALLS.

This is a very palatable dish for suppers, and its production
being so very simple, it only requires to be pointed out to become
popular.

Beard a dozen (more or less, according to the number you
provide for) small plump oysters, cover them singly with the
plain mashed potato paste, roll them with flour, or beaten-up
egg and bread-crumbs, into balls, and fry them in butter or
dripping.

Put into each ball when you make it up a teaspoonful of the
oyster liquor.

POTATO CAKE.

Mash the potatoes in the same way as for potato-balls, adding
the yolks of two beaten-up eggs; put the quantity you may
require for your cake into a tin, " glaze" the top with the white
of the eggs, and bake in a quick oven a quarter of an hour.

Having already given directions (at page 50) for " fried
potatoes" and potatoes à la Maître d'Hôtel, it is needless to
trouble you with more examples.   When you have mastered
the art of boiling, which is the " one thing needful," you may
be safely left to invent another hundred " other ways" for yourself.

I am now about to handle a very delicate subject—one which
in the process of manipulation is pretty sure to bring tears to
the eyes—which, from the pungency or nasal titillation, as certainly follows ; and moreover, when finally discussed, condemns
the tabooed epicure to the performance of quarantine so long as
he abideth not in the odour of " May Fair."   But this potent,
invaluable vegetable, this precious conglomerate bulb, needs no
evidence from me; its merits are acknowledged all the world

over ; therefore I will not attempt to "gild refined gold," or "add a perfume to the violet," but simply announce that I have to deal with

ONIONS.

Notwithstanding the ill-favour with which this fine vegetable is looked upon by what is called in America the "*Upper Ten Thousand*," who always associate it with beef-steaks and vulgarity, it is one of the most useful and valuable friends of all our kitchens, where it constantly appears either openly in its native succulency and "*haut-goût*," or subdued and civilized by artful disguises.

The following able defence from *The Cottage Gardener* of this *fashion-proscribed* vegetable will perhaps be found interesting to those who do not believe their love for it is incompatible with gentility :—

Whether it be the tyranny of fashion, or a morbid sense of delicacy which has all but banished this valuable bulb from the tables of the affluent, we know not ; but certainly it does not find its way thither to one half the extent we are told it does in other countries where it can be grown, and where a taste for the "useful" has been sufficient to overcome that "fastidious denial," which, we believe, is the only excuse for its less general use here. And as the highest authorities have pronounced the onion not only wholesome and nutritious, but likewise valuable for properties peculiarly its own, we trust the day is not far distant when our fair friends will deign to patronize this neglected vegetable, when sent to table prepared *à la Soyer;* for we rest assured that until we have their consent, we must not eat onions, but must content ourselves with the little of its extract that does find its way to our tables under the disguise of something else. Now, the farm labourer in most of our southern counties is not under such restraints. There he may be seen eating his bread and raw onions with a zest which the epicure in vain seeks for amongst his innumerable dishes, cooked and prepared in accordance with the most improved practice of the day ; and, though we have no doubt the rustic would willingly exchange his onion and salt for a beef-steak or mutton-chop, and benefit by the change, yet we should be at a loss to find a better substitute for animal food; and the healthy appearance the rural population have in the districts where this bulb is most grown and used, tells, in undeniable language, that their food agrees with them.

The late Mr. Read, in his Lectures on Cookery, fully corroborates these opinions, and, speaking of the great utility of onions in all shapes, observes :—

When used in moderation, onions are an indispensable adjunct to all good cookery, especially in soups, sauces, made dishes, and stuffings ; or, as Swift sang—

There is, in every cook's opinion,
No savoury dish without an onion.

And to youthful gourmands he gives this wholesome advice—

> *But lest your kissing should be spoil'd,*
> *The onions should be thoroughly boil'd.*

For making ragouts or sauces, the small white onions are the mildest and best. For this purpose cut off the two ends and boil them in plenty of water for a quarter of an hour, then put them into cold water; take off the skin and first coating, and stew them in broth or stock till tender. The stock may be then thickened with butter and flour, and seasoned with a little pepper, salt, and a small bit of sugar, and served with any dish you think proper; or, when boiled tender, the onions may, when cold, be eaten as a salad, with pepper, salt, and oil, or with the addition of cold boiled potatoes sliced. For stocks, soups, and broths, the larger onions may be used; and for these purposes they require to be merely peeled, slit in quarters, and boiled or "sweated" with the meat. In the preparation of all sauces (except onion sauce), made dishes, and soups, parsley should be used, as a corrective to the strong odour which the onions impart to the breath. The experience of ages has taught cooks the necessity of doing this, although there are but few of them who know why the best works in the culinary art recommend the two to be used together. Parsley, when eaten even after garlic, will prevent the breath from smelling so disagreeably as it otherwise would.

The mildness of Spanish onions induces many persons to prefer them to the common sort; they are consequently often eaten for supper with bread and butter, and with meats for dinner. They may be either baked, boiled, or roasted in a Dutch oven before the fire. When they are required of a very mild flavour, boil them in plenty of water, first taking off their skins; but when they are to be baked or roasted, their skins should be allowed to remain on. When done, take off one or two of the outer coatings of the onions with their skins, and serve them with cold butter, pepper, and salt. They are excellent served with baked or roast mutton, boiled or stewed beef; or when made into a sauce, with boiled rabbits, tripe, or mutton cutlets, or with hot roasted potatoes, as a supper dish. *Sauce soubise* is much approved of, even by ladies, when made with these onions.

It is quite as true as "union is strength," that *onions are strong;* but they are nevertheless toothsome, particularly when fried with a beefsteak; but although a taste for this savoury *"friture"* may, like Charles Lamb's "roast pig," have "grown" upon us, it is certainly not advisable to indulge in it just before going into genteel society. Still, "beefsteaks and onions" have been (Mayfair and Belgravia, cease to apply the vinaigrette to your aristocratic nostrils) patronized by royalty! There is a legend extant that that "Glass of Fashion," the late Count D'Orsay, and the Emperor of the French when he was in a chrysalis state, indulged in them at Gore House. George III. was fond of a roasted goose in which "violets" bore a prominent part in the stuffing; and "on the third day of the battle of Dresden," says Hoffman, the German novelist, who was in the town, "the Emperor's (Napoleon I.) energies were greatly impaired by the effects of a shoulder of mutton stuffed with onions," so we may live in hopes that some day, when the world is wiser, this poor man's delicacy will cease to be smuggled into our genteel kitchens, and its aroma will not be thought disagreeable, even though it "come betwixt the wind and our nobility."

As it would serve no purpose but to swell my book, to give directions for roasting, boiling, frying, and stewing a vegetable which the most inexperienced housewife knows when used by itself will almost cook itself, I will proceed to the next useful bulb, and say a few words on

TURNIPS.

The mention of turnips always conjures up in homely English minds an association of a "boiled leg of mutton and trimmings;" indeed, so national is the association, that it served as a knock-down blow to end an annoyance to which the late Charles Lamb, of facetious memory, was subjected to while travelling in a mail-coach, in the days when wits were in, and hard drinking went out, with a Yorkshire farmer.

"What dost ee think o' manglewurzle? how be beets wi' you? and will inguns and tatars go oop or down?" and a hundred other equally interesting questions, were put and vaguely answered with polite resignation; but, when after sixty miles of torture (at the rate of about seven miles an hour), "and how be turnips loikely to turn out this year in your parts?" was asked, the opportunity for a ".facer" couldn't be resisted by the humorist, who, gathering up all his *vis comica* of look and tone, replied, "Why, that, my good sir, will entirely depend on the boiled legs of mutton."

BOILED TURNIPS.

Pare them, taking care to remove all the inner rind, put them into the saucepan with the meat you are cooking, either whole or cut in halves; young turnips will require three quarters of an hour, and if they are middle-aged an hour and a quarter. Old ones should never be used when they are to be eaten with the meat, for they are stringy and bitter; indeed, they should be cautiously used even for soup.

MASHED TURNIPS.

Press the liquor from them by placing them between two plates, beat them up with an ounce of butter to about four middling-sized turnips, and half a teaspoonful of pepper and salt. Be careful to remove lumps, &c. You may, if you have company, add a spoonful or two of cream, then warm, and mix in a stewpan.

I will say nothing of stewing in butter, *Rissoles*, &c. &c., as they are extravagant varieties belonging to the French kitchen.

CARROTS,

When plain-boiled, form part of the leg of mutton trimmings, and "hold their own" with boiled beef and pork. Care should be taken that they are not too large or too old. It is, of course, understood that they must be scraped when at maturity, and rubbed when very young. To accompany delicate dishes, the small French carrot is in great favour.

N.B.—All kinds of carrots (excepting the small French, which require a full hour) must be boiled *two* hours.

CARROTS A LA MAITRE D'HOTEL.

Melt an ounce of butter in a stewpan, with a teaspoonful of chopped parsley, half a teaspoonful of salt, and a quarter of a teaspoonful of cayenne ; then put in half a dozen small (boiled) French carrots, and shake them into the butter and parsley.

SUMMER CABBAGE.

Before giving instructions for cooking this "sweet harbinger of summer," it is necessary to say a few words on its proper preparation for the saucepan.

Take as a rule that all kinds of "*pot* greens" harbour amid their leaves a large quantity of insects and dirt, or, not to mince the matter, grubs, caterpillars, slugs, small worms, mould, stones, &c.; these the clean and careful housewife must remove in the following manner :—

After cutting off the outer leaves and the stump, if you see small green or black spots on the stalks, or a number of holes in the foliage, you may be certain that undesirable tenants occupy the interior of the premises ; to ensure their ejectment, steep the vegetable tenement in salt and water for an hour, then pull open the leaves round the heart, carefully remove all *skulkers*, and wash well in two or three waters. If you do not perceive the above signs of the presence of disagreeable tenantry, examining and washing will be sufficient, for " steeping" is apt to destroy the freshness and crispness of the vegetable.

Another hint: " green water" should never be thrown down the sink, but be kept in a covered pan or jug until you have an opportunity of sending it out of the house, either to assist in nourishing the animals we make bacon of, or, if you live in London, to augment the turgid stream against whose unsavoury odours the *Times* has so energetically, and it is hoped (by the exertions of the sanitary commission which originated through its warnings) successfully, denounced. To return to the cabbages : put them, with a tablespoonful of salt, into boiling water, and the " *smallest taste in life*" of common soda—be careful to adhere strictly to the *quantity* of this direction, for if you over-do the *water-softening agent*, you will not only destroy the flavour of the vegetable, but cause the outer leaves to be boiled to pulp before the heart is half done.

You must regulate your time for boiling according to the season of the year and the size of the cabbages ; for instance, the spring plants being very tender, they will require but a quarter of an hour ; in the autumn, being larger and harder, they will take from five-and-twenty minutes to half an hour ; and in the winter, being stronger and tougher, they will want at least three quarters of an hour. Strain through a colander, and *press them quite dry* between two plates.

CAULIFLOWERS AND BROCCOLI.

Be very careful in your examination and washing before you put these in the saucepan, for their stalks and branches afford peculiar facilities for " squatting" to many insect settlers. The time required for cooking is (according to size and season) from twenty minutes to half an hour.

Put a little salt in the water, but *no soda*, for the latter will cause the flower to drop from the stem.

SPINACH

Must be picked leaf by leaf, then take off the stalks and thoroughly wash the leaves in *five or six waters*, or they will be, as is too often the case when carelessly prepared, *gritty.* When you are sure that every particle of mould, &c., is removed, drain in a colander, and put the leaves into a large saucepan with a tablespoonful of salt, and a pinch of soda sprinkled over them, then add a quart of *boiling* water, press the leaves down, and boil quickly ten minutes, stirring frequently. When done, strain and press carefully, as this vegetable retains the water more than any other.

This is the plain, and to my mind the best, way of sending spinach to table, as it preserves the true flavour of the plant ; but if you wish to make it richer, after straining and pressing, put your spinach on a board, chop it fine, and place it in a stewpan with an ounce of butter, half a teaspoonful of pepper and salt (in equal quantities), stir well until the butter is absorbed, turn into a hot dish, cut the pulp into small squares or diamonds, and serve with poached eggs and slices of fried bacon, garnishing with sippets of fried bread.

SPINACH IN THE FRENCH MANNER.

This, to many plain English tastes, is a scientific manner of destroying the flavour of a vegetable which, when simply cooked, is most agreeable. The process is as follows :—After picking, boiling, straining, and pressing, put your spinach into a pan of fresh water ; and when it is cold make it into balls, and squeeze them in your hands until all the water is expelled ; chop fine on a board with a wooden spade ;* then melt an ounce of butter in a stewpan, put the spinach into it, mix well for ten minutes, lightly dredge with a tablespoonful of flour and a teaspoonful of salt ; add gradually a quarter of a pint of boiling cream or the yolks of two beaten-up eggs, in which case omit the flour ; two tablespoonfuls of *velouté*, or strong white stock, and a teaspoonful of pounded sugar; mix well, and serve in a hot dish with light brown sippets of fried bread or puff-paste baked in fanciful devices.

* In France, where spinach is indigenous, not only this instrument, but many other ingenious utensils are used for its most perfect manipulation. Visitors to Paris cannot fail to be struck with the numerous ways in which this familiarly called "broom of the stomach" is served up by the *restaurateurs;* and its various "Protean shapes" on the boards of the vendors in the markets and the greengrocers' shops, when prepared with sorrel, garlic, saffron, and curd cheese, lead our unsophisticated countrymen to suppose it to be the "fresh laver" they see advertised in the newspapers, or the "caviare" alluded to by Shakspeare.

ASPARAGUS.

Scrape well, cut the heads to an equal length, tie them together in small bundles, and boil briskly twenty minutes, serve with a toast at the bottom of the dish, and butter-sauce à la Tickletooth.

Endeavour to cook this vegetable as soon as possible after it is cut; but it will keep well, if put on the stones in a cool larder, for three or four days. Do not keep it in water, or you will make it hard and destroy the flavour.

ASPARAGUS POINTS.

Chop the tender parts of the small green plants into small pieces, and boil them loose in the saucepan for twenty minutes —then put them into a stewpan with an ounce of butter, and brown them; add a tablespoonful of cream, and another of gravy, or, if you have it, Béchamel sauce.

GREEN PEAS.

Shell them at home, as there are obvious reasons against buying them ready shelled—when they first come in, being young, they will need no separation, but as the season advances, you must sort them in the shelling, and give the old, and the middle-aged, ten and five minutes' boiling before you put in the younger ones.

Boil with a good handful of salt, quickly, from twenty to twenty-five minutes, according to age and size; strain through a colander, and serve in a deep dish with an ounce or so of butter (according to the quantity of peas) cut in small pieces over the top.

It is the old English custom, to boil and serve with the peas, a few leaves of fresh mint; but as many have an objection to it, it is advisable to boil it in a separate small saucepan, and serve it as garnish round the dish, and so propitiate all tastes.

N.B.—*Never, under any circumstances, unless you wish entirely to destroy all flavour, and reduce your peas to pulp, boil them with soda.* This favourite atrocity of the English kitchen cannot be too strongly condemned.

GREEN PEAS A LA FRANCAISE.

If, according to Brillat Savarin, " the truffle is the diamond of the kitchen," in what category are we to place green peas? Is there in the whole of the vegetable creation any known root, pod, pulse, plant, leaf, or offshoot, that does not doff its cap and bow its head to the pride of the garden and the field; the native, the common, the to all classes, favourite luxury; the spring-tinted, saccharine, pulpy orbs, which are sold at Christmas to the millionaire at *ten guineas a quart*, and in July to the million at *fourpence a peck?* To go no further into the *garden* or *field* of pea poesie, green peas may be styled *our* kitchen emeralds, and when we see them in the hands of a French cook, we share the uncomfortable presentiment of the ducks, who, while feeding on their blossoms, have a vague consciousness that their fate will be governed by the method of cooking them. But, however, as tastes differ, and the French mode has many admirers, I will record it.

Put a quart of fresh-gathered and shelled young peas into a pan with a quarter of a pound of fresh butter, and two quarts of cold water, rub the peas and butter together with the fingers until well mixed, then pour off the water and put the peas into a stewpan with the hearts of two lettuces shred small, a small onion, and a sprig of parsley, a dessertspoonful of pounded sugar, and a quarter of a teaspoonful of salt—cover well, and stew gently half an hour. Next put about two ounces of fresh butter on a plate with a dessertspoonful of flour, and knead them together, put this into the peas, and toss the whole together until well mixed. When you serve, take out the parsley and onions, but let the lettuce remain.

BROAD BEANS,

When very young and served with parsley and butter and a piece of good bacon, are considered by many as one of the treats of the season. Simple boiling in hot water from twenty to five-and-twenty minutes, according to age, is all they require.

FRENCH BEANS AND SCARLET RUNNERS.

Wash well, and "top and tail" them, break them in half, put them into a basin (without water) and sprinkle a tablespoonful of salt over them, in about ten minutes put them with a *very* small pinch of soda into a saucepan full of boiling water; boil from ten to fifteen minutes, and strain dry.

When the beans are getting elderly, break off the pointed end, and string them down the back and front. When they are very old, you must split them down the middle and cut them in half; they will then require from twenty-five minutes to half an hour.

The French method is to chop them up (after boiling) and warm them with butter in the stewpan.

VEGETABLE MARROW.

Choose them young and of a moderate size, divide them longways in the centre, if they are large, cut them in quarters, take out the seeds, and put the pieces into boiling water, with a little salt; boil twenty minutes, take out with a slice, and serve on a toast with melted butter.

Lettuces and spring radishes may be treated in the same manner.

Thinking the foregoing examples for the proper cooking of vegetables quite sufficient for the scope of my work, I will wind up the subject with the celebrated

RECIPE FOR A WINTER SALAD, BY SYDNEY SMITH.

Two large potatoes, passed through kitchen sieve,
Unwonted softness to the salad give.
Of mordent mustard add a single spoon;
Distrust the condiment which bites so soon;
But deem it not, thou man of herbs, a fault
To add a double quantity of salt.
Three times the spoon with oil of Lucca crown,
And once with vinegar procured from town.
True flavour needs it, and your poet begs,
The pounded yellow of two well-boiled eggs.
Let onion atoms lurk within the bowl,
And, scarce suspected, animate the whole.
And, lastly, on the favoured compound toss
A magic teaspoonful of anchovy sauce;
Then, though green turtle fail, though venison's tough,
And ham and turkey are not boiled enough,
Serenely full the epicure may say—
Fate cannot harm me—I have dined to-day.

I cannot quit this portion of my labour without strongly urging the great importance of procuring every kind of vege-table as soon as possible after it is cut or dug up; the reason of this is obvious, for when the "milk" has left the plant and the air has dried the "pores" of the bulb, the flavour becomes greatly deteriorated ; consequently those who live in towns, and are obliged to make their purchases in markets or of green-grocers, know but little of the mellowness, crispness, and sweet-ness of " our garden" produce.   Careful town housewives should therefore make their purchases *early on market days ;*   or, instead of having the articles they require but *a day or two old,* which from their being gathered for loading a day beforehand is *always* the case, they will in all probability be put off with withered, sapless plants, and roots kept in water in a cellar for perhaps a week or more.   To know when vegetables have been "*refreshed*" is no easy task, but after paying for a few practical lessons, a pretty certain judgment may be formed, and bitter asparagus, sticky turnips, decomposing cabbages, diseased pota-toes, and tasteless peas and beans, may be avoided.   In all cases, I would advise the housekeeper to market for herself.

PUDDINGS AND PIES.

In approaching this very important subject, so wide is the field to be traversed, and hydra-headed are the prejudices I have to combat, that nothing but boldly *pinning* each kind of paste to the board, and by *floury* arguments insidiously *kneading* butter, dripping, suet, and lard into civilized *fatuity*, will ever enable me to *roll* out my system, and *manipulate* my recipes.

The first point to ascertain is, when does pastry cease to be digestible ?   Some eminent doctors tell us that in any form it is the most destructive and unwholesome thing we can eat, in-asmuch as it generates bile, dyspepsia, and gout, and when it is allied to fruit, and eaten constantly, inevitable decay of the teeth.   On the other hand, equally eminent practitioners as strenuously advocate a moderate indulgence in it as advisable for its nutritious qualities, as well as its digestibility.

On the " fallacies of the faculty" I will not pretend to argue, for the mole-like working of medical science so closely re-sembles the navigation of a ship in a fog, that it is entirely a matter of chance whether the port be reached or a rock be run upon.   A piece of sponge charged with acids, thrust with a strip of whalebone down the throat, *may* be a cure for every-thing, from consumption down to a refractory chilblain ; mes-meric passes *may* eradicate the gout and tic-douloureux, and give vitality to a wooden leg ; being taken out of bed and wrapped in wet sheets *may* consolidate the nerves, and sweat away chronic rheumatism; and infinitesimal doses of subtle poisons *may* restore a shattered constitution to its pristine vigour; still, *clever men have been known to make mistakes.*

In a few years many of our present " bubbles of the day" will be found, like Abernethy's " blue pill "—which, after he had prescribed it, in firm belief of its curative excellence, for more than twenty years, he himself denounced as " the very worst thing that could be taken*—*scientific delusions.* But, despite of all time and all opinions, there is one kind of pastry which stands boldly forward to give the " loud lie" to all invidious assertions against its digestibility and nourishing properties.

DUMPLINGS

Will always maintain an important position on the tables of our labouring classes; in fact, the taste for them may be considered national, particularly in the agricultural counties.

Let them be mere flour and water "chokers," as hard as paving stones, or sad and heavy "yeastys," were they ever known to qualify Giles Scroggings or Simon Snaggers for the waters of Vichy? or when did cherries, gooseberries, damsons, or mulberries, wrapped in plain paste, ever destroy the white and solid nutcrackers of Kitty Clover or Sally Cowslip?

It is clear, then, that at least *that* branch of pastry is wholesome; Yorkshire puddings, suet dumplings, and meat pies and puddings, may also be placed in the same category; but when we approach the higher walks; when puff, flaky, and short crusts are ventured upon, there's the rub! They may challenge controversy, and sometimes *richly* merit every objection that can be urged against them.

---

* This is a well-known fact. A patient being asked by the Doctor in his peculiar brusque manner what medicine he had been taking, replied, "Your blue pill, sir," received, to his astonishment and dismay, the following alarming confession of error:—

" I thought so, I thought so; it's the worst, the very worst thing in the world, sir! Make your will, sir, make your will; for it will kill you, sir, kill you."

" But," urged the trembling patient, " you yourself prescribed it for me ten years ago."

" Very likely, very likely," answered the Doctor, repentantly rubbing up his hair, and nervously twirling his watch-chain; "I believed in it *then*, know better now; poison, sir, rank poison. If you wash your shirt with oxalic acid, though it may whiten it, it will rot it—rot it, sir. Your stomach is like your shirt, the blue pill's worse than the acid; it will kill you, sir, it will kill you. I was a fool to recommend it."

It shall now be my endeavour to show you how, by a little care and skill, you may make your paste both light and digestible.

Taking each of the three above-mentioned kinds under its proper head, I will first proceed to show the best method of producing what is technically called

FLAKY PASTE.

In the first place, have your hands, your pasteboard or marble-slab, your dredging-box, your rolling-pin, and all your other utensils, in "*working order*" (it is some time since I used that expression, but you'll remember it); next, having decided on the size of the pie or pudding you wish to make (allowing a quarter of a pound of butter to half a pound of flour), put half the butter, with the whole of the flour, into a paste-basin, rub them well together with the tips of your fingers *as quickly and lightly as possible;* then in the same manner mix with cold water until you have formed a loose paste, then flour your board or slab, and, also quickly and lightly, roll the paste upon it to the substance of a thin pancake, upon this spread with a knife over its entire surface a third of the butter you have put aside; fold the paste in three, and roll it again to the thin pancake, coat it as before with half of the remaining butter, fold and roll again, spread the remainder of the butter, then roll for the last time.

It may be thought that if the quantity of butter and flour be correct, and strict attention is bestowed on spreading, folding, and rolling, that everything necessary has been done for the production of a fine light paste; but there is something yet needed: unless the hand that forms it be " as light as a feather," and the whole process is performed with celerity, it will be " as heavy as lead." How often have I seen the flour and butter " squashed" together with both hands, the rolling-pin used as a beater, and the whole force of a stalwart pair of arms thrown upon it when employed in rolling the pancake. The three essentials in the preparation of all kinds of pastry are, to mix well, so that perfect smoothness may be obtained, to roll and spread lightly, and never to dwell long on any portion of the work.

As the success or failure of your paste will depend a great deal on the temperature of your oven, be careful to get it up to the heat you require, which, though brisk, should not be too fierce.

SHORT PASTE

Is formed by mixing *all* the butter with the flour in the basin, making the paste a little firmer, and rolling out but once. If a richer paste be required, add to each half-pound of flour an ounce of powdered sugar, half the yolk of a beaten-up egg, and a quarter of a teaspoonful of salt.

PUFF PASTE.

The butter and flour must be in equal quantities, and the yolk of a beaten-up egg, half a teaspoonful of salt, and half a pint of cold water should be used with every pound of flour and butter. Mix the flour with the egg, the water, and the salt, lightly and quickly, with the tips of the fingers, making the paste moderately firm. Then place it on the slab, and put the butter (which should be pressed in a cloth to expel the milk) in one piece in the centre, fold the paste over it, and set it aside, on ice (if possible) in the summer, or on the stones in a cold cellar, for a quarter of an hour; then place it on the slab, with a dredging of flour over and under it, and roll it out to the thickness of about half an inch, observing that you keep it square at both ends, as much of the success depends on due attention being paid to the turning and folding; then lay it in three folds, and roll it out again in the opposite direction; fold as before, and put it back on the ice or stones for another quarter of an hour, then roll out and fold once more. This paste, which is very rich, is principally employed for savoury patties, fruit puffs, and delicate tartlets. When carefully made, and well baked, it will rise several inches.

SUET CRUST.

For boiling, chop into *small* pieces six ounces of good beef or veal suet, mix it with a pound of flour and sufficient water to form a firm paste.

For baking, shred the suet, and rub it well into the flour before you put in the water. This paste should also be firm.

LARD AND DRIPPING CRUSTS

are produced in the same manner as the " flaky paste," lard or dripping being used as economical substitutes; for in these, as well as in the foregoing pastes, lightness of hand and rapidity of execution are equally essential.

Presuming that you are now in possession of all the secrets of paste-making, I will, as I have directed in my receipt for the production of the "puff" variety, leave it for awhile to settle, and proceed to another branch of the subject—pudding-making—to which the following whimsical, yet withal philosophical, meditation, culled from Boswell's *Journal of a Tour to the Hebrides*, with Doctor Johnson, in 1785, will, I trust, be found a pleasant introduction. It is remarkable for conveying in a very few words the essence of a lengthy and learned treatise:—

MEDITATION ON A PUDDING.

Let us seriously reflect what a pudding is composed of. It is composed of flour, that once waved in golden grain, and drank the dews of the morning; of milk pressed from the swelling udder by the gentle hand of the beautiful milkmaid, whose beauty and innocence might have recommended a worse draught, who while she stroked the udder indulged in no ambitious thoughts of wandering in palaces, formed no plans for the destruction of her fellow-creatures—milk that is drawn from the cow, that useful animal that eats the grass of the field, and supplies us with that which made the greatest part of the food of mankind in the age which the poets have agreed to call golden. It is made with an egg, that miracle of nature, which the theoretical Barnet has compared to creation.

An egg contains water within its beautiful smooth surface; and an un formed mass, by the incubation of the parent, becomes a regular animal, furnished with bones and sinews, and covered with feathers.

Let us consider:—can there be more wanting to complete the meditation of a pudding? If more be wanting, more can be found. It contains salt, which keeps the sea from putrefaction—salt which is made with the image of intellectual excellence, contributes to the formation of a pudding.

On the principle that an artisan should know the quality and capability of the tools he has to work with, I think it necessary, before I specify the various kinds of puddings that can be made for the family table, to offer a few remarks on the properties of the articles that must be used in their production, together with a practical hint or two on the best manner of preparing them.

That the information I wish to convey may be perfectly clear and easy to be acted upon, I will, instead of generalizing, treat each article separately.

FLOUR, for fine pastry, should be dried in a slack oven, and sifted. Biscuit flour may be used for "puff paste," but it should not be boiled. For family pies and puddings, there is no need either to dry or sift.

MILK.—For this, if you do not keep your own cow, you are entirely in the hands of your purveyor. The London "sky blue" mixture is the most difficult to deal with, but it is not *always* as blue as it is painted. In the country, where you get it pure and fresh, a much smaller quantity is required than when it has been "stretched" with water, chalk, potato starch, &c. &c. In this experience can alone direct you.

"Scalding," particularly in warm weather, is to be recommended, as it not only prevents the milk from turning, but enables you to remove from it all the "stretching" impurities. The process is as follows:—put the milk into a jug or basin, and place it in a saucepan with just enough cold water to cover about a third of the vessel. As soon as the water boils, take out the jug or basin containing the milk, and set it aside in a cool place. When cold, the top will be creamed, and the impurities will remain at the bottom.

CREAM.—This is also greatly adulterated in London. By "scalding" you may remove the deleterious matter; but if the quality be poor and thin, a beaten-up egg should be used to give it consistency.

BUTTER, for fine pastry, should be fresh; but for general purposes, use good salt. It may also be clarified by pouring boiling water on it and leaving it to get cold; in this state it is nearly equal to the best fresh; it should, however, be used as soon as possible, for it will not keep.

EGGS vary considerably in size; judgment is therefore required to use more or less according to the quantity set down in the receipt. Duck eggs, which in general are larger and fuller flavoured than those of the hen, are greatly used for all kinds of puddings and pies. Be careful to break each egg separately in a cup, for if it should happen to be bad, you can put it aside, which you cannot do if you break your whole quantity in a bowl. Remember what I have previously said about "that will do;" one musty egg will flavour a large pudding; trust, therefore, to your nose as well as your eyes, and on no occasion hope a doubtful one "will do."

LARD.—It is best to purchase the pig's "flair" and "melt it down" yourself, as you will then be sure it is not whitened with arsenic or thickened with lime, both of which adulterations are still, in spite of Mr. Wakley's exposures in the *Lancet*, very prevalent: under all circumstances, never use it unless it is quite fresh. It may be mixed to advantage in small quantities with butter in the formation of "flaky" and "puff" pastes.

DRIPPING should be clarified before it is used, and carefully freed from gravy, cinders, &c. Be sure that it is fresh.

SUET.—To have it fresh is the main point, for should any portion be at all musty it will entirely destroy your pie or pudding. Beef is the best, veal the next, especially for making crust, but mutton is the lightest for dumplings.

The best method for keeping, is to wipe the piece carefully, sprinkle a little salt or flour over it, and *hang it up* in a cool place.

If the pieces are too small to be hung up, put them on a plate, and turn them every day, wiping the plate carefully, and adding a little fresh flour or salt.

You will, as matters of course, carefully wash and pick your currants and stone fruit, remove mouldiness from your preserves, and be *quite certain* of the "working" condition of your pudding cloths, moulds, basins, tins, &c. That your oven is at the proper heat when you bake, and the *water is boiling* when you put in your puddings and dumplings, must also form part of your "matters of course."

Having shown you the properties of your principal tools, I will now direct you how to use them. I will take as my first example the especial "pet" of all housewives, which each flatters herself she can make much better than any of her neighbours, a

CHRISTMAS PLUM-PUDDING.

This peculiarly national dish, which Lord Byron, during his sojourn in Florence, after devoting a whole morning to giving directions to his cook for its proper preparation, for an English treat to his friends on his birthday, had served up as soup in a tureen, is now so well known throughout the Continent, that in some guise or other, although it must be confessed our "home-bred youth" may often say with Hamlet, "Thou comest in such a *questionable* shape," it is to be found occupying a distinguished position among the *entremets* in the *cartes* of the highest and the lowest restaurateurs. "*Blom Budin*" au *Rhum* or *Vin de Madére* being considered, like "*Pal-al*" and red hair, a *Britannique spécialité*.

To "make assurance doubly sure," and give the inexperienced housewife an opportunity of perfecting her *own* pudding by adopting the good points and eschewing the bad of several "old masters" and mistresses of the culinary art (as a young painter will try to retain the beauties of a Turner or a Rembrandt, while he avoids their eccentricities), I will for once depart from my usual course, and give two or three "other ways" from the works of my most talented contemporaries.

CHRISTMAS PLUM-PUDDINGS.

SOYER'S RECEIPT.

Pick and stone one pound of the best Malaga raisins, which put in a basin, with one pound of currants (well washed, dried and picked), a pound and a half of good beef suet (chopped, but not too fine), three quarters of a pound of white or brown sugar, two ounces of candied lemon and orange peel, two ounces of candied citron, six ounces of flour, and a quarter of a pound of bread crumbs, with a little grated nutmeg; mix the whole well together, with eight whole eggs and a little milk. Have ready a plain or ornamented pudding mould, well butter the interior, pour the above mixture into it, cover a sheet of paper over, tie the mould in a cloth, put the pudding into a large stewpan containing boiling water, and let it boil quite fast for four hours and a half (or it may be boiled by merely tying it in a pudding-cloth previously well floured, forming the shape by laying the cloth in a round-bottomed basin, and pouring the mixture in; it will make no difference in the time required for boiling). When done, take it out of the cloth, turn from the mould upon your dish, sprinkle a little powdered sugar over, and serve with the following sauce in a boat:—Put the yolks of three eggs in a stewpan, with a spoonful of powdered sugar, and a gill of milk; mix well together, add a little lemon peel, and stir over the fire until becoming thickish (but do not let it boil), when add two glasses of brandy, and serve separate. The above sauce may be served poured over the pudding, if approved of. An excellent improvement to a plum-pudding is to use half a pound of beef marrow, cut into small dice, omitting the same quantity of suet.

MRS. ACTON'S RECEIPT.

To three ounces of flour, and the same weight of fine lightly grated bread-crumbs, add six of beef kidney-suet chopped small, six of raisins weighed after they are stoned, six of well cleaned currants, four ounces of minced apples, five of sugar, two of candied orange-rind, half a teaspoonful of nutmeg mixed with powdered mace, a very little salt, a small glass of brandy, and three whole eggs. Mix and beat these ingredients well together, tie them lightly in a thickly floured cloth, and boil them for three hours and a half. We can recommend this as a remarkably light small rich pudding. It may be served with German wine or punch sauce.

DOCTOR KITCHENER'S RECEIPT.

Suet, chopped fine, six ounces; Malaga raisins, stoned, six ounces; currants. nicely washed and picked, eight ounces; bread-crumbs, three ounces; flour, three ounces; eggs, three; sixth of a nutmeg; small blade of mace, same quantity of cinnamon, pounded as fine as possible; half a teaspoonful of salt; half a pint of milk, or rather less; sugar four ounces; to which may be added candied lemon one ounce, citron half an ounce. Beat the eggs and spice together; mix the milk with them by degrees, then the rest of the ingredients; dip a fine close linen cloth into boiling water, and put it in a hair-sieve, flour it a little, and tie it up close; put it into a saucepan containing six quarts of boiling water; keep a kettle of boiling water along side of it, and fill up your pot as it wastes. Be sure to keep it boiling six hours at least.

MY OWN RECEIPT A LA TICKLETOOTH.

One pound of muscatel raisins, stoned, and cut in half; one pound of Sultana raisins; one pound of best currants, washed, picked, and rubbed dry; one pound of fresh beef suet, chopped fine; one pound of moist sugar; two ounces of candied citron peel; two ounces of candied orange peel; two ounces of candied lemon peel, and half the rind of a fresh lemon chopped in small pieces—the candied peels should be cut in strips; two ounces of bitter and two ounces of Jordan almonds blanched, and cut in not too small pieces; three nutmegs grated; a small tea-spoonful of powdered white ginger, and the same quantity of salt; one pound of fine bread crumbs; three quarters of a pound of fine flour. Mix all well together in a large pan before moistening. Beat up nine eggs (if they are small, ten) for a quarter of an hour, add a wineglassful of good ale, beat up again and stir this well into the pudding until all be thoroughly mixed. Damp a close pudding-cloth in the boiling water, then flour it well, turn the pudding into it, tie it up securely, *very nearly* tight, for it should not have much room to swell—BOIL IT NINE HOURS. Remember the old adage,

> Plum-pudding hot,
> Plum-pudding cold,
> Plum-pudding in the pot
> Nine days old.

When done, lift it out of the saucepan, and put it in a pan of cold water, turn it over three or four times, take it out, stand it on a colander, untie the string, and carefully turn the pudding into a large hot dish.

Have ready four ounces of blanched Jordan almonds, stick them all over the pudding, make a hole in the centre with a spoon, pour into it two wineglasses of brandy, and a third over it.

N.B.—If you boil in a saucepan, before you put in the pudding, place a small plate, turned upside down, at the bottom.

This will prevent it from sticking. If you use a copper, this precaution is unnecessary. Keep the saucepan, or copper, continually boiling, and be sure to have plenty of water. This *I* (of course) consider the very best receipt in the world; at all events, it is the result of forty years' experience, and may be valued as a good " study" for a young housewife to improve upon.

As rhyme is sometimes more impressive than reason, to complete my examples on this subject I will give you

A METRICAL RECIPE FOR A CHRISTMAS PUDDING.

AIR—*"Jeanette and Jeanot."*

If you wish to make the pudding in which every one delights,
Of six pretty new-laid eggs, you must take the yolks and whites,
Beat them well up in a basin till they thoroughly combine,
And be sure you chop the suet up particularly fine.
Take a pound of well-stoned raisins, and a pound of currants dried,
A pound of pounded sugar, and some candied peel beside;
Rub them all up well together with a pound of wheaten flour,
And let them stand to settle for a quarter of an hour.
Then tie the mixture in a cloth, and put it in a pot—
Some people like the water cold, and some prefer it hot.
But though I don't know which of these two plans I ought to praise,
I know it ought to boil an hour for every pound it weighs.
Oh! if I were Queen of France, or, still better, Pope of Rome,
I'd have a Christmas pudding every day I dined at home;
All the world should have a piece, and if any did remain,
Next morning for my breakfast I would have it fried again.

Leigh Hunt's Journal.   F. J. S.

A PLAIN PLUM-PUDDING.

Mix half a pound of stoned muscatel raisins (cut in half), three ounces of bread-crumbs, four ounces of flour, a quarter of a teaspoonful of grated nutmeg, two ounces of moist sugar, and seven ounces of finely-chopped suet; then beat up the yolks and whites of three eggs (carefully removing all specks), and gradually add to them half a pint of milk; put this into the pan with the raisins, &c., and mix with a wooden spoon until you have formed a smooth *thick* batter; let this remain for half an hour in a well-buttered earthenware mould or basin, then tie a pudding-cloth tightly over it, put it into boiling water, and boil it three hours.

Serve with melted butter flavoured with sherry or vanille.

PLAIN SUET PUDDING.

Half a pound of flour, three ounces of beef suet chopped fine, two ounces of currants, or sultana raisins, mix to a thick paste, tie in a cloth, and boil an hour.

BLACK CAPS, OR COLLEGE PUDDINGS.

Put the beaten-up yolks and whites of three eggs into a basin with two ounces of flour, half a teaspoonful of grated nutmeg, an ounce of candied *lemon*-peel chopped in small pieces, and a quarter of a teaspoonful of grated ginger, mix well with a wooden spoon to a smooth batter, then add six ounces of beef suet (chopped fine), and six ounces of well washed and picked currants.

Boil in a cloth an hour, or in small cups (tied in a cloth) three-quarters of an hour. Serve with melted butter, flavoured with white wine or a little rum.

BOILED BATTER PUDDING.

Beat into a smooth batter three tablespoonsful of flour and a pint of milk, then add the beaten-up yolks and whites of three eggs; boil in a well-buttered basin, with a damped and floured cloth tied closely over it, one hour and a half.

Serve with melted-butter and sugar, flavoured with wine, rum, vanille, &c. &c.

N.B.—All batter-puddings must be put into boiling water immediately they are made, or the flour will sink to the bottom. Boil briskly.

BOILED RICE PUDDING.

Parboil (technically called "swell") three ounces of rice in a pint of cold water ten minutes, strain quite dry, then, having well-floured a cloth, spread the rice over it, and put in the centre two ounces of well-washed and picked currants or sultana raisins, cover them with the rice, tie the cloth securely (leaving a little room for swelling), then put the pudding into *boiling* water, and boil an hour and a half. Serve with melted butter and sugar, flavoured with anything you may fancy.

BAKED RICE PUDDING.

"Swell" two ounces of well washed and picked rice, and six bay-leaves, in a pint and a half of milk, a quarter of an hour;

take out the bay-leaves, and add to the milk and rice a smooth batter composed of the yolks and whites of three beaten-up eggs, an ounce and a half of beef or veal suet finely shaved, or the same quantity of butter cut in small pieces, two tea-spoonsful of arrowroot, a quarter of a pound of moist sugar, and half a pint of milk; mix well, and bake in a dish in a brisk oven three quarters of an hour.

PLAIN RICE, COMMONLY CALLED POOR MAN'S PUDDING.

Mix a teacupful of well-washed rice, a pint and a half of warmed milk, one ounce of chopped beef suet, two ounces of moist sugar, and a " grate" of nutmeg; put the pudding into a well-buttered dish, and bake an hour in a brisk oven.

A PLAIN BREAD PUDDING.

Break into a basin the crumb of a French-roll, pour upon it a pint of milk, in which has been boiled two cloves, a small blade of mace, and two bay-leaves (remove the cloves, mace, and bay-leaves), then add the yolks and whites of three beaten-up eggs, two tablespoonsful of moist sugar, and the same quantity of well-washed and picked currants; mix well, and bake in a well-buttered dish in a brisk oven three-quarters of an hour.

A FAMILY BREAD PUDDING.

Soak any pieces of bread you may have in the house in a pint of boiling milk, beat them up, and add to them another pint of milk boiled, with two cloves, a blade of mace, and a shred of lemon-peel; then " mix in" the yolks and whites of two beaten-up eggs, two tablespoonsful of currants or sultana raisins, put on the top of the pudding thin slices of bread and butter, sprinkled with currants, and a little grated nutmeg. Bake in a brisk oven an hour.

YEAST, OR NORFOLK DUMPLINGS.

Roll as much bread dough as you may require into small balls with your hands, drop them into boiling water, and boil for fifteen minutes.

In Norfolk they are eaten with gravy *before* the meat, but they are equally popular served *after* it, with melted butter and sugar, flavoured with wine, &c. The butter-sauce may be advantageously replaced by treacle.

HARD OR SUFFOLK DUMPLINGS.

Mix six ounces of finely chopped beef suet with a pound of flour and the whites and yolks of two beaten-up eggs; add just milk enough to " wet the dough," and put it into a " pudding poke" (a bag half a yard long and about six inches in circumference); tie up the end, and boil with salt beef or pork an hour and a half. Serve cut in slices, an inch thick, with gravy. This dumpling is also used as an *appetite damper* at the commencement of the dinner, and is generally made without eggs.

It is often rolled into balls about the size of a walnut, and browned in the dripping-pan under roast meat, or added as " floats" like forcemeat, to stews and soups.

YORKSHIRE PUDDING.

Make a stiff batter of the beaten up whites and yolks of three eggs, half a pound of flour, a pint and a half of cold milk, a small teaspoonful of salt, and *two tablespoonsful of ale*. Pour it into a shallow tin which has been put to get hot under the joint that is roasting.

In Yorkshire it is made firm, and always about half an inch in thickness (when done), but in the Southern Counties it is made *thinner* (lighter) and thicker. It will take two hours before a good fire. In the Yorkshire mode it does not need turning; but when it is thick, as soon as it is lightly browned on one side, it should be turned on the other. This is best effected by dividing it in quarters.

ROWLEY POWLEY, OR BOLSTER PUDDING.

To make this schoolboy's luxury, familiarly called " a dog in a blanket."—Mix six ounces of flour and two ounces of finely chopped beef suet, with cold water, into a stiff paste. " Roll it out" twice; then spread the whole surface with a quarter of a pound of raspberry or any other kind of jam. " Roll round" into a pudding of about eight inches long and six inches in circumference. Tie at both ends in a floured cloth, and boil an hour.

CRUST FOR FRUIT AND MEAT PUDDINGS.

Allow to each pound of flour six ounces of beef or veal suet, finely chopped, and half a teaspoonful of salt. Mix smoothly with the tips of the fingers, pouring in gradually as much cold water as will form a stiff paste. " Roll out" *twice* with the same lightness of hand and rapidity as for pie-crust.

APPLE PUDDING.

Line a well buttered basin with the above paste (reserving a piece for the cover); put into it as many " cored" apples (be careful that they are of the boiling kind), the number of which will of course depend on the size, cut in pieces, as you may re-quire to fill it. Add a little minced fresh lemon-peel or two or three cloves, according to the size of the pudding. Cover with the reserved paste, pinching it carefully all round. Tie in a floured cloth, and boil from an hour to an hour and a half, according to size.

When done, turn carefully into a hot dish, and cut a small piece out of the top of the pudding for the steam to evaporate, or it will be heavy. Put into the opening a piece of butter and a small quantity of moist or pounded sugar, and grated nutmeg.

As apples vary much in their sweetness, you must be careful how you use your sugar. It is better to put in very little, and leave the provers of the pudding to sweeten to their own tastes.

APPLE DUMPLINGS

Are made in the same way as puddings, the only difference being that each dumpling is formed with a single apple, peeled, but not cut open. It is usual to remove the core when served, and put in a small slice of butter, with a little sugar and nutmeg. Baked apple dumplings have many admirers; they should be put into a moderate oven and turned frequently, for they are very apt to burn.

BOILED CUSTARD OR EGG PUDDING.

Mix a tablespoonful of arrow-root or flour with a tablespoon-ful of cold milk and the beaten-up whites and yolks of four eggs; gradually add a pint of hot milk, flavoured with a blade of mace and two cloves (removed, of course), three ounces of powdered white sugar, ten drops of the essential oil of almonds. Stir well with a wooden spoon; boil gently in a well buttered basin or mould, tied in a floured cloth, three-quarters of an hour.

Serve with plain butter sauce, à *la* Tickletooth.

BOILED CUSTARDS FOR TARTS.

Boil a pint of milk with a laurel leaf, a blade of mace, and about an ounce of lemon or Seville orange peel—take out the flavouring, and dissolve in the milk three ounces of powdered white sugar. Gradually add the beaten-up whites and yolks of *six* eggs, mixed (to prevent curdling) with two tablespoonsful of *cold* milk.

Put the custard into a basin which exactly fits the top of a saucepan, that has been previously put on the fire (half full of water), and is *boiling*. Stir *continually* with a wooden spoon for twenty minutes, taking care to *keep* the water boiling. Fill into glasses or cups, grate a little nutmeg over each, and set them aside to cool.

BAKED CUSTARD PUDDING.

Border a pie-dish with "flaky" or puff paste; make your custard in the same manner as for boiling, and bake in a moderate oven twenty minutes.

BAKED PLUM PUDDING.

Mix well in a large pan half a pound of muscatel raisins, half a pound of carefully picked and washed currants, half a pound of bread crumbs, half a pint of boiling milk, half a pound of suet chopped fine, the yolks and whites of three beaten-up eggs, a quarter of a pound of moist sugar, an ounce of candied lemon or orange peel, and half a grated nutmeg. Bake in a slow oven, in a well buttered dish or mould, one hour.

BREAD-AND-BUTTER PUDDING.

Put three layers of very thin slices of bread and butter into a well buttered dish; sprinkle each layer with currants and a little fresh or candied lemon peel. (Two ounces of the former and one ounce of the latter will be sufficient for the whole pudding.)

Boil three-quarters of a pint of milk with two bay-leaves and a blade of mace ten minutes; then take out the bay-leaves and mace, and having in the meantime beaten up the yolks and whites of three eggs with three-quarters of a pint of cold milk, add the hot with an ounce and a half of moist sugar.

Pour this custard gently in at one end of the dish (to prevent the currants and lemon from being disturbed); grate half a nutmeg over the top, and bake in a brisk oven three-quarters of an hour.

RICE, BOILED IN THE INDIAN FASHION.

Wash it well in cold water two or three times, then put it *loose* into a saucepan with a large quantity of *boiling* water; boil very fast for twenty minutes. Strain through a colander, and pour over it a teacupful of cold water; shake the colander until all the water is gone, then lightly shake the rice into a hot dish, let it dry for a few minutes before the fire, and serve.

N.B.—Many English cooks, after straining the rice, replace it in the saucepan, and either cover it with the lid or a cloth, like potatoes, and set it on the hob to dry; but the method which I give, from Indian experience, will be found the best, as it makes the rice "rocky," which is the great point of "native" cookery. "Sticky rice, beat wife," is a well known Hindustanee maxim. It is not necessary to give more examples of "sweet" puddings, as the foregoing are quite sufficient for "foundations."

FRUIT PIES AND TARTS

Vary only in the kinds of fruit employed, their crusts being made, according to taste, of either of the three pastes. I will, therefore, dismiss them, with a caution to be very attentive to their baking. The oven should be brisk, but not fierce, and the pies should be carefully watched and turned *every ten minutes*, or they will be burnt and spoiled. It is necessary to place a small cup, turned upside down, in the centre of the dish, to collect the juice, without which it will "bubble up" round the edges and be wasted. A *little* sugar should be sprinkled over the fruit, but abstain from the usual "half teacupful" of water, as it serves no purpose but to "stretch" and impoverish the juice.

FLAVOURINGS FOR PUDDINGS AND PIES AND SWEET SAUCES.

Essential oil of almonds, although a poison when taken otherwise than in minimum quantities may be safely taken to the extent of a few drops.

Vanille, rum, brandy, as well as sherry, Madeira, Muscatel,

and any kind of sweet or white wine, fruit vinegars, bay and laurel leaves (be careful of the latter, for they are poisonous when more than one or two are used), orange-flower, and rose-waters, attar of roses (by drops), pineapple, lemon and orange-peels, fresh or candied, and every kind of sweet essence may be employed to flavour either the puddings and the pies or the butter sauce that is served with them.

GENERAL REMARKS ON FRUIT PUDDINGS AND PIES.

Every kind of fruit, raspberries in particular, should be carefully picked for insects, &c.; gooseberries and currants should be topped and tailed; plums should be wiped (not washed); many remove the stones, but it is an extravagant practice, and greatly impairs the flavour.

As there are many kinds of apples which will neither boil nor bake, care should be taken in selecting them. They are generally peeled; but when used for a family table, wiping with a soft cloth is sufficient. A few pieces of quince may be advantageously used to flavour apple-pies and puddings, but they must be discreetly dealt with, or you may realize the Irishman's idea, and make your apple-pie or pudding "all quinces." Cloves should also be sparingly used. Lemon-peel gives the most delicate flavour.

The quantity of sugar both for pies and puddings must entirely depend on the kind of fruit employed. For instance, raspberries and currants require more than plums, and gooseberries more than apples. Rhubarb and damsons are tarter than cherries or apricots. It is best in *all* cases to be under the mark rather than overdo the sweetening, and serve raw, or, as it is technically called, "live" sugar (either moist or powdered white) for the guests to sweeten to their own tastes. Treacle is often boiled with family puddings, and is very much in favour, particularly with juveniles, poured over dumplings, &c.

OMELETTES.

Although strictly belonging to the French kitchen, are becoming so popular at our English tables, that the following plain receipts may be considered acceptable.

The leading features of all *egg pancakes*, for omelettes are nothing more— *must* be lightness, freeness from grease, thickness (if they are thin they'll be like Jack of Newbury's old hare, "naughte but shoe leathere"), and a *light* brown appearance.

To obtain this combination is by no means an easy task, particularly if attempted without the proper tools and clear instructions for *pan*-ipulation. Let me try to remove the difficulties. First, let your pan be small, and, if possible, keep it for this purpose alone. Taking six eggs as your medium quantity,* you will see at once that if they are beaten up and poured into the large pan used for general purposes, the batter will spread all over its surface, and the omelette will not only be too thin, but very likely to be burnt. Purchase, then, an "omelette-pan" (they are known by that name at the iron-mongers), just large enough to contain (according to your likely requirements) six, nine, or twelve eggs at the utmost. Understand, however, that the batter must not cover the whole of the surface. Allow about two inches margin. This you can effect by slightly inclining the pan towards the handle when you pour in the eggs, and beating the ends to the centre with a fork; the instant the batter is set, you can easily shake it into the centre of the pan. You will thus give your omelette its proper elongated form, and have space for turning, &c. The next essential tool is what is technically called a "salamander." This is a small iron shovel which is made red hot, and held for a minute or so over pies, puddings, and omelettes, to give a finishing-touch to the browning; it is besides useful to complete the cooking of the parts that may have escaped the heat of the pan or the oven. For omelettes it is particularly useful, as their centres generally require additional heat. A thin slice, a three-pronged steel fork, a moderate fire, a light hand, and your *batterie de cuisine* is complete. Warning you that you must bestow undivided attention on your work, or disasters will certainly happen, we will first attack a

HERB OMELETTE.

Beat well, in a basin, the yolks and whites of six eggs, and two tablespoonsful of cold water (the latter will dilute the eggs

---

* Brillat Savarin says: "If you wish your omelette to be perfect, never (however numerous your guests) let it be made of more than twelve eggs. It is much better to have two or three composed of that quantity than one of twenty-five or thirty, for in the latter case, instead of a light crisp omelette, you will produce nothing but a heavy, tough, leathery pudding."

and make the omelette more delicate); then add half a teaspoonful of salt, a quarter of a teaspoonful of ground black
pepper, a teaspoonful of chopped parsley, half a teaspoonful
of chopped onion, and an ounce of butter or lard cut in small
pieces. Mix well with a wooden spoon.

Dissolve in your omelette-pan two ounces of butter or lard;
then tilt *at once* the beaten-up eggs, &c., into it, inclining the
pan to the handle for an instant; then shake the omelette into
the centre, turn up the right and left edges, and fry quickly
about five minutes, the *exact* time cannot be given, as it will
greatly depend on the force of your fire and the size of the
omelette.

SWEET OMELETTES.

These are prepared like the above, omitting the herbs, and
adding, when ready to serve, pounded sugar, or preserves—
when the latter are used, the best way is to spread them lightly
over the surface *in the pan*, the instant before the omelette is
taken out, and roll them up with it. Sugar is merely sprinkled
over when served.

On the Continent, rum is in great favour for flavouring, a
little being used when the eggs are beaten up, and about half
an ordinary wineglassful poured over. At the instant of
serving, a light is put to the spirit, and the omelette appears on
the table enveloped in " blue flames."

OMELETTE SOUFFLEE.*

Beat well the yolks (I will presently tell you what to do with
the whites) of six eggs with four tablespoonsful of finely-
powdered white sugar, and a tablespoonful of rose, orange, or

* A *Soufflée*, which may be described by a poetical cook as a substance
of gossamer lightness that may almost float in the air, has long been a
great triumph of the French kitchen, and is employed to "give an air" to
the most extraordinary nothings. Carême, in his *Maître d'Hotel Français*,
speaking of the exertions of the cook of Marshal Davoust during the siege
of Hamburg, to vary the, by dire necessity, horseflesh dinners of his master,
expresses supreme contempt for his contrivances, which he terms "*filets
de bœuf à la boot-heel*," and " *soups à la wooden leg.*" What should he
say to the wondrous *soufflées* of some of the present " little great" hangers-
on to the edges of his imperial apron, who form them of crystallized snow,
the dew of violets (not onions), and the pinions of butterflies preserved in
their flour; indeed great efforts are being made by a new candidate for
kitchen honours, to *souffle*, by a photographic process, a lady's smile, a
lover's sigh, and a poet's imagination.

elderflower water; or, if other flavours be preferred, plain water, and half the rind of a grated lemon, or two ounces of vanille sugar, chocolate, coffee, or three or four pounded macaroon cakes —or, in fact, any flavouring essence that may be selected.

Then whisk the six whites to froth, and lightly mix them (without too much incorporation) with the yolks.

Dissolve four ounces of butter or lard in your omelette-pan, tilt in the batter at once, and, when one side of the omelette is set, take it out quickly and carefully with your slice; turn it (the under side up) into a well-buttered dish (which will stand the fire), form it into a dome, powder it with sifted white sugar, set it in a brisk oven, and bake it from five to ten minutes, according to size. Remember it must be served the instant it rises, which, if it be well made and cleverly cooked, it will do to a great height.

The dish may be garnished with any kind of preserved fruit, jam, jelly, or marmalade. There is no end to the varieties of *soufflées*. Some are made with rice boiled in milk or cream, others with cheese and arrowroot, or potato flour, &c. &c.; but the *one* example I have given is quite sufficient as a good foundation to work upon, the different articles used in the varieties being merely added at the last beating up.

PANCAKES.

Mix three tablespoonfuls of flour with half a pint of milk, half a teaspoonful of salt, half a grated nutmeg, and a wine-glassful of good ale; then beat up the whites and yolks of four eggs with another half pint of milk, and mix with the other batter, adding, if necessary, a little more milk to bring it to the consistency of good cream.

Dissolve in a small fryingpan an ounce of butter or lard (butter is the best) for *each* pancake, and pour into it a teacupful of the batter, which will form itself into a thin cake over the entire surface. N.B. You must lift up the edges all round with your slice, or they will burn. Fry quickly for two or three minutes, or *till it is a light brown;* then turn with your slice (experienced cooks "toss," but as that is a manœuvre which requires great practice, it is safer to use the slice*), and fry the other side two minutes.

---

* Apropos of amateur "tossing," the following anecdote of Napoleon's failure in giving the artistic twist may be appropriately quoted: "The

Set each before the fire in a hot dish until *half* the quantity of batter is used, then serve, and while the first three or four are being consumed, fry the remainder, as it is essential they should be eaten quite hot.

They are usually served with sprinkled sugar and a squeeze of lemon, but occasionally with preserves.

APPLE FRITTERS.

These are generally made smaller than pancakes, with the same kind of batter and treatment, apples chopped in small pieces being the only addition. A little good cream with pounded sugar may be served with them. Currants and other fruits are sometimes substituted for apples.

CABINET PUDDING.

Butter a mould or basin, and place in it layers of sponge-cakes, ratafias, or macaroons; then fill up the mould with a lemon custard made with the yolks of eight eggs, a pint of milk or cream, six ounces of sugar, a glass of brandy, and the grated rind of a lemon. This custard must not be set, but merely mixed up. Cover the top of the mould or basin with a piece of buttered writing-paper, tie a cloth tightly over it, and steam for an hour and a half, either in a large potato-steamer or in a saucepan, with the water reaching about half-way up the mould or basin. Serve with custard, melted butter flavoured with wine, rum, vanille, pineapple, or preserves.

MINCEMEAT A LA TICKLETOOTH.

Half a pound of stoned muscatel raisins, half a pound of sultanas, and one pound of currants, well washed, picked, and rubbed dry; six ounces of beef-suet, half the rind of a lemon,

---

Empress Josephine was amusing herself one day with her ladies of honour with the manufacture of an omelette, and at the most critical moment of the operation Napoleon entered unexpectedly. Seeing the embarrassment the Empress experienced in turning the omelette, he took the pan from her hand, saying, 'I will show you, ma *bonne amie,* how to turn an omelette: this is the bivouac method'—and at the same time he gave the pan that little twist so well known to all cooks; but the disobedient omelette, instead of returning to the fryingpan, fell right into the fire, to the great delight of Josephine, who, turning to her august spouse, said to him, with a charming smile, ' Your Majesty is not at the bivouac now: you understand much better how to gain battles than to turn omelettes.'"

one ounce each of candied orange, citron, and lemon-peel; two good-sized apples peeled and cored, and a quarter of a pound of lean and tender rump-steak. Chop all these as fine as possible, mix well, with two grated nutmegs, half a teaspoonful of grated ginger, a quarter of a teaspoonful of salt, and a quarter of a pound of pounded white sugar.

Put them into an earthen jar, and set it in a brisk oven for an hour and a half, turning and stirring occasionally; then add a wineglassful of brandy and another of sherry; stir well, cover close, and set the mincemeat aside (in the jar) in a cool place until you are ready to make your pies, which may be formed with either of the pastes, according to taste. Butter some small tins, and cover them with a thin layer of paste; then put into each a tablespoonful of the mincemeat; cover with another layer of thin paste, carefully pinch round the edges, and bake in a brisk oven half an hour.

This mincemeat will keep twelve months, if put aside, with a piece of bladder tied over the top of the jar.

MEAT PUDDINGS AND PIES.

Make a good suet crust according to receipt, page 122 (for pies use butter and lard, or suet, in equal proportions); butter well your basin if for boiling, and line it with paste, keeping a piece for the cover. For baking, your dish does not require it. Put in the meat in layers in both cases, cut in pieces about three inches broad, and half an inch thick; lightly season each layer with pepper and salt mixed together. For boiling: cover with paste, pinch the edges, and tie tightly a cloth over the top of the basin, and boil from two hours to two hours and a quarter. For baking: place a thin layer of paste round the edge of your dish, extending half way into it; then put in the meat and seasoning and slices of hard-boiled eggs; cover with the paste, and make a small hole in the top. Ornament the edge of the crust by "crimping" it with the back of your knife.

For a centre ornament for fruit pies, flour well your board and roll out a small piece of paste as thin as a wafer; then lightly fold it into a small compass, and pinch one of the ends together with your fingers; put it into the opening in the centre of the pie, and cut it through with your knife four times across; it will then fall and form leaves.

The above receipt will serve for all kinds of mutton, beef, and kidney puddings and pies.

VEAL AND HAM PIES.

Cut the veal in pieces of about four inches square, and half an inch thick; put it in layers in the dish with thin slices of uncooked ham, mild bacon, or pickled pork. A little chopped parsley should be added to a seasoning of pepper and salt in equal quantities; and a few slices of hard-boiled eggs. Bake according to size, in a moderate oven, from an hour to an hour and a quarter. A little stock gravy may be poured into the hole (which must be made in the top) when about to serve. If you wish to make the pie very savoury, add a little veal stuffing (see receipt, page 137) made into small balls.

PLAIN CHICKEN PIE.

Cut off the neck, feet, and scaly part of the legs, the heart, liver, and gizzard, clean, and put them in a saucepan with two button mushrooms, a small shalot, a quarter of a pound of gravy beef, half a teaspoonful of salt, and eight peppercorns. Let them stew in half a pint of water for an hour before you make your pie. Form your crust with flaky, short, or puff paste, according to taste; border the dish on the edges and half way down with it; put a layer of bacon or ham at the bottom. Cut up the fowl and place the back (in four pieces) on the bacon; strew over them a little chopped parsley and lemon-peel mixed with bread crumbs; then put the breast (whole) in the centre, a leg at each end, and the wings at the sides, and fill up the corners with small rolls of thin slices of ham or bacon. Pour in the gravy you have made with the giblets, cover with your paste, make a small hole in the top, and bake in a moderate oven one hour.

CHICKEN PIE A LA TICKLETOOTH.

Remove the giblets (as in the foregoing receipt) from a plump chicken, put it in a deep dish, and pour over it a quart of boiling water; cover closely with a larger dish, and let it remain five minutes; then put it on the chopping-board, and, with a sharp knife, cut it up in the manner a boiled chicken is carved at table; then put the pieces together, fill the interior with veal stuffing (for which see page 137), and put the fowl, which will appear not to have been dismembered, into a dish, bordered with either of the three light pastes, upon a thin slice of veal or rump-steak. Fill up the ends and crevices with slices of sweetbread which has been boiled five minutes and lightly browned, and thin slices of ham; cover with the paste, make the usual hole at the top, pinch round the edges, ornament according to taste, and bake in a moderate oven one hour.

When done, have ready a savoury gravy composed of a dozen button mushrooms browned, with an ounce of butter, and stewed twenty minutes with a small piece of chopped shalot, a shred of lemon-peel, to which must be added, *a few minutes before serving,* a dozen bearded oysters cut in two or four pieces according to size, two teaspoonfuls of flour mixed with the oyster-liquor, and a sprig of minced parsley.

Cut the crust of the pie all round, take off the top, pour the gravy over the chicken, replace the top, and serve. Slices of hard-boiled eggs may accompany the sweetbread, and the neck, feet, liver, and gizzard should be stewed an hour, and the liquor strained from them added to the mushrooms while they are stewing.

PLAIN PIGEON PIE.

"Border" a dish (in the manner I have shown you) with flaky, short, or puff paste, and put at the bottom a rump or well-beaten beef-steak about three-quarters of an inch thick, cut in three or four pieces (allowing a quarter of a pound to each pigeon). Place your two, three, or four pigeons upon the steak, with their breasts upwards, each covered with a thin slice of ham. Sprinkle them with a seasoning composed of a teaspoonful of salt, a quarter of a teaspoonful of pepper, a little chopped parsley, and *half* a clove of shalot. Fill up the corners and crevices with slices of hard-boiled eggs; pour in a teacupful of cold water, cover with the paste, and bring the feet of the pigeons through the hole in the centre. Ornament according to fancy. Bake in a moderate oven an hour or an hour and a half, according to size.

SAVOURY PIGEON PIE.

Having made your pie in every particular according to the above receipt, either fill the birds with button mushrooms browned for ten minutes with an ounce of butter in a stewpan, or veal stuffing (see receipt, page 137) in which the livers (previously boiled) should be chopped; or you may mince them with a small slice of ham, four button mushrooms, and a small piece of lemon-peel, rubbed well together with a little salt and cayenne and the yolks of two eggs. To give a pleasant form to this savoury adjunct, cut the hard-boiled eggs in two, long ways; take out the yolks, fill the cavity with the stuffing, and close the whites over it. These savoury eggs should then be placed at the corners of the dish, to be cut when served. The remainder of the forcemeat should be put into the birds.

An oyster cut in small pieces may be mixed with the stuffing in each egg.

A TOAD IN A HOLE.

Make a batter of a pint of milk, three tablespoonfuls of flour, a tablespoonful of ale, and the whites and yolks of two beaten-up eggs. Pour it into a deep dish, and put upon it a thick rump steak; sprinkle a little pepper and salt, and bake in a brisk oven (according to the weight of the steak) about an hour.

I have found that half cooking the steak on the gridiron before putting it on the batter is advantageous, as it not only adds to its crispness (on both sides), but prevents the pudding from being dried before it is done. The gravy should be carefully saved from the gridiron, and be put on the steak when it is placed in the oven.

A CORNISH RABBIT PIE.

Cut off the legs and shoulders of a rabbit; cut the back into four pieces. Split the head and stew it in a little more than half a pint of water, with a quarter of a pound of beef and a shalot. Put part of half a pound of pickled pork, cut in thin slices, at the bottom of the dish; strew over them a chopped roasted onion and a little parsley. Then add a layer of the rabbit, filling up the vacancies with hard-boiled eggs; cover this with a layer of the pickled pork, parsley, and eggs; then another layer of rabbit.

N.B.—Slices of turnip are frequently added to the eggs and parsley. Moisten with a teacupful of cold water; and when done, which in a moderate oven will be in about an hour, cut round the top of the crust, and put into the pie the gravy made with the head, and half a pint of warm cream. The same kind of pie is made with veal, slices of bacon, and leeks; in fact, there is nothing, as they say in Cornwall, which "will *not* pie;" and it is no uncommon thing to see them made of an *olla podrida* of fish, flesh, and fowl.

CRUST FOR RAISED PIES.

Put half a pound of lard into a saucepan, with three-quarters of a pint of water; when it boils, pour it gradually into two pounds and a half of flour which you have heaped together on your paste-board; mix well with a spoon, and then knead with your hands till you have formed it into a stiff paste. Then roll it with your hands (not with the rolling-pin) into a sugar-loaf shape, put it upright on the board, then also with your hands flatten the sides of it. When you have equalized it all round, and it is quite smooth, squeeze the middle of the point down to half the height of the paste, then hollow the inside by pressing it with the fingers; and in doing this be careful to keep every part of equal thickness. Then put in the meat in layers, and fill the corners and interstices with the forcemeat; put on the cover, trim it with your knife, pinch the edges, crimp them, make a hole in the centre, and place round it any ornamental paste device your fancy may dictate.

PORK PIES.

Form your raised crust according to the quantity of the meat, which should be cut in small pieces about half an inch in thickness, and an inch square. It is advisable also to mix a little beef or veal with the pork; put over each layer of meat (which should not be too fat) a sprinkling of seasoning made of pepper, salt, and a small quantity of dried or green sage. Bake it in a moderate oven an hour or an hour and twenty minutes, according to size. When done and nearly cold, pour in a gravy made of the bones stewed, with a little salt and a small onion.

GAME PIES.

"Raise" a crust to a size corresponding with the quantity of your game. Cut with a sharp knife the flesh from the best parts; keep each kind separate, and set them aside for a moment. Then split the heads, break the bones, and put them with the inferior parts into a stewpan, with a roasted onion, a carrot, a teaspoonful of salt, twenty black peppercorns, sprigs of winter savory, marjoram, lemon and common thyme, two bay leaves, *half* a clove of garlic, and half a pound of gravy beef. Stew in a very little water (according to the quantity of the meat, &c.) five hours. When done, skim and strain, and set it aside to cool. Line the whole of your raised crust with a thin layer of *short* paste, then a layer of fat bacon or ham, cut in thin slices. Now put in your different kinds of game in layers (not round, but from the bottom), filling up the corners and crevices with hare forcemeat stuffing, according to receipt, page 138. Having mixed together two teaspoonfuls of salt, half a teaspoonful of cayenne, and half a grated nutmeg, sprinkle a little of them over each layer. Livers may be chopped in small pieces and baked with the game, or mixed with the mincemeat. Finish the filling with a layer of the ham or bacon, put over it a layer of the short paste, then cover with the raised crust. Pinch round the sides, ornament, by crimping, leaves, &c., according to fancy, and bake in a moderate oven an hour, an hour and a half, or two hours, according to size and weight. When both pie and gravy are *nearly cold*, put the point of a funnel into the small hole (which, by the way, you must make in the top of the pie before you bake it), and gently pour through it the gravy you have prepared.

N.B.—I have found it advantageous to line the bottom of these, as well as every other kind of meat, game, or poultry pies with a moderately thick rump-steak.

A word to the wise !

GIBLET PIE.

Prepare the giblets in the same manner as for soup (see page 75). The crust may be either flaky, short, or puff. Place a rump or well-beaten beef-steak at the bottom of the dish ; put the giblets in in layers, season each with pepper and salt, chopped onions, a sprig of parsley, and half a clove of shalot ; add a few forcemeat balls of either kind of stuffing, moisten with a teacupful of water or stock, and bake an hour.

As fish, and all other " light crust" meat pies are made with but little variation from the foregoing receipts, it would be encroaching too much on my space to particularize them. I will therefore conclude the pudding and pie " question" with a receipt for a very savoury " holiday" treat.

OYSTER PATTIES.

Cover some small tins, technically called patty-pans, with puff paste, cut it round, and put in the centre a small piece of bread (to prevent the top and bottom from collapsing), cover it with paste, slightly pinch the edges together, and bake in a brisk oven a quarter of an hour. Then, having bearded and parboiled (which will take but three or four minutes) a dozen large oysters, cut them in quarters, and put them into a stewpan with an ounce of butter, a teaspoonful of flour mixed with their liquor, and the broth from the beards (which you must stew in a small saucepan, with a little stock gravy and two or three shreds of lemon). Season *with a very little salt*, a quarter of a teaspoonful of powdered mace, and the same quantity of cayenne; then gradually add three tablespoonfuls of cream. Mix well; then with a thin knife open the patties, take out the bread, put in a spoonful of the oysters and cream gravy; put the covers on again, and serve hot.

This receipt will serve for lobster and all kinds of savoury patties, the oysters of course being left out.

STUFFINGS.

As these are in constant use, and the flavour of the meats, &c., they accompany being greatly influenced by their good or bad construction, I will give you particular directions how to produce each kind. I will commence with

VEAL STUFFING.

Three or four sprigs of parsley, two ounces of beef suet, and a small piece of lemon-peel, chopped fine; two teaspoonfuls of dried marjoram, one teaspoonful of common thyme, half a teaspoonful of lemon thyme, a teacupful of fine bread crumbs, half a teaspoonful of salt, a quarter of a teaspoonful of black pepper, a sprinkle of cayenne, and a grate of nutmeg. Mix with a well-beaten-up egg.

PORK STUFFING.

Roast a small Spanish onion, peel, and chop it with a dessertspoonful of powdered sage, two tablespoonfuls of bread crumbs, a teaspoonful of salt, and half a teaspoonful of pepper. Mix well, and moisten with two tablespoonfuls of walnut catsup.

HARE STUFFING A LA TICKLETOOTH.

Boil the liver of the hare slowly five minutes; roast a middling-sized onion ten minutes; then chop them with an ounce and a half of beef suet, two ounces of lean ham, a handful of parsley, a strip of lemon-peel, the *quarter* of a clove of garlic, two pickled mushrooms, and half a teaspoonful of French capers; add four tablespoonfuls of bread crumbs, one teaspoonful of salt, the same of black pepper, and a quarter of a spoonful of cayenne, one teaspoonful of dried marjoram, the same of lemon and common thyme, and the same of tarragon vinegar, two tablespoonsful of walnut and the same of mushroom catsup. Beat up the whites and yolks of two eggs, mix well, put it in the body of the hare, and sew the skin over it.

N.B.—If the stuffing be too moist, add a few more bread crumbs.

GOOSE STUFFING A LA TICKLETOOTH.

Roast a large Spanish onion three-quarters of an hour, peel and chop it with two good-sized pared apples, and three mealy potatoes boiled and mashed; mix these in a large bowl with one tablespoonful of dried mace, and the same of dried marjoram, both rubbed to powder; one teaspoonful of mustard flour, two teaspoonfuls of salt, one teaspoonful of moist sugar, and another of pepper, a quarter of a teaspoonful of cayenne, and six ounces of bread crumbs. Mix well together, and moisten with two tablespoonfuls of mushroom catsup, one teaspoonful of shalot vinegar, and three tablespoonfuls of strong stock.

Put this into the body of the goose, and skewer it up.

N.B.—Roasting the onions for stuffing greatly improves their flavour.

As I wish this work to embrace every section of the question it purposes to illustrate, I will leave for a moment the "*Family Kitchen*," and turn to another most important branch of our system of feeding.

DINING OUT,

Or, as the French call it, *en ville*, which implies that we either dine by invitation with our friends, or at a tavern or some other place of public entertainment.

The times when merchants and tradesmen lived at their places of business, and dined with their families at one o'clock on a plain joint and a pudding, and their clerks and shopmen bought half a pound of mutton-chop or beef-steak at a butcher's hard by, and cooked it for themselves on a gigantic common gridiron for a penny, which included salt at " discretion," or for an extra twopence they could have a thick slice of bread and a couple of baked potatoes;* these "good old times," when " Templers" and other " limbs of the law" were contented with a basin of mock turtle, a cut of the joint, and a pint, or as it might be a *bottle*, of old port at Dicks' or the Grecian, and the denizens of the West-end had no other public feeding-places than the expensive coffee-rooms of large hotels ; these very steady " pig-tail " times have long since, like watchmen and coach travelling, become curious matters of history. The merchant now dines at eight on three courses, in his mansion in Belgravia or at his villa in the country. The tradesman has his cottage at Richmond or Notting-hill ; and clerks and shopmen, despising the gipsy mode of feeding, take their dinners at Ishaut's, in Bucklersbury, or at some other equally renowned " Dining Room," where for fifteen pence they can have a sufficing plateful of fine, well-cooked meat, bread, and vegetables, with a slice of pudding or pie, a pint of porter, a " skim" at the *Times*, and " thank you, sir," from the bland waiter for his customary fee into the bargain.

Nowadays " Templers" more frequently dine at the West-end by the *carte à la Française*, at palatial clubs " *en Prince*."

* " The Fleece," in Old Threadneedle-street, two doors from Leman's, the famous biscuit baker, had a butcher's shop adjoining it, and it was no uncommon thing for a thousand chops and steaks to be cooked there in a morning, besides a large quantity of sausages and kidneys. No customer taking *less* than a pint of beer, the quantity consumed in the course of the year was enormous.

So profitable was this system of dining to the landlords, that the proprietor of the " Excise Coffee House," opposite the Excise-office in Broad-street, left it in his will that at the end of every seven years each of his children should in turn succeed to the business, as in that time they could, as he had done, retire with a fortune.

At another well-known tavern, " The George and Vulture," in George-yard, Lombard-street, I have been told by an old gentleman, that about half a century ago any one taking half a pint of wine could walk into a room on the ground floor, and partake freely of the cold meat of the preceding day, which was set out on a large table for the purpose. This was a sort of decoy to attract customers to the house, which had a great reputation for its soups and club dinners.

As the "Reign of Terror" introduced "*plats de résistance*" and potatoes "*au naturel*" into French cookery, so the Battle of Waterloo was the epoch for introducing *entrées* and *soufflées* into our middle-class kitchens.*

By slow degrees "John Bull" became sobered down, and was well content to swallow some of his anti-Gallican prejudices, and a succulent French dinner at the same time.

Our countrymen, indeed, have not only for many years been conspicuous as the chief supporters of the Parisian *restaurants*, but have succeeded in beguiling from their allegiance many of the most talented of the French *chefs*, able and willing as we are to pay "any money" for everything that France can produce. In short, we have been long aware of our inferiority in the art of cookery, and with our palates propitiated and our eyes opened to the necessity of reform, we have had the good sense to turn our foreign travel to advantage.

In the establishments of our "grandees," of course the old English plain roast and boiled only wait on the more *récherché* efforts of the French kitchen; but our middle classes, however, in their over-anxiety to be genteel, are too often too prone to attempt, without either knowledge or proper appliances, to make a display of dishes, which, purporting in name at least to be French, would sadly puzzle a Francatelli or a Soyer to identify.

Yet, although we are still far behind our continental friends in the higher acquirements of the culinary art, we have managed successfully to grapple with some of its realities; witness the immense improvement of our club dinners, and the superiority of hotel cookery generally, to what it was a few years ago, to say nothing of those more ambitious establishments under the especial management of a French *chef*.

To come down to places of more modest pretensions, we question whether there is in Paris a *restaurant* of its class to match with the "Wellington," in St. James's-street; Simpson's, in the Strand; or Sawyer's "London Dinner," in Fleet-street,

---

* As some compensation for the injurious influence of the Revolution in its first stages upon cookery, it is right to mention that it contributed to emancipate the *cuisine* from prejudice, and added largely to its resources. *Pièces de résistance*, says Lady Morgan, on Carême's authority, came in with the National Convention—potatoes were dressed *au naturel* in the Reign of Terror—and it was under the Directory that tea-drinking commenced in France.—*Hayward's Essays.*

which we particularize as types of their class. In all these houses, which are fitted up with all the elegance and comfort of their Parisian models, a better dinner can be had for less money than in the close *entresols* and profusely mirrored *salons* of the more pretending " *Cercle des Étrangers*," " *Diners de Paris*," &c. &c., of the Palais Royal, the Rue Vivienne, and the Boulevards, where, in spite of their voluminous *carte*, the " dishes of the day" are generally found to be very limited in variety," and often far from satisfactory to an English palate. In fact, it may be safely predicted, that if we steadily pursue the course of culinary reform now happily initiated in the more respectable and popular of our public refectories, that with our greatly superior viands and our greater command of the fruits of the earth from our unbounded wealth, we shall ere long distance our rivals in this art, as we have in so many others.

The late Count d'Orsay, in a letter written a few years since, gives the following classification and description of the then principal *restaurants* in Paris. The graphic sketch is now the more curious, inasmuch as it shows the transitory nature of gastronomic popularity; for we find Véry—the descendant of the world-famous Véry of 1814, who contracted to supply the table of the Allied Sovereigns at the moderate sum of 3000 francs (£120) a day, exclusive of wine—is degraded to the second class.* But let us hear Count d'Orsay himself:—

" Paris, May 1st, 1852.

" I must confess that the culinary art has sadly fallen off in Paris, and I do not clearly see how it is to recover, as there are at present no great establishments where the school can be kept up. At all the first class *restaurants* you have nearly the same dinner; they may, however, be divided into three categories. Undoubtedly the best for a great dinner and good wine are the " Frères Provençaux" (Palais Royal), " Philippes"

* The two brothers of this name once stood at the very head of the first class, and so long as their establishment on the Tuileries was left standing the name of Véry retained its talismanic power of attraction, the delight and pride of gastronomy—

" Whilst stands the Coliseum, Rome shall stand ;
And whilst Rome stands, the world."

But when the house in question was removed to make way for the public buildings which now rest upon its site, the presiding genius of the family deserted it. Death, too, intervened, and carried off the most distinguished of the brothers. A magnificent monument was erected to his memory in *Père la Chaise*, with an inscription concluding thus :—*Toute sa vie fut consacrée aux arts utiles.—Hayward's Essays.*

(Rue Mont Orgueil), and the "Café de Paris;" the latter is not always to be counted upon, but is excellent when they give you a *soigné* dinner.* In the second class are Véry (Palais Royal), Véfours (the "Café Anglais"), and Champeaux (Place de la Bourse), where you can have a most *conscientious* dinner, good without pretension; the situation is central, in a beautiful garden, and you must ask for a *bifstek à la Châteaubriand.*

"At the head of the third class we must place Bonvallet, on the Boulevard du Temple, near all the little theatres; Defreux, chiefly remarkable for public dinners; Durand, Place de la Madeleine; Ledoyen, in the Champs Elysées, where is also Guillemin, formerly cook to the Duke de Vincennes. The two best places for suppers are the "Maison d'Or," and the "Café Anglais;" and for breakfasts, Tortoni's, and the "Café d'Orsay," on the Quay d'Orsay. In the vicinity of Paris the best *restaurant* is the "Pavillon Henri Quatre," at St. Germain, kept by the old cook of the Duchess de Berri.

"At none of these places could you find dinners now such as were produced by Ude; by Soyer, formerly with Lord Chesterfield; by Rotival, with Lord Wilton; or by Perron, with Lord Londonderry.

"I must not forget to mention the two great contractors for dinners and suppers; these are Chevet, of the Palais Royal, and Potel, of the Boulevard des Italiens.

"The best possible materials may be procured at these establishments; but the dinners of Chevet and Potel are expensive and vulgar—a sort of *tripotage* of truffles, cocks'-combs, and craw-fish mounted on the back of a fillet of beef, and not a single *entrée* which a connoisseur can eat; the roast game always *tourmenté* and cold, for their feathers are stuck on again before they are served up.

"You are now *au fait* of the pretended French gastronomy. It has emigrated to England, and has no wish to return. We do not absolutely die of hunger here, and that is all that can be said."

This was the state of the most celebrated dining-houses in Paris in 1852, since when they have all pretty nearly retained the same relative positions. But a multitude of smaller establishments of a much lower grade has meanwhile sprung up (particularly during the time of the Great Exhibition) in every quarter, and in most of these bad cookery and bad materials struggle for the mastery. But we must except from this censure "Tavernier's," "Moreau's," and "Richefeu's," in the Palais Royal, where the charge is two francs for soup, four dishes (at Tavernier's and Richefeu's only three), dessert, half a bottle of wine, and bread at discretion; there are no other places in Paris where for that price (I will say nothing of the thirty sous houses) a hungry man can get anything like a satisfactory or sufficient dinner.

As an almost universal rule, the small plate of soup is thin

* The "Café de Paris" was closed in September, 1856, but its place is well supplied by "Vachettes," on the Boulevard Montmartre, which is making rapid strides to come up with "Philippes."

and flavourless ; the wine reveals its *log-wood* consanguinity by making a black stain on the table-cloth.   Your first dish, a fried sole, is merely a diminutive dab, fried to a chip, or they give you about two inches of plaice covered with a little cloudy paste called " *turbot à la sauce;*" your second dish, your "*plat de résistance,*" a *bifstek* " *aux pommes de terre,*" three inches of some unrecognisable kind of brown meat ("where ignorance is bliss," &c. &c.) done to a cinder or scarcely warmed through, the potatoes being the only endurable part of the dish; your third, a "*poulet aux cressons,*" the drum-stick of a warmed-up fowl (these houses buy up all the " *left*" legs of the large establishments), garnished with two or three sprigs of water-cresses.   By this time you are very anxious for something really eatable, in order to appease your appetite, and when the fourth dish is to be produced, you hesitate between *macaroni au gratin,* as being tolerably substantial; and *civet de lievre au vin de Madère :* but, on seeing a portion of the latter served up to a fellow-countryman at a table near you, and which appears not objectionable, in a fatal moment you make choice of that, and attack it with gusto, until looking up by chance you see an old gentleman, seated opposite, watching you with a strange look of pity, you pause, and ask for an explanation ; he bows, shrugs his shoulders, and politely replies, " Monsieur has not been long in Paris, or he would not venture on *that* dish !"   " Why not?" you say, with rising misgivings.   " Merely," replies the old gentleman, with a mysterious look of aversion at your plate, " that the *hares cooked in these cheap establishments have in general short ears, and are apt to mew.*"

Your dessert is an apple or a pear, or a beggarly melange, most appropriately styled " *mendians,*" consisting of four almonds, four raisins, four Barcelona nuts, and four very small figs.

This is a fair sample of the two franc Parisian dinner so eagerly sought after by our cockney excursionists on their first arrival ; but after one or two trials they cannot fail to discover that the fare of an ordinary dining-room in England is immeasurably superior, and they are consequently soon driven to " Byron's," in the Place Favart, where they can get a " cut of the joint," too glad to exchange " make believe" dinners for something wholesome and substantial.

Owing in some measure, no doubt to a little continental experience, the young men of the City nowadays display no want of critical acumen in discussing the stereotype viands prepared for their delectation and sustenance, at the more humble dining establishments ; in these, you will hear a "fast" young fellow with an incipient moustache, from a ship-broker's or a banker's, say depreciatingly to the damsel in attendance, "Now, Sarah, my dear! do you call *this* a stewed steak ?" turning over with his fork the very pale cutlet of a watery hash. " It ought, you know well enough, to be brown, plump, and tender, with lots of thick flavoury gravy, besides carrots, mushrooms, and onions, and not a sickly, consumptive, warmed-up slice of yesterday's cold ribs ; you can't deceive *me*, Sarah, you little gipsy ; so bring me half a plate of roast goose, with plenty of stuffing and apple-sauce; and tell old Kidneybean from *me*, if he does not educate his cook up to the knowledge of his customers, he'll come to grief, for the *men* of the present day have travelled, and know a thing or two in the cookery line never dreamed of by their fathers."

Besides the London "dining out" establishments I have named, there are hundreds of other excellent and well-conducted luncheon and dinner-houses of every grade in every quarter of the great metropolis, particularly in the neighbourhood of Cornhill and the Mansion House, whose skilful cookery and attendant comforts in the appropriate decoration of their rooms and their table-service are daily becoming more conspicuous ; as an example I may mention Simpson's "fish dinners," in the Poultry (removed from Billingsgate), where, at the *"table d'hôte,"* both at one and at four o'clock, for *eighteen-pence*, you have three or four kinds of the freshest and best sorts of fish, and as many joints, all plainly, but well cooked, together with bread, butter, cheese, and celery ; and one of the best features of the establishment is, that you are not expected as *a matter of course*, by the usual hint of a wine-glass being placed beside you, to drink for "the good of the house;" and although supplies at hand of Bass's pale ale, Guiness's stout, and pine-apple punch, are of tempting quality, you may drink water if you please, and leave the table with the cheese. This, although quite unpretending, is perhaps the cheapest *good* dinner in London, for everything brought to table is as excellent in quality as it is in its cookery.

Until within the last few years a comfortable, well-served, and withal genteel *table-d'hôte* at a moderate cost was not to be found in all London. Shilling ordinaries at one, or at the latest two o'clock, where the fare consisted of our proverbial "gory joints" and badly cooked cheap fish, served on a second day's tablecloth, with steel forks, and leaden spoons, in a dingy room with a sanded or sawdust-strewed floor, garnished with spittoons, and reeking with the fumes of stale tobacco, were the only attempts at *social* dinners in public, and their frequenters were nearly all coarse feeders of a vulgar stamp, careless of everything but the *quantity* of meat and pudding they could swallow for their shilling. But now, having seen how much better "they manage these things in France," we have reformed our "ordinaries" with other things, by banishing the sand, the spittoon, the tobacco reek, and the coarse, ill-dressed fare, for the best of everything in season, plainly yet skilfully cooked, and served in a properly ventilated, well-furnished room, replete with comfort. The result is, that instead of being patronized by *one* class as formerly, various grades are mingled at these public places of resort; the clerk, the merchant, the lawyer, and the "man about town" from the West End, may be seen elbowing each other at the ever-crowded table, and not seldom exchanging civilities with the ease and freedom of manners of our more social neighbours.

The Wellington in St. James's-street takes higher ground, and invites the patronage of a more wealthy, and in culinary matters certainly a better informed class of customers. The dinners are divided into four grades:—1st, *à la carte*, up to whatever price you please; 2nd, "The French Dinner" for *five* shillings; 3rd, "The English Dinner" for *three* shillings; 4th, the "joint and vegetables' for *two* shillings. The dining-room is large and lofty, the attendance and table service unexceptionable; all the French dishes are to be *depended upon*, and the quality and cookery of the joints, fish, and poultry of the English kitchen, are equally commendable. After dinner you can ascend to the drawing-room (once "Crockford's" grand saloon), which is well supplied with newspapers and periodicals, and take your coffee.

"Sawyer's London Dinner," in Fleet-street, follows the Wellington in its style, but confines itself to but two divisions of its entertainment, viz., The joint and vegetables, cheese, and salad for *eighteen-pence;* fish, soup, and *entrées à la carte;* and THE LONDON DINNER, consisting of two soups—

K

two fish—two entrées—joints—two sweets—cheese and salad, for *half-a-crown*, attendance three-pence each person.

This bill of fare will bear comparison with the best that can be offered in Paris for the same price, and when it is considered that every dish is of the finest quality, and everything connected with the establishment is of the first class, it may be naturally inferred that "The London Dinner" does not lack customers.

At Simpson's, in the Strand, there is but *one* dinner, but that is a right good one, and fully deserves its high reputation.

The charge is *two shillings*, for the joint, two kinds of vegetables, bread, cheese, butter, and celery. Fish and soup may be added for another shilling, and a *few* well-composed made-dishes *à la carte*. This is *par excellence* the DINNER OF THE DAY. Its fare is purely English, and those who have once had a cut at its "saddles" or "surloins, turbot or salmon," never fail to come again.

Coffee-room dinners at two shillings, and three-and-sixpence, are also to be had at the "Café de l'Europe," next door to the Haymarket Theatre. The choice wines and the good cookery at this establishment promise to secure for it as great a reputation as "Vachettes," on the Boulevard Montmartre, at Paris, whose *cuisine* and cellar it professes to rival.

The *restaurant* of the St. James's Hall is taking a good position among the *English* French houses, treading closely on the heels of Regent-street Véry.

Evans's under the Piazza of Covent-garden still holds its place for "chop" suppers, which with its theatrical portrait gallery* and superior musical entertainment, nightly draw crowds of the best company in town.

In the neighbourhood of London (to match the Pavillon Henri Quatre at St. Germain) we have "HIGHBURY BARN,"

---

* This is a very rare and interesting collection of all the "celebrities" who have "fretted their brief hour on the stage," from the time of Garrick down to the present day. It reflects great credit on the taste and "*esprit du corps*" of the worthy proprietor, Mr. Green, who has expended a large sum of money upon it; but it is a great satisfaction to him when he looks upon the "counterfeit presentments" of his old friends, and the revered master-spirits of the dramatic art, to say in the words of Charles Surface, in the *School for Scandal*, "Here I sit of an evening surrounded by my family."

the time-honoured *hostelrie* dating from the reign of Queen Anne, and celebrated for its "Corporation" and "Company" feasts. Here the City *bon vivants* still delight to congregate, and are in no way displeased to find the "foreign travel" of its proprietor has given him ideas in French cookery which are by no means at variance with their views of the march of improvement.

At the Crystal Palace, good and cheap dinners are also to be obtained; while the "Star and Garter," the "Castle," and the "Roebuck," at Richmond; the "Trafalgar," the "Crown and Sceptre," and the "Ship," at Greenwich; the "Brunswick," at Blackwall; "Waite's" and the "New Falcon," at Gravesend, are names which will live in "Little Dinner" and "White-bait" story, and convince our "lively neighbours" that we *can* cook something beyond a joint of meat and a pudding.

By the foregoing descriptive details of "Tavern Dining-out," I have endeavoured to show how great has been our recent progress in that department of "plain cookery," that it may be placed in strong contrast with the old-fashioned, unimproved, I may almost say, retrograding state of family kitchens.

Surely if our public *cheap* eating-houses can keep pace with the times, the same amelioration should find its way into our private establishments, yet *the old evil still remains*.

THE CULINARY ART IS BUT LITTLE UNDERSTOOD, AND, CONSEQUENTLY, GREATLY UNDERVALUED BY THE GENERALITY OF ENGLISH HOUSEKEEPERS, which is the more astonishing, when on every side they turn, they must see, from the superior manner in which every article of domestic consumption is prepared for the market, and the numberless novel appliances of steam-ranges, gas and charcoal stoves, hot plates, &c. &c., and a host of cleverly contrived kitchen implements and utensils, that a new era of gastronomy and cookery has dawned upon us.

I will now suppose that, having profited by my instructions, the "lady of the house" is competent to superintend the arrangements of her kitchen, and is anxious to display her new accomplishment by giving a little unostentatious dinner to a small party of her friends.* To enable her to carry out her

---

* For a "set dinner" for a large party, although it does not come strictly within the range of the present work, it may be recommended to follow as

intention without either parsimony or luxurious excess, I will
endeavour by a few useful hints to point out what the guests
will expect at her hands, and how she can best minister to their
comfort and satisfaction.

For these ends there are several very important points to be
considered : first, the number of persons to be entertained; next,
what extent of expense may be incurred; then, how is the dinner
to be served; and lastly, how is your table to be arranged and
lighted.   Let us take each point separately.

Eight or nine should be the limit of the party, for if you
should exceed that number, it generally happens that, instead
of an agreeable flow of conversation and easy mutual interchange
of ideas among the guests for the advantage of the whole company, coteries are formed, making all beyond their small circle
a desert, and resisting the united efforts of the vexed host and
hostess to lead their members into general sociality.

Especial care should be taken to avoid all "flints and steels,"
collisions likely to occur between persons who are at enmity, or
are opposed in political sentiments.   Nothing is more hazardous
to the harmony of your party than inattention to this rule.

Avoid "bores" of every kind, the parliamentary, the literary,
and scientific varieties above all; and do not, as many eccentric
persons often do, congregate oddities together.   A party composed of one-eyed or humpbacked men and women cannot pass
off satisfactorily; neither can a *réunion* of bluestockings or
"inspired idiots" of any class be productive of anything pleasant.
Observe, therefore, the happy medium; eschew "lions," and ask
none but those who are likely to assist in promoting a well-
tempered general hilarity, so that each guest may have his fair
share both of the general enjoyment and the satisfaction arising
from contributing to it.

Endeavour also to secure more than an equal proportion of
ladies, for it may be taken as a general maxim that no dinner
is so pleasant as that which is eaten under the harmonizing
influence of female society.

Never, from the fear of giving too little, be led into giving
too much ; neither, as is too frequently the case for the sake of
making an imposing show, crowd your table with " kickshaws "

closely as possible the bill of fare and general arrangement detailed in the
letter of " G. H. M." at page 8, as it is scarcely possible to produce anything
better for the class to which it appeals.

and side-dishes (often very costly), which in all probability will never be touched. *Have enough for your party, and no more.* By following this golden rule, you will never have to lament over wasteful expenditure; besides which, by having but few dishes and sauces to prepare, you will be able to give them better attention, and nothing (which is too often the case) will be done "anyhow."

The absurd pride of feeling it necessary to "astonish the Browns" when a party is given, is a great check to genial hospitality, while it entails on the silly entertainer more expense than he can afford, to say nothing of the toil that attends the preparation, and the mortification that follows the failure of the unsatisfactory display.

The late Lord Dudley truly said, "A good soup, a small turbot, a neck of venison, and an apricot tart, is a dinner fit for an emperor." Let, then, your dinner be based on this principle, for in proportion to its smallness ought to be its excellence both as to the quality of its materials and its cookery.

Without proper "appliances and means to boot," it is madness to attempt *entrées* and *entremets*. A simple, inexpensive dinner well cooked and served will be certain to give more *real* satisfaction than the most elaborate and costly banquet produced under difficulties and put on table amid bustle and confusion.

With good management and patient drilling, everything for a small party can be cooked and served by two female servants, and you will thus be spared the annoyance of the usual "butler" for the nonce in the person of an occasional waiter, who is generally a small greengrocer in white cotton gloves, who comes to his work in "mellow mood," and gets fairly half seas over before the dessert is put on the table, his fixed belief being that his especial mission on earth is to drink the bottoms of bottles (often the tops), and to stagger about among the guests with a vase of ice, portions of which he will insist on thrusting with a long spoon into your glass, or missing it (which often happens), over your arm, whether it be required or not.

The arrangement and lighting of your table call for the exercise of much of your taste and judgment. Your table should not be too broad nor too profusely ornamented; be sure in the cold season to have a good screen before the fire; let the tablecloth, napkins, plate, and every article of use or ornament, be scrupulously clean, fresh, and bright. Have a few *real* flowers in tasteful, delicate vases in the centre of the table, and place by the side of each guest three wineglasses: for sherry or Madeira, claret, and hock; the latter should be coloured. If you give champagne, substitute either the long or broad glass it is the fashion to use for it, for the claret or hock glass.

Do not crowd your guests, for nothing is more annoying to them than to have to use their knives and forks with their elbows pinioned to their sides; it is also inconvenient for the servants in changing plates and offering dishes. Endeavour as far as possible that every accessory of your dinner be placed on the table before your dishes; for the want of this foresight, I have known salmon and turbot grow cold while waiting for lobster sauce, and lamb and ducks become the vassals of their vegetables. Do not send round bread or " cruets," but have both on the table within reach of every one, for many often " do without" rather than give trouble. Let wine also be placed within easy reach, on both sides of the table, for it is very unpleasant to ask for it to respond to a challenge; and perhaps, after waiting, glass in hand, for it being brought to you from the farthest end of the table, to find it sherry, when you want hock or champagne.

Do not fill up the centre of your table with too many large ornaments, such as vases and épergnes of artificial flowers, and heavy candelabra, for they often so divide the party that you can scarcely see your second neighbour, while those on the opposite side are totally invisible.

If you have any delicacies to offer, do not, because " it is fashionable," delay their appearance until the appetite of your guests has been satisfied, or at all events blunted by a variety of solids. I have known partridges "picked," grouse, woodcocks, and wild ducks scarcely tasted, and pheasants sent away untouched, all of which, if they had been served at an earlier period of the dinner, would have been resolutely attacked and keenly relished by the whole company. The excuse for this barbarity is, that to provide enough to make them the *substantial* part of the dinner would be too expensive. This may be true in reference to a grand banquet for eighteen or twenty persons; but for small parties, depend upon it, if you serve your game or any other of your especial delicacies very soon, if not *imme-*

diately after your fish, your guests will swallow the affront without for an instant reflecting on your taste for leading them out of the " pale of fashion," particularly if you complete the atrocity by allowing light wines to appear with them.

In set dinners you *must* run on the usual grooves, and give punch after turtle, and dry Madeira, *à la* Talleyrand, after every other soup; Burgundy with *rotis*, claret with grouse, &c., reserving champagne, as Francatelli recommends, according to the custom in France, " until the latter part of the second course, as by that time the palate has become more fit to appreciate the delicate *bouquet* of this delicious and exhilarating beverage."

To have everything " hot and hot," directly it is taken from the fire, is a luxury that can only be enjoyed at small parties; let, then, each dish and *its proper vegetables* appear simultaneously;—we will say, for instance, after a few minutes' pause (which will materially assist digestion), while the soup-plates are being taken away and the glass of sherry or Madeira is going round, the cook dishes the " delicacies" or the substantial portions of the dinner, and sends them up so " smoking hot" that when the covers are removed the " *aroma*," " *fumet*," " *bouquet*," or savoury odour of each, may give a zest to the appetite which is totally lost when they are served *à la Française* by being placed on the table with the soup and fish, or cut up at a side-table and handed round in portions, *à la Russe*.

To *see* our dinner in its integrity in all its parts, is an English comfort we still cling to; and although it may involve a little trouble to the host in the carving, I am convinced, though a few travelled or fashion-loving exclusives may pretend to prefer " *service à la Russe*," with a *menu*, " neatly written in a lady's hand," to guide their choice, the majority of rational diners must feel much greater satisfaction in beholding their host, and hostess also, carving the smoking saddle, haunch, or sirloin. I say hostess advisedly, for when ladies have learned this very useful accomplishment and are not afraid to exhibit it, they lend a grace to the operation; and moreover, as all diners-out at tables where a lady " *carves their (palate's) destiny*," can avouch, by the peculiar nicety and neatness of the slices they dispense, greatly add to the individual comfort and general satisfaction of the guests. No jagged, uneven, clumpy, veiny pieces, superabundance of fat, or forgetfulness of gravy; no backs and drumsticks of poultry, no carelessness of any kind; in fact, nothing can be more true and valuable than the advice an old dinner-giver, who understood the art in all its phases, gave to his son on commencing housekeeping :—

" Let your wife learn to carve, my boy, for it is an accomplishment which will enable her to secure you a host of friends; for the man who knows that his little gastronomic partialities are remembered and will be delicately ministered to by the lady of the house, will always be anxious to find himself at your table."

A " liver wing" of a chicken, a couple of succulent slices from the breast of a goose or a turkey, a cut of the haunch or sirloin just done enough, dexterously carved, and sent with a hospitable smile, conveying, " I know you like that part," to each individual whose taste it will gratify, have cemented many friendships and made the plainest dinners Apician feasts.

Think of this, ladies, and lose no time in qualifying for the important office of " grand carver." You can try your " 'prentice hands" on your family dinners, and with a very little attention and practice will be soon able artistically to " hit the joint," and make the most of everything that comes before you.

I give the same advice to gentlemen, particularly to those who are nervous or bashful in society; they should learn to carve at *any cost*, for to men who dine out it is as much a matter of necessity as learning the polka or the figure of the quadrille. If you wish to spare yourselves many wretched moments, make yourselves carvers; you can never escape being called upon at some time or other to dissect something, and the fear that it may be a goose or a hare is ever at your heart; next to being called upon to return thanks for the ladies (by the way, if you are not blessed with oratorical powers, study some pretty flowerets, and keep them ready for accidents), and making an oration on the occasion of glasses being drained to your own health and prosperity, it is the greatest bore in the world.

Mr. L. F. Simpson, in his clever translation of Brillat-Savarin's *Physiologie du Goût*, whimsically, but at the same time with great truth, observes—

" The unfortunate man who has had the honour of taking down the lady of the house to dinner is like a culprit going to execution. He has a presentiment when going down-stairs that he will have to carve two fowls smothered in white sauce: he is seldom deceived, and gets no dinner until the third course."

To court rather than to shun the articulation of the wings of a pullet or the breast of a partridge, and when asked, to grapple with the sinuosities of a hare or a goose, to attack them with a certainty of subduing them without splashing the gravy, turning the edge of the carving-knife, overwhelming yourself with perspiration and confusion, your host and hostess with agitation, and the whole company with terror or laughter, should be the accomplishment of every man who wishes to dine out with comfort to himself and, what is equally important, usefulness to his entertainers.

Finger-glasses (although when applied to their original intention are cleanly comforts) are frequently so disgustingly abused that they should be banished from all civilized tables.* A little rose-water may, however, be handed round on a silver saucer or a glass vase, in which the corner of the napkin may be dipped to wipe the fingers and mouth.

On the best mode of lighting a dinner-table there are many opinions. Should the light be *on* the table or *over* it, or should rays be thrown *upon it* by strong reflectors from the walls ?

Let me, to justify my opinion, which is in favour of the illumination being *on* the table, quote the testimony of a most reliable authority, the writer of an article in *Fraser's Magazine* for April, 1859, entitled " Russian Dinners:"

" The lighting of the dinner-table is always a matter of importance. Light and enjoyment ever go together, while discomfort at the dinner-table is as surely wedded to the darkness visible that is sometimes inflicted upon a miserable set of unoffending fellow-creatures by a parsimonious or ill-judging entertainer.

The light should be as much as possible concentrated on the table; and in a small party it will be desirable to shade the eyes of the guests by semi-transparent reflectors of some kind, which will throw nearly all the light on the table. This, of course, only applies to lamps; the more diffused light of several candles requires no such caution. In some rooms, including the famous dining-room of the late Mr. Rogers, the light has been made to proceed from lamps arranged with opaque reflectors in front of pictures on the wall, so that no direct rays shall enter the middle of the room from the lamps; and the room is lighted by the rays reflected on the surface of the pictures, and from these again reflected into the room, so that the pictures themselves are the apparent sources of illumination.

---

* It is said of Brummel, who was particularly sensitive on this subject, that on a servant presenting him with one at the conclusion of a grand dinner, he declined it, saying, while he fixed his eyes on a gentleman opposite who was *audibly* gargling his mouth, " No, thank you; I cleaned my teeth and washed my mouth before I came out."

This naturally would only be done with works of art of the highest character, and such as can afford to challenge criticism in the conversation which is sure to turn upon them. But with all deference to great authorities, we hold that the presence of such pictures in a dining-room at all is a mistake, and the mistake is aggravated by making them conspicuous objects for attention.

The proper study of the dining-room is dining, and whatever tends to divert the eyes from the table is wrong in principle.

As in a theatre, where the looks of the spectators should be riveted by every artifice upon the scene of performance, so in a dining-room should all the accessories of necessary furniture be subordinated to the great object which occupies its centre. Here there can hardly be too much light. The table and the faces of the guests round it alone demand attention, and for them the greatest amount of illumination should be reserved.

How to obtain this general light is the great desideratum. Everybody who is in the habit of giving dinner-parties feels it is a great difficulty, and all kinds of expedients are resorted to to arrive at some perfect method. Gas is of course entirely out of the question, especially in London, now the companies are consolidated and stringent agreements are necessary to be made, upon which the supply can at any moment be cut off.

Lamps are exposed to more casualties even than gas: the very best will sometimes prove untractable, and should they go out, leave very unpleasant reminiscences of their motive power. Wax has consequently been long in the ascendant as affording a clear, steady, controllable, uncasualty-liable light; but it has two disadvantages—it is expensive, and (unless a great number of candles are used) not sufficiently brilliant to impart that warm, genial, sunlight glow which is so much prized and so difficult to secure. Within the last few years, however, a "new light" has appeared, which is gradually making its way, and bids fair, when its properties become better known, successfully to rival, if not eclipse, time-honoured wax. I allude to Price and Co.'s "Belmontines," or patent sperm candles, which possess every quality that the dinner-giver wishes to combine in the illumination of his table, viz., elegancy and delicacy of appearance, immunity from accident, brilliancy, and, which is a very strong feature, saving of cost, for the plaited wicks being closer and firmer, and the material from which the glycerine has been expelled more luminous in its effect than wax, a lesser quantity is found to suffice. By reducing the number of lights, moreover, the temperature of the room is greatly benefited, as each flame necessarily throws out a large amount of heat.

Added to their superior illuminating quality, the "Belmontines" are very ornamental, from their long slender shape and
from their transparency, affording a strong contrast to the
short, thick, opaque wax candles in general use, which being
large in diameter, are certain to flicker and flare with the
slightest breath of air, while the flame of the "Belmontines"
being stronger, and concentrated in a narrower space by its
intensity, repels everything but a strong current. I would
therefore recommend you to light your table with them placed
upon it in light candelabra, the sockets of which being
generally made large for wax, can be easily reduced by a cork
with a hole cut in it to the size of the thinner candles. The
French, who are always on the alert to avail themselves of
anything that can improve their dinner comforts, have already
discarded their four to the pound wax *bougies*, and adopted the
form, although they have not been able to arrive at the
brilliancy and transparency of the new English material. The
rapidly-increasing popularity of these candles is proved by the
following extract from a lecture delivered before the Society of
Arts by G. F. Wilson, F.R.S., son of the original proprietor,
and the present manager of the Belmont Works:

"In the month of October, 1840, from which time I can speak from
personal knowledge, we employed 74 men and 10 boys, and manufactured
about 20 tons of cocoa-nut candles, value £1227. In the corresponding
month of 1855, we employed 1098 men and 1191 boys and girls, and
manufactured of stearic and composite candles and night lights about 707
tons, value £79,500, in the month."

This leaves no doubt of the utility and perfect success of the
invention, which, but for a patriotic bias in the decision of the
"Council of Presidents," would have received (*as awarded by
the Jury and Group of Juries*) the first instead of the second
class "*Médaille d'honneur*" at the Paris Exhibition in the
*Palais de l'Industrie.**

* Mr. Wilson, in the course of his very interesting lecture (published by
W. H Smith and Son, 136, Strand), after dilating on the early struggles
with and subsequent triumphs over numerous difficulties which attended
the progress of his discoveries, says: "Connected with the manufactures
of the company are the endeavours which have been made to raise up a
set of improved and contented work-people, originated by my brother and
managed by him, aided by liberal grants from the Company. I rejoice to
say, that the educational and improvement work is going on most happily
in our London factories, and in our recently established colony on the
Mersey—the New Bromboro-Pool Works." Thus, in addition to the

The next point to be considered is, the best method of serving your dinner. Here a great deal of forethought and management are necessary, in order that you may *have everything in its proper place, at its proper time, and in proper condition.* Simple as these words may appear when written, in what a " mass of reticulated meshes" do they involve the dinner-giver, should any of the requirements they involve *not* " run smooth." Who has not seen a poor hostess, with flushed face and anxious eyes, trying hard to smile and appear happy, while she is nearly distracted by the carelessness or impertinence of the cook, and the awkwardness of the bewildered Susan, who is everywhere where she should not be, and does everything she ought not to do.

The host also comes in for his share of annoyances; the best of husbands and mildest of men have been known to exchange anything but kind glances with their partner in misfortune when cold plates have been brought for the hot turkey, and sweet pudding sauce has been given by mistake for plain butter for the salmon. How many moments of torture have been endured by the corkscrew being mislaid, and the filling of the cruets having in the hurry been forgotten! How many Jawkins's have struck consternation into the bosoms of their entertainers by asking for absent currant jelly or bitter beer; and how fatal has been the influence not only on the success of the dinner, but the comfort of the entire company, by bad management of the fire and the lights, and inattention to the suppression of draughts of cold air from the door and windows ? Let, then, every lady who would make sure of her dinner going off without mishaps, personally superintend every detail connected with the arrangement of her table, her dining-room, and her kitchen ; let her draw out a plan of the table, and mark on it the spot where every dish is to be placed, and *show* Jane and Susan how to act in concert. With a very little good and careful drilling it is astonishing how cleverly the whole affair can be managed. As an example of what can be done with few hands, *if the mind of the master or the mistress be given to it,* I will quote the bill of fare for a party of twenty, every dish of which was cooked at home, and served by two female servants.

general benefit arising from a very valuable invention, Mr. Wilson and his colleagues have been enabled to sow the seeds of goodness amid a part of the community whose welfare is too often neglected by their employers.

It affords a good illustration of substantial English fare blended with just sufficient of the French kitchen to give it piquancy and lightness. It may serve as a model for inexperienced entertainers to form smaller dinners upon :—*

First Course.

| Curried Lobster. | Turbot. Lobster Sauce. Salmon. | Stewed Eels. |

———

Entrées.

| Stewed Pigeons. Lamb Cutlets. Tomato Sauce. | Potatoes. | Curried Rabbit. Beef Olives. |

———

Second Course.
Fore-quarter of Lamb.

| Roast Ducks. | | Roast Fowls. |
| Potatoes. Boiled Fowls. | Bacon and Beans. | Peas. Tongue. |

Sirloin of Beef.

———

Third Course.
Cream Pudding.

| Blancmange. Currant Tarts. Jelly. | | Jelly. Raspberry Tarts. Blancmange. |

Salad.   Cheese.

———

Dessert.
All Fruits in season, and Dried Fruits.
Pine Apple.
Cream and Water, Ice.

———

Wines.
Hock, Champagne, Sparkling Hock, and Moselle, Port,
Sherry and Claret.

———

* This well composed and excellent dinner was given by Mr. Benjamin Webster, the highly respected actor and proprietor of the New Royal Adelphi Theatre, on the occasion of his being elected President and Governor of the Drury Lane Theatrical Fund, founded by David Garrick for the support of aged and infirm actors and actresses. Mr. Webster is also the President of the Royal Dramatic College, another benevolent theatrical institution, which was originated by him, and owes much of its prosperity to his untiring efforts to befriend his poorer histrionic brothers and sisters.

As a contrast to this plain English entertainment, and at the same time to show the great reliance now placed by the foreign cooks (particularly those who have conducted any of our establishments) on our national dishes in the composition of their dinners, I will quote from *"Hayward's Essays"* the bill-of-fare of a grand French banquet, given to Lord Chesterfield on his quitting the office of Master of the Buckhounds. It took place at the Clarendon, was ordered by the late Count d'Orsay; the party consisted of thirty, and the price was six guineas a head :—

First Course.

Soups.—Spring; à la Reine; TURTLE.

Fish.—Turbot, with lobster and Dutch sauces; Salmon à la tartare (cutlets broiled with sharp sauce); Trout à la Cardinal; fried Cod; WHITEBAIT.

Removes.—Filet de Bœuf à la Napolitaine; Turkey à la Chipolata; Timballe (a mould or saucepan in which anything is baked with a crust) of Macaroni; HAUNCH OF VENISON.

Side Dishes, or *Entrées.*—Croquettes de Volaille (minced poultry with a bread-crumb coating); Oyster Patties; Lamb Cutlets, Puree (pulp) of Mushrooms; Lamb Cutlets with asparagus points; Fricandeau of Veal, with sorrel; Larded Sweetbreads, with tomato sauce; Pigeons à la Dusselle-Chartreuse de Légumes aux Faisans, (this is a mixed preparation, consisting of vegetables symmetrically and tastefully arranged in a plain mould, the interior of which is filled with game, &c.; in this instance it was pheasants); *"Filets"* of Ducklings à la Bigarrade; Puddings à la Richelieu; sauté de volaille aux truffes (cutlets of poultry lightly fried in butter with truffles); Savoury Mutton Pâté.

Side Dishes.—ROAST BEEF; Ham; Salad.

Second Course.

Roasts.—Capons, Quails; Turkey Poults; GREEN GOOSE.

Side Dishes.—Asparagus; Haricot Beans à la Française (with cream); Mayonnaise d'Homard (lobster salad); Macédoine Jelly; Plover's Eggs with aspic jelly; Charlotte Russe (this is composed of "lady's-finger" biscuits placed in a mould and filled with fruit or preserves, iced, and garnished with whipped cream); Maraschino Jelly; Marble Cream; Corbeille (fancy basket) of Pastry; Vol au vent de Rhubarb (rhubarb tart, with very light puff-paste); Apricot Tart; Corbeille of Meringues (light cakes, garnished with whipped cream); Dressed Crab; Gelatine Salad; Mushrooms, with sweet herbs.

Removes.—Vanille souflé; Nesselrode Pudding; Adelaide Sandwiches; Cheese Souflé; Savoury Patties, &c. &c,

The number of dishes of which the dinner is composed will, I have no doubt, strike many of my readers with astonishment, and probably some thrifty housewives may moralize over the quantity of "garnish" that must have been entirely wasted; but this is but a simple luncheon compared with some of the gorgeous repasts at the Albion in Aldersgate-street, the London Tavern, and the Trafalgar at Greenwich, where occasionally as much as twenty guineas a head has been paid; indeed, in the days of the late Sir William Curtis, it is said that the enormous charge of forty guineas a head has been incurred. All dinners of this description are silly mistakes, as they are not given for the sake of hospitality, but for ostentatious display; to send a special messenger to Westphalia to choose a ham, to the West Indies for turtle, to New York for canvas-backed ducks, or to Florence for ortolans and beccaficoes, seems an act of pure insanity; yet such extravagances have been recorded, and at this very hour equally reprehensible follies are indulged in, not only for tavern feasts, but for private dinners, where very large sums are often paid for delicacies out of season, merely to show that the entertainer's purse can bear the cost. How much better would it be for all classes to give their dinners for their proper objects, and entirely abandon empty display in *all* its branches. Instead of a crowd of servants, who by their numbers impede rather than promote the comfort of the guests, why not be contented with a few who are well trained, and have sharp eyes and quick ears, and let nothing be put on the table which does not form part of the *body of the dinner*.

Let but one great Amphitryon " take the bull by the horns," and show that even at a grand banquet it is possible to entertain liberally without senseless extravagance; and although the number of the dishes may be reduced from the ordinary standard, by the cook's talent being concentrated on a few *chef-d'œuvres*, the delicacy of the cookery will be increased, and *every* dish will become an " object of interest;" this would at once remove the evils so long complained of; and none but vulgar upstarts would attempt to outvie their neighbours by ostentatious and wasteful display.

The influence of this gastronomic revolution at great tables would rapidly extend to those of the middle-class; and then, instead of a dinner-party being a source of great trouble and anxiety alike for the preparation and the expense, and looked upon as one of the evils attendant on a comfortable position in society, it would become, from its moderate requirements, a pleasant social gathering of friends, who, by showing themselves pleased with their entertainment, would make their host and hostess happy in the success of their unpretending efforts to combine the true elements of hospitality, good cheer, and mutual sociality.

I will not attempt to direct you in the choice of the dishes you should provide for your party, as their number and cost must entirely depend on your means; but lest you should, in your ignorance of the seasons of the various good things at your disposal, think of giving pork in July, or ducks and green-peas at Christmas, I will subjoin a table of THE SEASONS OF EVERY KIND OF MEAT, FISH, POULTRY, GAME, VEGETABLES, AND FRUIT.

JANUARY.

Winter is the most agreeable season of the year to the lovers of good cheer; and January is one of the months most favourable to it, being the period when family parties are generally prevalent, and *nearly every kind of provision, meat especially, is in full season*, green and young vegetables and fruit excepted. This month, from the copiousness of its supplies, needs no list.

FEBRUARY.

This month has little occasion to envy its predecessor; game perhaps may be less plentiful, but it has lost none of its good qualities; and every description of poultry is still in prime order; spring chickens and ducklings may be added to the list, although their prices are in general beyond the means of thrifty housekeepers; cod is getting a little on the wane; and salmon is beginning to make its appearance.

MARCH.

In this month there is a slight decrease in the flavour of beef and veal, and mutton is beginning to be replaced by house lamb; pork, however, is still in its prime; game is loosing its flavour, and is preparing to take wing; cod continues to decline, but oysters, lobsters, crabs, crawfish, prawns, shrimps, turbot, plaice, skate, eels, flounders, soles, whiting, and every other kind of sea and river fish, excepting mackerel, are still in full season and flavour. In addition to the winter vegetables, seakale is now plentiful, hinting the approach of asparagus.

APRIL.

" Come, gentle Spring," sings the gourmand, longing for

early vegetables; and heartily doth he hail the advent of showery April, for now many of the *primeurs,* or harbingers of summer, are *forced* to appear in the market. Lamb is rapidly displacing mutton; pork still keeps its ground, although the sometimes warm breath of spring gives warning that its reign is drawing to a close; game is getting out of season; chickens and ducklings are now plentiful; cod, knowing that oysters, its *saucy* satellites, are about to vanish, has withdrawn his head and shoulders, politely making way for mackerel, which towards the end of the month begin to make their appearance; salmon, although still dear, is daily increasing in quantity in the market, and promises shortly to be within the reach of " the million."

MAY.

With the flowers which usher in this month, so dear to the poets, come most of the summer vegetables ; first asparagus, then potatoes, then the " emeralds of the kitchen," green peas, summer cabbages, broccoli, cauliflowers, lettuces, young onions, and carrots, small salad, cucumbers, and kidney beans ; mutton is getting " woolly;" and beef, which, though *always* in season, is now a little in the shade; while veal courts the sunshine, in which grass lamb now revels with all its youthful attractions ; pork, to use a sporting phrase, is beginning to be " nowhere." Although here and there a leveret may be seen, game is quite out of season, but its place is well supplied by chickens, capons, fowls, pullets, pigeons, ducks, ducklings, and *green geese,* Mackerel and salmon are now within the reach of the thrifty housewife, who has still at her disposal carp, chub, eels, crabs, crayfish, John Dory, flounders, gurnet, brill, haddock, halibut, herrings, lobsters, plaice, prawns, shrimps, skate, smelt, soles, trout, turbot, and whitings.

Rhubarb now betokens the advent of green gooseberries ; and currants, forced cherries, strawberries, raspberries, and peaches are now plentiful.

JUNE.

This, in spite of all that has been sung and said in praise of " blooming May," is the most genial month of the whole year, for the sun is of dazzling brilliancy without sultriness, and everything not only *looks,* but seems to *feel,* gay. Beautiful month ; and yet a distinguished *gastronome* has ventured to assert in print that it is the most miserable one in the calendar to a dinner-giver ; for from so many delicacies being out of season, he is compelled to feed his company on vegetables !

There is no denying that many of the superior kinds of fish, excepting salmon and " WHITEBAIT," which latter delicacy we are warned by the circulars of the Greenwich, Blackwall, and Gravesend tavern-keepers, is " now in season," are not so plentiful nor so prime in quality. To make up for the absence of game, venison is plentiful, and turkey poults, ducklings, green-geese, chickens, capons, and fowls, with leverets, too, " woo the spit," and wait upon the young vegetables, all of which are now in their best days.

JULY.

In this month butcher's meat is not so much cared for as in the winter season, while ham and bacon, in mercantile language, are " looking up ;" green peas, now in their zenith, suggest rashers ; and young broad beans, which are beginning to show themselves, naturally turn us towards the streaky ribs or well-smoked gammon. Poultry is plentiful, and salmon is cheap, but mackerel are preparing to take leave. Fruit of nearly every kind is now in full season ; and vegetables, although many of them have lost the bloom of youth, are still attractive in their maturity.

AUGUST.

Butcher's meat is still " at a slight discount," but every kind of poultry continues to be plentiful and in good condition. Game is now beginning to make its appearance, and quails, wheatears, leverets, wild ducks, wood-pigeons, and wild rabbits, are, after the twelfth of the month, followed by grouse and black-cock. Mackerel go quite out this month, and oysters come in on the fourth. Turbot, soles, skate, brill, salmon, shrimps, prawns, crabs, crayfish, John Dory, lobsters, mullet, trout, eels, and flounders, are also in good season. Peas are going, and beans of every kind are succeeding them. Stone fruits are now in full season, and at the latter end of the month cob-nuts and filberts come in with a few *foreign* walnuts.

SEPTEMBER.

This month, which in England is, according to the *Times*, devoted to " St. Partridge," restores butcher's meat to its popularity, while partridges, hares, grouse, black-cock, and venison begin their reign. Pork also puts in an appearance. Fish continues the same as last month. Whitebait, however, which immediately after the ministerial dinner grows larger and larger, now forsakes its bread and butter. The same fruits as last month, with the addition of English walnuts, which come in about the middle.

OCTOBER.

This month is pleasantly ushered in by pheasants, and now that the spring and summer vegetables are gone, we have in their places, artichokes, sprouts, winter spinach, and truffles. Fish is generally plentiful, and cod, turbot, brill, crabs, John Dory, eels, gudgeons, cockles, haddocks, mussels, oysters, salmon-trout, shrimps, smelts, soles, and whitings, are all in prime season. Every kind of meat is now in demand, the game season is at its full, and poultry begins to grow dear.

Grapes, apples, pears, and dried fruits replace wall fruit, and plums are only represented by damsons. Walnuts are still good, and filberts and cob-nuts are in their prime.

NOVEMBER.

This month brings us up to the winter season, the days draw in, but dinners are greatly lengthened, there are so many good things to discuss. With the exception of salmon, mackerel, and whitebait, every kind of fish may be now said to be in prime season. Game is plentiful, and in full flavour. There is a great falling off, of course, in fruits and vegetables; but store potatoes, winter spinach, endive, celery, and sprouts make a good show. A great variety of foreign fruits flow in to enrich the dessert-table—delicious Jersey pears, French plums, raisins, &c. &c.

Early in this month sucking pigs come in, and on Lord Mayor's day, mince pies foreshadow plum-pudding, and sprats make a noise in the world.

DECEMBER.

This is the cardinal month for feasting and goodfellowship, and he who does not welcome its approach with joyful feelings, must have a very poor heart indeed. Scarcely has November run its course before preparations are made for the great fête of all classes, Christmas-day—poultry is fattened, the ingredients for the pudding are purchased, arrangements for the dinner party discussed. What packings in the country, and unpackings in town! Members of " Goose Clubs " are to be seen in flocks carrying home gigantic birds. Morel, and Fortnum and Mason, are unable to execute half their orders for " truffled turkeys," Strasbourg pâtés, and all the thousand other *wonders of the gastronomic repertory.* In short, in this month the tocsin of " war to the knife " is sounded in all quarters against everything that swims, flies, and grazes, or is pickled, preserved, potted, and pied, or collared and kippered. With its manifold enjoyments are associated the compliments of the season, so, with the wish that every succeeding Christmas may bring to every home increase and comfort, I will conclude my calendar.

The time has now arrived to give my promised examples of

FRENCH COOKERY.

Strange though it may appear, the French pre-eminence in cookery is comparatively modern, and may be traced to England! but it is nevertheless true; the comfort of the English taverns and coffee-houses, which came into vogue towards the end of Queen Anne's reign, and reached their apogee during the days of the second George, was so extolled by every traveller who had partaken of their solid hospitality, that at last a great gastronomic mind burst through the shackles of prejudice and routine, and gave to Paris what it had long wanted, a public dining establishment, where a good dinner could be enjoyed in the midst of good society, without the diner being compelled to shake hands with any one, nor eat anything which was not quite agreeable to his palate; in short, a place where a man could choose his dinner, and be always sure, whether it was a moderate or an expensive one, of having it well cooked and well served. The name of this national benefactor, for such he deserves to be called, was Lamy, and he opened his modest *salon* in one of the dark and narrow passages leading to the Palais Royal, towards the end of the year 1774. Over his door he had the following inscription in kitchen Latin :—

O vos qui stomacho laboratis, accurite,
Et ego vos restaurabo.

O you, whose empty stomachs moan in pain,
Come to me, and I'll restore you again.

Whence was originated the name of *Restaurateur.* Two years, however, before this time, in 1772, *tables-d'hôte* were provided by the *traiteurs-rôtisseurs,* who then only kept public kitchens for cooking and *sending out* dinners, which were composed either of articles supplied by themselves, according to order, or of meat, game, poultry, fish, &c. &c., sent in to them from private houses to be cooked, both of which customs, by the way, exist in Paris up to the present time. The establishment of these *tables-d'hôte* was also the result of a happy idea. One of the *traiteurs* having a large commodious room attached to his kitchen, thought he might turn it to advantage by giving a public dinner at a fixed hour, for a small price, to those of his customers who, from a press of business, or any other cause, could not conveniently go to their own homes to dine. The idea was a good one, and it prospered, so it was adopted by his brother *traiteurs,* and in a very short time *tables-d'hôte* of every grade became popular; but it was reserved for Lamy to make the great leap to fortune by introducing dinners *à l'Anglaise à la carte,* which at once, as the French phrase it, put every man "*dans son assiette,*" or proper position, by enabling him to choose the dishes which pleased him, and enjoy in the midst of a lively crowd the privacy of his own house. As in everything else, perfection is only arrived at by slow degrees, and great patience and exertion; Lamy at the commencement of his enterprise had a hard battle to fight; the whole body of the *traiteurs* conspired against him, and compelled him to confine himself to the strict letter of the municipal law, which, besides obliging him to open and shut his doors at particularly inconvenient hours, and keep a register of the names and addresses of every one frequenting the house, levying heavy duties on the wines and provisions consumed on the premises, prohibited the use of silver spoons and linen cloths, and exacted that every article he served in his "eating shop" should be upon tables covered with green or jasper-coloured oil-cloth.

Still he struggled on bravely, and finally triumphed; the municipal restrictions were removed, the "eating shop" was

called a *restaurant*, he made a princely fortune, and retired
to make way for Robert (the inventor of the famous sauce),
Beauvilliers, Béchamel (another great "*saucier*"), and at a
later time Carême, the fame of whose genius spreading far
and near, made the establishments they presided over the
resort of the choicest company. To improve the various
dishes, many of which were even now imperfectly produced,
more gastronomic minds went to work, and their labours
meeting on all sides with liberal encouragement from wealthy
gourmets of both sexes, a gastronomic college was established,
which effectually revolutionized the dinners of Europe, and
elevated cookery to a science.[*]

The establishment of *Restaurateurs* was a great social fact;
before their fortunate advent the enjoyment of delicate cookery
was confined solely to the opulent; the *Restaurateurs* placed it
within the reach of almost every one. He who could spend
twenty or five-and-twenty francs for his dinner, and *knew how
to choose his dishes*, could dine in one of the first-class *salons*
better than in the palace of a prince; while he who could not
afford to launch out so far, had for his five, or even three francs,
in less pretending establishments, a repast which the resources
of his domestic kitchen could not in any way compete with; in
fact, the *Restaurateurs* were the missionaries of civilization,
and their efforts did for French cookery what the seventeenth
and eighteenth centuries did for literature—they rendered it
universal. And this happy, useful reformation, tending to social
equality, really had its birth in England, its first nurseries
having been the Mitres, Turks' Heads, Cocoa Trees, Grecians,
White's, Will's, Buttons, &c. &c., whose glories are so graphically recorded in the pages of the *Spectator*, the *Tattler*, and
the *Guardian*, and at a later date in Boswell's gossiping *Life
of Doctor Johnson*, which latter *weighty* authority emphatically
gave it as his opinion that "a tavern chair was the throne of
human felicity."

Since these bygone days, while *we* have been gradually

[*] Monsieur Henrion de Pensey, late President of the Court of Cassation,
says: "I regard the discovery of a dish as a far more interesting event
than the discovery of a star, for we have always stars enough, but we can
never have too many dishes; and I shall not regard the sciences as sufficiently honoured amongst us until I see a cook in the first class of the
Institute."

weaned from our fondness for taverns, and *away from home enjoyments,* the French have taken up our bad habits, and have made tavern comforts their particular study. To prevent the fire on the domestic hearth from being entirely extinguished, and coax erratic husbands *sometimes* to dine at home, prudent housewives became pupils of the great *chefs,* and under their instructions made themselves " *cordon bleus,*"* or female adepts in the arcana of cookery; thus the French family kitchen, or *La cuisine Bourgeoise,* which is now so renowned as offering the happy medium of delicate dinners, where real enjoyment is not trenched upon by empty state, gathered its first laurels. It was this wise movement of the French housewives that raised the standard of French cookery, and fully established its European pre-eminence.

Not having the same stimulus for exertion, and *the growing wealth of the middle-class rendering domestic accomplishments unfashionable,* our English wives have, during the last half century, taken but little interest in their kitchens, leaving to their servants the superintendence which their grandmothers were educated to consider the imperative duty of the mistress of a family; but all is getting right again; *the establishment of clubs has given English wives the same fright which the restaurateurs introduced by Lamy gave to the Parisian dames; and English domestic cookery is now making rapid strides to compete with the best efforts of the so long-vaunted foreign school;* in aid of which national movement I humbly beg to contribute my mite, by giving receipts for a few of the most popular French dishes which are quite within the compass of the family kitchen's ordinary appliances; I would, however, advise the addition of a charcoal-stove, and a *bain-marie,* as they are very valuable agents for the acquisition of the peculiar delicacy of finish and flavour so much esteemed in the French kitchen. The great advantage of the charcoal-stove is, that by the exact amount of heat being attained *before* the stewpans are put upon it, everything is cooked gradually, which is very necessary for delicate

---

* This title belongs exclusively to *female* artists. The first so ennobled was the *cuisinière* of Madame Dubarry, who cooked a dinner for Louis XV. so exquisitely, that the royal voluptuary, whose confirmed opinion was that it was morally and physically impossible for a woman to obtain the highest perfection of the culinary art, declared her to be worthy a *cordon-bleu.*

sauces, ragouts, &c. &c. The expense of such stoves is not great, and the outlay for erecting one would soon be repaid by the saving in fuel. The "*bain-marie*," or hot water-bath, is a broad, flat, shallow saucepan, made expressly for the purpose, and kept continually on the stove. Into this bath, which should be *hot*, but *not* boiling, the stewpans are placed when the ragouts, sauces, &c., are completed, and their contents can *be kept hot without affecting their flavour or quantity*, which is a great advantage ; for if the pans are set aside on the hob in a common range, as the stewing will continue, the gravies will waste and thicken, the side next the fire will burn, and the delicacy of the flavour is very apt to be injured, if not entirely destroyed.

Soup being always the "leading article" in a French dinner, my first "*pas en avant*" shall be

SOUP A LA REINE.

Cut up two good sized young fowls, put them into a stewpan with three quarts of strong white stock (in which carrots and onions alone have been stewed), or, if that be wanting, let three pounds of knuckle of veal, half a pound of lean ham, two middling-sized carrots and onions, a blade of mace, and twenty black peppercorns, be previously stewed down to the same quantity of liquor ; stew with a close-fitting lid for an hour, then take out the pieces of fowl, strip off all the white meat, and pound it in a mortar with three tablespoonsful of "swelled" rice. Put the bones and skin of the fowls into the stewpan again, simmer for ten minutes, then skim *carefully*, and strain through a fine sieve. Mix the chicken and rice pulp with the strained broth over the fire in the stewpan, and "*lift*" (I've come to the grand secret again) until it becomes quite smooth and moderately thick.

N.B.—If it be too thick, add a little more stock or broth ; if too thin, a little arrowroot, mixed smooth in a cup with a little *cold* stock.

Keep hot on the hob, or in the *bain-marie* (if you have one), until wanted ; and at the moment of serving, stir in gradually a pint of hot cream. Garnish with sippets of bread cut in dice and fried in butter. Let it be but moderately salt.

Monsieur Gogué, generally a good authority, says that this soup may be made with the relics (*débris*) of cooked poultry and veal, instead of fresh fowls; but I have tried his receipt, and find it far from satisfactory for *holiday* occasions.

POTAGE A LA BISQUE.

This very popular soup is erroneously supposed by many to be made *entirely* of crayfish, but mussels, crabs, whelks, cockles, and every kind of shell-fish excepting oysters, are very often used, even in the kitchens of the most celebrated *restaurateurs*, for the foundation, a few crayfish being added as garnish.

The mode of producing the real soup is as follows :—

Wash in several waters, and carefully pull away the black portion (the gall gut) of sixty crayfish, then brown in a stew-pan for five minutes with two ounces of butter, a small carrot, a middling sized onion, a head of white celery cut in slices, three sprigs of chopped parsley, a bay leaf, a sprig of thyme, a teaspoonful of salt, half a teaspoonful each of black and cayenne pepper; add to them the crayfish, a bottle of white French wine, and a quart of strong white or fish stock (for the receipt see page 77). Simmer gently (on the charcoal stove) half an hour, then take out the crayfish, and strain the broth through a tammy, pressing well to obtain the essence of the vegetables. Remove the flesh from the claws and tails of the fish, reserve half of the latter for garnish, and put the rest into a mortar, with four ounces of butter cut in small pieces, the spawn of a cooked lobster, six well washed anchovies, and the crusts of two small French rolls (previously fried with butter light brown); pound thoroughly, and put the paste into the stewpan with the strained broth; mix, and " lift" over the fire for a few minutes, then, having placed the reserved fish, cut in pieces in the tureen, pour the soup over them, and serve hot. This, from the quantity of wine used is a very expensive soup, but when well made it is perhaps more popular than any of its aristocratic relations. When wine is not to be had, the juice of a lemon, added at the moment of serving, may be substituted, and as I have already observed, crab, and other cheap shell-fish may re-present the *river lobster*, but their flavour is very inferior to that of the " real Simon Pure."

There are many other *bisques* of lobster, crab, prawns, chickens, game, &c., some of which are served with cream *à la Reine*, but as they are but fanciful variations of the receipt I have given, it is not necessary to notice them.

BOUILLABAISSE A LA MARSEILLAISE.

This is the dish for which Marseilles is as much renowned as Greenwich is for whitebait, and is thus immortalized by Thackeray in his " Miscellanies," under the title of " The Ballad of the Bouillabaisse."

This Bouillabaisse a noble dish is—
  A sort of broth, or soup, or brew,
Or hotchpotch of all kinds of fishes,
  That Greenwich never could outdo ;
Green herbs, red peppers, mussels, saffern,
  Soles, onions, garlic, roach, and dace ;
All these you eat at Terré's tavern,
  In that one dish of Bouillabaisse.

Indeed, a rich and savoury stew 'tis,
  And true philosophers, one thinks,
Who love all sorts of natural beauties,
  Should love good victuals and good drinks ;
And Cordelier, or Benedictine,
  Might gladly, sure, his lot embrace,
Nor find a fast-day too afflicting
  Which served him up a Bouillabaisse.

Although this soup contains several kinds of fish peculiar to the Mediterranean seas procurable only at Marseilles, a very excellent soup, similar in character, can be made with red mullets, soles, small turbots, whitings, gurnets, lobsters, and crayfish, in the following manner :—

Slice up two large onions, place them in a good-sized stewpan large enough to contain all your fish at the bottom—a flat wide pan is preferable ; add to this two tablespoonfuls of olive oil, and fry the onions pale brown ; next place the fish, cut in pieces of about three inches square, in the pan, with just enough *warm* water to cover them. To each pound of fish sprinkle about half a teaspoonful of salt, an eighth of a teaspoonful of pepper, half a bay leaf, half a lemon without the pips or rind, cut in dice, also two tomatoes in dice (having extracted the seeds) ; add three glasses of sherry or light wine, twenty peppercorns, and half a clove of garlic—set on a fierce fire, and boil very fast from ten to twelve minutes.

By this time the liquor should be reduced to a third of its original quantity ; add a small portion of saffron, according to taste, a tablespoonful of fresh chopped parsley ; let all boil one minute longer, and remove from the fire, as it is then ready for dishing up.

Line the tureen with slices of French rolls about half an inch in thickness.

N.B. Serve as soon as taken from the fire, as the shortest delay will injure the flavour.

SAUCE SOUBISE.

Mince a dozen small onions, and put them into a stewpan with a quarter of a pound of fresh butter, over a slow fire (or a charcoal stove), add two tablespoonfuls of *Velouté*, or if you have none prepared, mix the butter with two tablespoonfuls of flour, and half a pint of cream: when the onions are soft, squeeze them through a fine sieve, and put the pulp into the sauce again by little and little, stirring and "lifting" according to previous directions. This sauce should be thick.

MAYONNAISE SAUCE.

Put into a large bowl two *raw* yolks of eggs (be careful that they are very fresh), half a teaspoonful of salt, the same of ground and sifted black pepper, turn and mix (one way) with a wooden spoon, then add by degrees four tablespoonfuls of the best olive oil, and two of French vinegar. When the sauce begins to thicken, thin it with a little lemon juice, and keep on mixing until it is quite smooth, and of the consistency of good cream.

N.B.—This sauce must not be put on the fire, being merely a dressing for salads, cold poultry, fish, &c.

MAYONNAISE D'HOMARD, OR FRENCH LOBSTER SALAD.

Break a boiled lobster, take out the flesh of the tail and claws, and cut them in pieces of about an inch and a half long and an inch wide; then pound the spawn or coral (if there be none in the lobster, it is to be bought separately at the fishmonger's) with the cream, two ounces of butter, a boned anchovy, and half a teaspoonful of cayenne. Rub this paste through a hair sieve, and cover the bottom of the dish you are going to serve your salad upon with it, reserving a small quantity to connect the pieces of lobster, which you must now pile in layers round the dish, leaving the centre hollow, to be filled with the salad of lettuces, cresses, endive, and beet-root. Raise the salad into a dome, and garnish it with slices of hard-boiled eggs, beet-root, and pieces of boned anchovies. Pour over it a good quantity of *mayonnaise* sauce.

SAUCE ROBERT.

Here is the receipt for this once " wonder of the gastronomic world." Cut six middling sized onions into dice, brown them lightly in an ounce of butter, and moisten them by degrees, first with a tablespoonful of vinegar, and then as much *Espagnole* sauce (for receipt see page 56) as you may require to make for your *entrée;* mix, and lift, until you arrive at the thickness of cream (if too thick, add a little more vinegar or lemon juice), then *take the pan from the fire*, shake in a tablespoonful of mustard; mix, and lift again (off the fire), and serve. This sauce is greatly esteemed all over the Continent for *entrées,* particularly of pork.

SOLE AU GRATIN.

Clean, skin, and scrape, a good-sized sole ; lightly crimp the back, and place it in a well-buttered metal dish (a silver or plated one, if you have it) large enough to allow it to lie in the centre, the back upwards, with at least an inch of margin; put *over and round it,* a quarter of a pound of fresh butter cut in small pieces, a teaspoonful of shalot, a tablespoonful of parsley, and two tablespoonsful of button-mushrooms, all finely chopped, a quarter of a teaspoonful of cayenne pepper, the same of salt, a " grate" of nutmeg, and two glasses of sherry, or any other white *dry* wine ; add two tablespoonsful of *Espagnole* sauce (for receipt see page 56); strew *in the margin* half a dozen button-mushrooms cut in quarters, and a tablespoonful of picked shrimps ; bake in a brisk oven ten minutes ; then turn the fish, baste it with the gravy (without disturbing the mushrooms and shrimps), sprinkle a good tablespoonful of dried, or baked, bread-crumbs over it ; bake from five to ten minutes longer (according to size) ; then serve *in the dish it is baked in.* At the moment of sending to table, flavour with a slight squeeze of lemon. The same receipt will serve for " *Filets de Sole.*"

N.B.—All kinds of fish can be dressed in this manner, or simply in a common baking-dish, with an ounce or two of butter, or good dripping, plain bread-crumbs, and chopped herbs ; ale may be substituted for the wine ; and if you do not serve in the baking-dish (which is by far the *best* way), gently slide the fish into a very hot dish, and pour the gravy *round*, but *not over* it, or you will destroy the crispness of the bread-crumbs.

SOLE A LA NORMANDE.

This is nothing but a variety of the " *sole au gratin*," the only difference in its preparation is that a *matelotte sauce l a Normande* (see receipt below) is used in the place of the *Espagnole*, and parboiled oysters, and mussels, small crayfish, fried gudgeons, truffles, and champignons (browned in butter), and sippets of fried bread are added to the garnish. It is served in the dish it is baked in, with a squeeze of lemon, and a sprinkle of cayenne. As the matelotte flavour should predominate, use *three* tablespoonsful of the sauce. Dutch sauce (see receipt, page 88) is often used in place of the " *matelotte*."

MATELOTTE SAUCE A LA NORMANDE.

Take the flesh from the tails of a dozen small crayfish, a quarter of a pint of mussels, a dozen and a half of oysters (there is no need to beard them), half a tablespoonful of button-mushrooms, two anchovies, two glasses of white wine, the oyster liquor, and a tablespoonful of *Velouté* sauce; simmer with a close lid one hour; strain through a tammy, and set the sauce aside in a cool place until it is required for use.

This is a very rich sauce, and may be used for all kinds of fish ragouts.

POULET A LA MARENGO.

Cut up two plump pullets, and put them into a stewpan with four tablespoonsful of the best olive-oil; brown the legs first for two or three minutes, and then the other pieces; season with a teaspoonful of black pepper, and the same quantity of salt; add two small green onions, a clove of garlic, two shalots, and two sprigs of parsley, all chopped fine, half a tablespoonful of tomato sauce, a wineglassful of sherry, Madeira, or any other dry white wine, two tablespoonsful of *Espagnole*, a small piece of ice (to give smoothness), and a very small pinch of pounded sugar (to correct acidity), half a dozen button-mushrooms, and half a pound of truffles cut into small squares; mix the gravy, &c., with a wooden spoon, and baste well the pieces of the pullets with it; simmer on the charcoal-stove, or a slow fire, with a close lid, from twenty to five-and-twenty minutes, according to the weight of the meat; put the pieces on a hot dish in the form of a pyramid; pour the sauce over it; add a squeeze of lemon, and a sprinkle of cayenne; garnish with sippets of a French roll, and eggs fried in oil.

FRICASSEE DE POULET.

Having carefully plucked, drawn, singed, and chopped off the scaly legs and feet of your chicken, cut off the thighs and wings, and divide each into two pieces; then separate the breast from the back, and cut them into four pieces; wash well the liver and gizzard, and put them, with all the other pieces, into a pan of cold water; move them to and fro several times with the hand to bring away any blood or small vessels which may have been overlooked in the drawing.

Now dissolve in a stewpan an ounce of butter cut in small pieces, lightly brown in it half a small carrot, a small onion, half a head of white celery cut in thin slices, a blade of mace, a sprig of parsley, two cloves, a teaspoonful of salt, and a dozen black pepper-corns; then put the pieces of chicken upon them; add to them a quart of white stock, or if that be not at hand, the same quantity of boiling water; stew gently with a close lid three-quarters of an hour; then skim, and strain off the vegetables, and put the pieces of chicken aside in the pan, and the broth in a basin, until you have made your sauce, which you must do as follows :—Melt two ounces of butter in another stewpan, and shake into it by degrees (mixing with a wooden spoon) two tablespoonsful of flour, taking especial care that the thickening does not " colour ;" then *take off the pan*, and pour in the broth by degrees ; mix and lift with the wooden spoon until you have formed a smooth sauce; then, having beaten up the yolks of four eggs with half an ounce of butter cut in small pieces, and two tablespoonsful of good cream, add them also by degrees to the sauce ; mix and lift as before for about five minutes ; then pass the sauce through a tammy into the stewpan in which you have placed the pieces of chicken, with two dozen button-mushrooms stewed, and cut in half.   Warm up over a brisk fire, and serve on a hot dish, the pieces of chicken being fancifully piled in the centre with the mushrooms round them, and the white sauce poured over all.

Truffles cut in squares and stewed in *Velouté* sauce, artichoke bottoms, cucumbers, small onions, pieces of fried sweetbread, ham, and savoury forcemeat, are also used for garnishing.

FRICANDEAU DE VEAU.

This savoury dish, so long the pride of the French kitchen, is, strange to say, fast going out of fashion, being seldom seen in Paris but at the *restaurants* frequented by the English, with whom it is still in high estimation as a *plat de resistance ;* in fact, it may be regarded as a French veal cutlet. It is prepared thus :—

Procure a cutlet from the fillet, weighing a pound and a half: about eight inches in length, three inches thick, and from three to four inches broad. Smooth it with two or three smart blows with your " meat bat ;" pare off the skin and gristle, and lard it thickly on the top and sides (according to the instructions at foot) ; then select a stewpan just large enough to hold the cutlet and vegetables with but little margin, and cover the bottom with two middling-sized carrots and onions cut in thick slices, three sprigs of parsley, two blades of mace, two sprigs of lemon thyme, a quarter of a teaspoonful of cayenne, half a teaspoonful of salt, and twenty white peppercorns ; add first a thin layer of fat bacon, and then the cutlet ; moisten with as much white stock as will *just cover the vegetables and bacon, but not the meat.* Stew gently with a close lid three hours on the charcoal-stove or a slow fire ; baste frequently with its own gravy ; about a quarter of an hour before it is done, strew the top of the pan with live charcoal, to brown and crisp the larding ; if, however, it should happen not to be sufficiently deep in colour (it should not, however, be *too* dark), hold the " salamander" over it for a minute or two. Strain off the vegetables, and having placed the *fricandeau* in a hot dish upon spinach, pea, or any other vegetable *purée*, pour the gravy, which ought to be moderately thick, over it.

LARDING.

This process is very generally used in the French kitchen to impart succulency and flavour to meats which have but little natural juice, such as veal, turkey, rabbits, capons, pheasants, &c. All that is required for it is a larding-needle, which can be bought at almost any ironmonger's, and some fat bacon.

The mode of operation is simply to pinch up with the finger and thumb a piece of the flesh; then force the needle, charged with thin strips of bacon, through it; withdraw the spring, and leave the "larding" in an equal length (about a quarter of an inch) on each side.

A very little practice will enable you to cover your *fricandeau*, or your bird, with "*lardons*" as thickly and fancifully arranged, as "the quills of the fretful porcupine."

PUREES.

These are simply vegetables of various kinds, boiled, or browned and stewed; then pounded in a mortar, incorporated with two or three spoonsful of either *Espagnole*, *Velouté*, or *Béchamel* sauce, and formed in a pulp by being squeezed through a fine sieve or a tammy. As this preparation is very savoury, and affords a pleasant change to the plain English style, I will give a few examples of the principal varieties.

PEA PUREE.

Boil for twenty minutes in a pint and a half of water, a quart of green peas, with the *young* leaves of three sprigs of fresh mint, a handful of parsley, and a dozen spring onions. Strain off the water, and pound the vegetables in a mortar; then put them in a stewpan with two tablespoonsful of either *Velouté* or *Béchamel* sauce; mix well over the fire for two or three minutes; then beat the pulp through a fine sieve; when required for use, warm in a stewpan with an ounce of fresh butter. The same receipt will serve for young French bean *purée*.

SPINACH PUREE.

Pick and boil the spinach in the usual manner—pound it, add half a teaspoonful of grated nutmeg, a quarter of a teaspoonful of salt, the same of sugar, and a tablespoonful of *Béchamel* sauce, mix over the fire, pass it into a pulp through a sieve or tammy—warm before serving, with two ounces of fresh butter.

POTATO PUREE.

Peel and cut in slices half-a-dozen good-sized potatoes, put them in a stewpan with two ounces of butter, twenty corns of black pepper, half a teaspoonful of salt, the quarter of a grated nutmeg, and a pint of white stock. Stew, with a close lid three-quarters of an hour; then stir in gradually (over the fire) half a pint of cream; stir and lift with a wooden spoon, then pulp through a sieve or tammy; warm when about to serve, with an ounce of fresh butter.

YOUNG CARROT PUREE.

Instead of being boiled the carrots must be cut in slices and fried with two ounces of butter, a little salt, grated nutmeg and sugar, and turned occasionally until they are a light brown; then moisten with a teacupful of white stock, and stew for ten minutes, next pound and beat through a sieve, or squeeze through a tammy; when required for use, warm with an ounce of fresh butter.

TURNIP PUREE.

The turnips should be sliced and put into the stewpan with two ounces of butter, a little sugar and salt, stewed gently for a few minutes, and turned occasionally (taking care that they do not burn), when they are nearly melted, add half a tea-cupful of either *Velouté* or *Béchamel*, stir over the fire until it arrives at the consistency of soft paste, then add gradually half a pint of good cream, mix and lift again, squeeze through the tammy, warm with an ounce of butter. Celery, onion, cauliflower, broccoli, cabbage, Brussels sprouts, and a great number of other purées are treated in the same manner. I give these receipts, that the *family housekeeper* may take a useful hint from them, *without incurring the expense of cream and meat sauces.*

The vegetables plainly boiled, pulped through the sieve, and *then* mixed with a little gravy, milk, or butter, will be found very tasteful; indeed, the whole of the foregoing French dishes can be produced by an intelligent cook (*who will well consider them*), for far less expense; I give them only as " holiday dishes," to be adopted in their integrity, or modified according to the taste and circumstances of those who are inclined to try them.

My last example shall be an *English holiday dish,* and in recording it, I shall bring to light a mystery that has hitherto

M

been confined to the bosoms of a few "*chefs*" who direct the preparation of the piscatorial delicacies of the famous " baiting houses " on the banks of London's river; it is

HOW TO DRESS WHITEBAIT.

Spread a clean napkin upon a table, cover it within half an inch of the edge with fine sifted flour (say half inch thick), next sprinkle lightly, by small handfuls, about a pint or more of the bait, taking care that it is spread all over the flour; have ready about three pounds of good and sweet lard in a *deep* frying-pan; let this be getting hot while you proceed as above. Observe carefully when the least vapour rises from the lard, for it then is hot enough. Now hasten to toss the flour and bait together from end to end upon the napkin; have ready a coarse cane sieve, throw the whole into it, sift away the flour quickly and throw the bait into the hot lard, or rather shake it in by degrees, but quickly, or part will be dressed and the other not, moving the frying-pan backwards and forwards to spread the whole, and prevent the fish from adhering, keeping the pan upon the fire. Have a wire slice or ladle ready at hand, apply this cautiously among the fish, and if they sound crisp and hard, remove them quickly into a colander, drain one minute, sprinkle lightly with fine salt, toss them over, and serve upon a dish, with a napkin, *instanter*. The whole process should not take more than six or seven minutes.*

I am indebted for the above to the kindness of Mr. Edmund Pallister, of Pallister's Hotel, Gravesend. It is the composition of his principal cook, Mr. Skilleter, and may be looked upon as the best practical receipt for the preparation of this delicacy that has ever been published.

---

* In the 28th number of the *Naturalist*, Mr. G. Pulman, of Crewkerne, Somersetshire, has clearly shown that whitebait (*clupea alba*), which has generally been supposed to be produced by the Thames only, swarm in incredible numbers in the river Dart, especially in that part of the river which extends from Totness Weir to Dartmouth, a distance of about twelve miles. These delicate fish feed upon shrimps, and when in pursuit of their prey, their gambols are very remarkable. Whether they remain in the Dart throughout the year, has not been ascertained; but they have been observed in March, and in every succeeding month till the end of November. They are also found in large quantities at Antwerp.

CARVING.*

The following brief hints on this subject will I trust be found to embrace the most essential rudiments of the art; but practice, constant practice, alone can bring about ultimate perfection; without it all the treatises you may read, with the help of their diagrams, will avail but little; you must, like a surgeon, obtain your " facility in operations" by constant experiments on the "subject." If, then, your early education on this little considered but very important branch of knowledge may have been neglected, lose no time in taking practical measures to remove the disability. As one simple method by which young married ladies who take the head of their table, and young gentlemen who " go into society," might be spared much annoyance from not possessing the necessary qualifications for the performance of this duty, I would recommend ladies who have young families, instead of carving the dishes sent into the nursery themselves, or deputing the office to a servant, to make it a rule that all the little ones, when they are old enough to handle a knife and fork safely, shall take their turns to carve, *beginning with the puddings*. In this manner, the art would be easily acquired, and, like swimming learnt in early youth, can never be forgotten.

If the mind be given to the matter, there are few persons who cannot find good *private* practice at home, or at the tables of their relatives; to them we say, seek to have a " cut" at everything that comes from the kitchen; and instead of dreading to encounter a goose or a hare, look out for favourable opportunities of cultivating their acquaintance. Follow with observant eyes all the little master slices and twists of a practised operator in table anatomy; and forthwith, if you have not an opportunity of " trying your wings" at a friend's table, have the bird, joint,

---

* In the latter part of George the First's reign (1720) it was the fashion for ladies to carve every dish that came to table, and so important was this accomplishment considered, that " professors of the knife and fork" gained fame and good profit by giving lessons in the art. Some of their preliminary exercises were very ludicrous: wooden effigies of meat, fish, and birds, with the " cuts " indicated, and the joints articulated, and put together like a child's puzzle, had to be operated upon before the real " subject" came under the knife, which subject was always provided at the pupil's expense. Indeed, so great was the vogue of a professor who held his court in Tavistock-street, then the " Emporium of Fashion," that the carriages of his titled patronesses often stopped the way, to the great detriment of the millinery and Indian curiosity establishments.

M 2

hare, or fish, cooked at home, and with bolted doors, as an alchemist would try a grand experiment, tuck up your sleeves, and go to work, armed with a long-handled " carver," with a broad, well-sharpened blade having a keen point to it.   With this and a two-pronged steel fork with a secure guard, attack your enemy; your remembrance of the "practised hand's" method of commencing with a shoulder or leg of mutton will direct you where to make your first incision ; but, if you should happen to have forgotten it, *one failure will cause you to understand which side is the proper one to be turned towards you as you cut*, and you will never afterwards find your knife hacking the bone when it should be slicing the flesh.   To carve poultry requires greater knowledge and practice ; you know that birds have wings, legs, breasts, backs, merry-thoughts, side bones, &c., and a very slight consideration of their structure and relative position will lead you to the main joints ; but you will hack and hack, and splash and splash, many and many times before you can hit them with any certainty and cleverness ; still, don't be daunted; try again and again ; as in the army the " goose-step" *must* be learned, don't flinch from *yours*.   But by all means get if possible some practised hand to give you a hint or two at the outset, and you may be sure that ere long the light will break upon you, and you will be able fearlessly to attack anything that comes to table.

Limited space will not permit me to give examples for carving meat and fish ; they are comparatively easy, and may be best learned from careful observation ; all that it is necessary to say in this place is, endeavour to cut *from* rather than *to* your fork, for by so doing you will be less liable to accidents from the knife slipping, and it moreover gives you a firmer " cut" and greater mastery over all parts of the bird, joint, &c. ; but, you must *take particular care to have your knife very sharp.*

HOW TO CARVE POULTRY AND GAME.

As the leading points are nearly the same for each, I will give one fundamental rule, appending to it a few observations where any variation be requisite.

Place the bird within easy reach, with the neck to your *left* hand.   Insert the fork firmly in the breast just above the merry-thought, then make a sharp cut (to the bone) in a direct line from the *inner* side of the pinion to the rump—do the same with the other side; by this you will mark out your wings; then with the point of the knife *touch* the pinion joint and cut through the sinew, incline the knife outwards on each side, and the wings will be ready for separating, which should be effected by *steadying* the body with the knife, *placing the fork at the top of the joint and pulling them away;* replace the fork in its former position, and carry the point of the knife sharply down each side of the breast-bone (as close to it as possible), and make two, or if the fowl be large three, slices on each side (the latter must be *pulled* away, like the wings); then take off the merry-thought, by cutting through its gristle at the top of the breast, forcing it back with the knife towards the neck, and cutting through the sinews at the back with the point.

Then, inserting the knife at the top of the shoulders, make a sharp cut towards the right, and pull away the side-bones; then, steadying the body with the fork, cut towards the back joint of the legs, and with the point of the knife *feel* for its centre; when you have found it, cut through the sinew, turn the legs outwards, cut them from the body, and divide them at the thigh-joint; then slice and pull away the good pieces on each side of the rump—scoop out the "epicure's bits" on each side of the centre of the back, hold the back firmly with the fork, bend it back in the centre with the knife, it will easily divide, amputate the "parson's nose," and your fowl is carved.

As geese and turkeys have large breasts, instead of beginning to carve them by taking off the wings, cut the breasts in handsome slices from the left to the right (always to the bone) until you arrive at the pinions, then attack the legs, &c. A hare should also be sliced down the back (keeping his head on your left hand), then take off the "legs and wings."

Wild ducks are sliced like geese, but tame ducks are treated like fowls.

Partridges are generally cut in half, but sometimes the legs are taken off, and the whole of the breast is separated from the back; to do this cleverly requires a good deal of practice—don't blunder in the dark, *look for the joints,* sever the sinews, hold the back firmly with the fork, and turn the breast from you with the knife.

Grouse and woodcocks are winged and sliced like fowls, or cut down the centre. Pigeons, snipes, and quails, are either cut in half, or served whole.

In dismissing the subject, I repeat the advice I started with; take good note of the dexterity of experienced carvers, never be ashamed of gaining information, but above all, seek every opportunity for practice.

HOW TO MAKE COFFEE.*

How many thick volumes have been written on this apparently insignificant subject! how many wonderful receipts are known for it! and how opposite are the various theories regarding it!

"If you boil it," says Professor Maresnest, "you spoil it; the aroma is entirely destroyed, and you might as well drink a decoction of mahogany sawdust." "If you *don't* boil it," says old Mr. Brownwig, who has almost lived upon it for fifty years, "you lose all its strength." "A *percolater* is the thing, my boy," says Mr. Fitzjones, of Pelham-crescent; "it's genteel, and clear; and I'm told by Lord Sniffle we get nothing but the true *ah-ro-mah,* just as we do in Paris." "Give me the old-fashioned black coffee-pot," says Mr. Ginger, the grocer (who in spite of the fashion for migration to a suburban villa still lives at his house of business in the City), "and plenty of the berry well roasted and fresh ground, and I'll back myself to turn out as fine a cup as any one can produce by *any* process, not excepting the French chaps, who I *know* always mix theirs with lots of chicory."

The Turk roasts and *pounds* the berry at the moment he requires it, *stews* it with a very small quantity of water, and drinks it boiling hot, *with the grounds*, without either milk or sugar.

Which method is the best?

How do they make it in France?" perhaps some one may ask; "for it is only there we drink it in perfection."

---

* The first coffee-house opened in England was in George-yard, Lombard-street, by one Pasqua, a Greek, who was brought over in 1652, by a Turkey merchant named Edwards. In 1674, it was petitioned against in Parliament, and termed "a base, black, thick, nasty, bitter, stinking puddle water," and the Rainbow Coffee-house in Fleet-street was indicted for the *nuisance* of selling it.

I am prepared to answer the question and give the French receipt; but in doing so, I am afraid my revelations will do for you what the microscope did for the Brahmin, *dispel all your long-cherished illusions*, for *French coffee is very seldom either fresh or pure*, the liquor from the boiled-up grounds of the preceding day being very generally used, and not only chicory, but in many cases *Spanish liquorice* is employed to give colour and flavour, as well as seeming strength. Startling as these assertions may appear, there are few English house-keepers in France who cannot corroborate them.

The French method is as follows :—Half an ounce of chicory (called *chicorée café*) is mixed with each ounce of coffee, and put either in a broad bottomed iron-pot, or an earthenware pan with a close-fitting cover; the strained liquor from the boiled-up grounds is then poured over them, with as much boiling water as, when reduced by stewing, will make the quantity of coffee required; the pot or pan is set on the stove over a slow charcoal fire, or on the hearth before the fire, with the hot wood embers and ashes piled round it; it is then left to simmer during the night, or day, as may be most convenient. When wanted for use, the coffee is boiled up quickly, strained through a fine cloth, put into a warmed metal pot, and served as hot as possible, with boiling cream or milk in a separate pot. The best lump sugar or sugar-candy is used for sweetening. When very strong flavour and colour are required for *café noir*, a small piece of Spanish liquorice is added at the concluding boiling-up; indeed, the use both of chicory and liquorice is very general throughout the Continent, particularly in the *Cafés* and *Restaurants*.

Having thus brought to light the secrets of the French coffee makers, I will now give my own method, which I will call

ENGLISH COFFEE A LA TICKLETOOTH.

Begin by procuring *good* berries (the Mocha are the best), for there is never anything saved by using an inferior article ; roast them at home (a cylinder made expressly for the purpose can be purchased for about five shillings), open the little door in the cylinder frequently during the process, to see that the berries are not getting too dark a brown, for the strength of the coffee does not depend, as many imagine, on its being highly coloured. As the roasting takes some time, and it may be inconvenient to repeat it on every occasion the coffee is required, you may prepare enough for three or four days, and set it aside in a *well-closed* tin canister. Next, grind the quantity you deem sufficient, allowing a *full* ounce to each breakfast-cupful required; put it into a broad-bottomed block-tin or iron coffee-pot, pour upon it as many cupfuls of *boiling water* as you wish to have of strong coffee, with the addition of a cup of water (more or less, according to the quantity of coffee) for wasting; stir well with a wooden spoon, then put the pot on the fire, and *boil quickly*, stirring all the while. As soon as the bubbles begin to rise, take the pot from the fire, pour out a cupful, hold it a couple of feet above the pot, and pour it back again; repeat this three or four times, as its effect is similar to the lifting practised with sauces; give the pot a smart knock, to cause the grounds to settle, as you set it on the hob, where you must place it at a sufficient distance from the fire to keep warm, but not to simmer. If you have a *bain-marie* put it in that. If you do not like the black coffee-pot to appear in the breakfast parlour (although it possesses many of the good qualities of the black-bottle), let the coffee be strained through a piece of muslin, put into a *warmed metal* coffee-pot, and served the moment it is ready.

Fining with isinglass, salt, egg-shells, or sole-skin *always* destroys the flavour, and is quite unnecessary if the person who pours the coffee into the cup from the black pot, or through the muslin strainer, be careful to do so *gently*, so as not to disturb the settlement or grounds at the bottom.

In straining into the warmed pot, *do not squeeze the muslin*, and endeavour to pour from the black pot so steadily that nothing but the clear liquor will have to be filtered.

Although Soyer and many other French cooks recommend that the grounds left from a previous brewing should be boiled up, and their strained liquor added to the fresh coffee, I perfectly agree with Mrs. Acton that it destroys the aroma, and should never under any circumstances be resorted to.

The bad quality of the chicory used in England is another great cause of our coffee gaining so bad a name, for the dirty trash sold for it by the generality of grocers (see Mr. Wakley's exposures in the *Lancet*), is not only destructive of flavour, but poisonous besides. I believe that a little pure chicory, *prepared at home,* may be advantageously used to obtain the French flavour, but never be tempted to try the deadly mixture sold at the grocers.*

The preparation of the endive, which is really " chicory," is very simple. Procure some fresh heads, wash them well, and thoroughly dry them by wiping them with a soft cloth, cut them in pieces, put them in a tin or pie dish, and bake them until they are quite crisp and brown; then rub them to powder with your fingers, or pound them in a mortar, using a teaspoonful of the powder to each ounce of coffee. I give the receipt for those who, like Sancho Panza, wish for " better bread than is made of wheat;" but for my own part, I think that *nothing can improve the pure coffee.*

As a dinner naturally terminates with the cup of coffee and its *chasse,* so will I conclude my book.

The bill of fare I have offered does not profess to display extraordinary novelties, nor give undue importance to anything that is already familiarly known; neither have I, on the other hand, supposed that *every one* is so well informed as to need no advice or instruction.

What I have aimed at has been to demonstrate to all classes the advantages arising from a practical knowledge of cookery, and the general management of a house. In adopting *The Dinner Question* for my title, I have taken advantage of the famous controversy that appeared in the columns of the *Times,* and whilom attracted so much public attention, thinking it a topic of such universal importance that it might well be

---

* Among the " adulterations of food " brought to light by the Sanitary Commission, recorded in the *Lancet,* that of chicory has a most unenviable prominency. It is not enough that a variety of deleterious compounds known as " Black Jack," " Coffina," and Hambro' Powder (roasted peas coloured with Venetian red or calcined copperas) are resorted to, but mahogany sawdust, and the used-up oak-bark powder from the Bermondsey tan-yards, charred and ground, are also largely employed. If these adulterations are stigmatized as atrocious frauds, what epithet should be employed to designate the admixture with chicory of baked horses' and bullocks' livers ?

In a useful little book by Mr. P. L. Simmonds, entitled *Coffee as it is, and as it ought to be,* occurs this startling piece of information :—" In various parts of the metropolis, but more especially in the east, are to be found liver-bakers. These men take the livers of oxen and horses, bake them, and grind them into a powder, which they sell to the low-priced coffee-shop keepers, at from fourpence to sixpence per pound, horses'-liver coffee bearing the highest price. It may be known by allowing the coffee to stand until cold, when a thick pellicle or skin will be found on the top.

enlarged upon. Instead, however, of compiling another mere cookery book, crammed with a vast number of impracticable or worthless receipts, I have preferred rather to condense my information, and to give a brief, comprehensive review of every useful phase of "The Art of Dining and Giving Dinners," combined with A PRACTICAL GUIDE TO YOUNG HOUSEKEEPERS TO THE RUDIMENTS OF PLAIN COOKERY, the want of knowledge of which I take to be one of the principal causes of the reproach that has been so long attached to English housewives and cooks, that the dinners they produce are like the attempts of amateur actors—mere superficial, unsatisfactory efforts, alike devoid of study and artistic training.

In almost every work I have read professing to teach ladies how to cook, the authors, instead of endeavouring to ground their pupils in *principles or causes,* devote their whole attention to *effects.* By giving a large number of receipts, which are often bewildering, and saying nothing of many of the essentials of preparation, manipulation, &c. &c., those who endeavour to cook from them often fall into errors which entirely destroy both the flavour and appearance of their dishes. By taking each branch separately, explaining thoroughly "the reason why" everything is done, and at the same time showing *the right way of doing it,* I have tried to make my book an unpretending but useful primer to the practical knowledge of cookery, so that any lady who will give it serious attention, and *commit to memory its most important hints,* will very soon be completely familiar with everything appertaining to the Family Kitchen, and at no distant period will be able fearlessly to venture on higher ground.

The great point I wish to inculcate is, self-reliance : *do not work with the book in your hand.* Study it carefully, and *be well possessed of its rules before you attempt to put them into practice;* and, as I have before observed, "when you know how to fry a sole, to make a matelotte, to hash, mince, roast, broil, bake, and stew, beef, mutton, veal, pork, and vegetables, and make pies and puddings on *proper principles,* you are in possession of the stem from which all the more elaborate and costly varieties branch."

In laying down my pen, let me relate a little anecdote.

The Prince de Soubise had one day the intention of giving a *fête;* it was to terminate with a supper, and he asked to see his bill of fare. His cook presented one with an estimate. The first article which caught the Prince's eye was *fifty hams.* "Eh ! what ?", said he ; " why, Bertrand, you must be out of your senses. Are you going to feast my whole regiment ?" " No, Monseigneur, only *one* ham will appear on the table ; but the remainder are indispensable to me for my *espagnoles,* my *blondes,* my *garnatures,* my ———" "Bertrand, you are plundering me; that article shall not pass." " Oh, Monseigneur," replied the indignant artist, " you do not understand our capabilities. Say the word, and *I will put all these fifty hams which confound you, into a glass bottle no bigger than the top of my thumb.*" What reply could be made to such a positive assertion ? The Prince smiled, nodded his head, and the item passed.

GENTLE READER,

I have stewed down *fifty cookery books,* and seasoned them with the practical knowledge derived from nearly *forty years' experience* in housekeeping, to form this little volume. Will you kindly imitate the Prince de Soubise, smile, nod your head, and sanction its adoption ?

INDEX.

THE END.